D1760671

# A Georgian Heroine

It is wrong to think that it is in the early days that a true loss is most painful. It seems then that one is not altogether sure about the nature of one's misfortune, one does not really know that there is no remedy, and the start of a most cruel separation is simply like a temporary absence. But when the passing days fail to bring back the person one needs, it seems that our sadness is constantly confirmed, and at every moment we say to ourselves 'it is forever!'

(*Histoire de Cécile Caliste par Mme Isabelle de Charrière*)

# A Georgian Heroine
## The Intriguing Life of
## Rachel Charlotte Williams Biggs

**Joanne Major and Sarah Murden**

PEN & SWORD
HISTORY

First published in Great Britain in 2017 by
Pen & Sword History
an imprint of
Pen & Sword Books Ltd
47 Church Street
Barnsley
South Yorkshire
S70 2AS

Copyright © Joanne Major and Sarah Murden, 2017

ISBN 978 1 47386 346 0

Printed and bound in England
by TJ International Ltd, Padstow, Cornwall

Pen & Sword Books Limited incorporates the imprints of Atlas, Archaeology, Aviation, Discovery, Family History, Fiction, History, Maritime, Military, Military Classics, Politics, Select, Transport, True Crime, Air World, Frontline Publishing, Leo Cooper, Remember When, Seaforth Publishing, The Praetorian Press, Wharncliffe Local History, Wharncliffe Transport, Wharncliffe True Crime and White Owl.

For a complete list of Pen & Sword titles please contact
PEN & SWORD BOOKS LIMITED
47 Church Street, Barnsley, South Yorkshire, S70 2AS, England
E-mail: enquiries@pen-and-sword.co.uk
Website: www.pen-and-sword.co.uk

To Hazel

# Contents

# Maps

Map of England, Wales and northern France, showing the locations central to Charlotte's story.

Lambeth and Westminster Bridge, leading across the River Thames to Westminster Hall and New Palace Yard.

# List of Plates

Fin tragique de Marie Antoinette d'Autriche reine de France, exécutée le 16 Octobre 1793. (*Getty Museum under their Open Content Program*)

Notre Dame, Abbeville, Charles J. Hullmandel, after J. Fudge, 1820. (*Yale Center for British Art, Yale University Art Gallery Collection*)

The Old Parsonage, Farrington Gurney, front view. (*Courtesy of Brian and Charlotte Murray, The Old Parsonage*)

The Old Parsonage, Farrington Gurney, rear view. (*Courtesy of Brian and Charlotte Murray, The Old Parsonage*)

Covent Garden Theatre from The Microcosm of London, 1808–1810, Thomas Rowlandson. (*British Library*)

The Rt. Hon William Windham, engraving after Sir Joshua Reynolds, 1787. (*Österreichische Nationalbibliothek/Austrian National Library*)

House of Commons from The Microcosm of London, 1808–1810, Thomas Rowlandson. (*British Library*)

William Wilberforce Esqr., James Heath after John Russell, 1807. (*Yale Center for British Art, Paul Mellon Fund*)

Portrait of Coster St Victor, in bust, profile directed right into an oval. Grautier and Dumontier, 1804. (*Bibliothèque Nationale de France/National Library of France*)

Miniature of Napoleon I, Jean-Baptiste Isabey, 1812. (*Metropolitan Museum of Art, gift of Helen O. Brice, 1942*)

Explosion d'une machine infernale. (*Bibliothèque Nationale de France/National Library of France*)

The Meeting of the Rivers Severn and Wye, near Chepstow, Edward Dayes, 1795. (*Yale Center for British Art, Paul Mellon Collection*)

The Eldest Princesses, print made by Gainsborough Dupont, after Thomas Gainsborough, 1793. (*Yale Center for British Art, Paul Mellon Collection*)

# Acknowledgements

Without the permission, support and amazing generosity of Marius Kociejowski, poet, essayist and travel writer this book could never have been written, so we would formally like to acknowledge his amazing work in initially piecing together Charlotte's *Testament* at a time when there was limited information available and his willingness (along with his lovely wife Bobbie) to meet with us to share information about Charlotte and allow us to see, for the first time, her original manuscript. We would also like to thank George Carey, documentary film-maker, who, at Marius's instigation, took time out of his busy schedule to meet with us.

We are extremely grateful to Sir Richard Head and the Bodleian Library for their assistance and agreement in allowing us to use the letters Charlotte wrote to Sir James Bland Burges, which have proved incredibly helpful when filling in many of the gaps in her life. Also, Graham Tratt and the team at Bristol archives, who answered some of our more obscure questions in an effort to establish where and why Charlotte was living in Bristol; we thank them for their patience and advice.

Dr Jacqueline Reiter, author of *The Late Lord: The Life of John Pitt, 2nd Earl of Chatham*, was a huge help in translating some tricky handwritten French documents.

We would like to thank SPL Rare Books who have been incredibly gracious in allowing us to use two of their images within the book and also Brian and Charlotte Murray for permitting us to include pictures of their bed and breakfast at Farrington Gurney in which Charlotte and Benjamin Hunt Biggs lived over 200 years previously.

Last, but of course by no means least, we would like to thank our respective families and all the staff at Pen and Sword for their continued support.

Joanne Major and Sarah Murden, 2017.

# Preface

The events in this story are, to the best of the authors' knowledge, true. Wherever possible the facts have been substantiated and proven in surviving records, but parts of the story come from information written in documents and letters left behind by the people concerned and where the facts contained in these documents and letters cannot be verified, we have to take them at face value and accept them for what they are: first-hand, word-of-mouth accounts left behind for history to judge their accuracy, whether the writer intended them to become public knowledge or whether they were written only for private consumption. Elements of this story seem far-fetched on first reading and indeed we had the same assumptions on first discovering Rachel Charlotte Williams Biggs, but we quickly realized that the truth was far stranger than fiction.

This is the incredible story of a brave and steadfast Georgian lady that history forgot and who broke the Georgian rulebook when it came to being a woman in what was, essentially, a man's world. She was a true enigma, both a helpless captive and an independent woman, respectable middle-class lady and adventurous spy, demure publicity-shy woman and propagandist author and, above all, a woman hopelessly in love with a man too far away for her to reach.

Journey with us while we explore the incredible life of Mrs Biggs.

# Introduction

A year ago, actually a bit more, I was pleasantly surprised to receive a letter to the effect that a couple of people were researching the life of a woman who, three decades ago, had me absolutely enthralled. I thought I had finished with her, or she with me, but clearly this was not to be the case. The letter was close to bursting with enthusiasm and of all the triggers in the universe enthusiasm is the most potent. This book is the product of two authors who came to their subject from an angle quite different to mine. They discovered Charlotte B— while investigating the history of Peterborough House in Fulham, whereas she came to me from the bottom of a cupboard in Long Acre, in central London. Sarah Murden and Joanne Major, Georgian scholars both, were very much on their own trail. Somehow, happily, we met in the middle. What for them has been an historical undertaking, involving much painstaking research, for me was a modern ghost story, one in which the events described might be said to have been subject to the extraordinary workings of chance. There's not much meat on a ghost, of course, which is not to say I didn't do a considerable amount of research but that Misses Murden and Major have on several fronts taken matters considerably further than I was able to. Whereas for them the mystery of Charlotte's existence had to be resolved in the historical past, for me it was inside the historical present. Ghosts will never be caught otherwise.

One might subscribe to any number of notions involving chance, from the idea that everything we do is to some degree governed by it to the very opposite view, so ably voiced by the poet Schiller: 'There is no such thing as chance and what seems to us merest accident springs from the deepest source of destiny.' When we talk about Destiny, however, we put at risk our common sense. I am rather more inclined to the idea, one that has governed much of what I write, that the air is full of connections waiting to be made, and that what is asked of us is that we have the sensitivity sufficient to such an enterprise. In this respect I think the historian and the imaginative writer go hand-in-hand down the same route. As one writer of things real has put it, it takes imagination to see things as they are. If we are to speak of 'merest accident' then a sceptic might argue that the subject of this study was more than a little accident-prone. I mean just how many blunders can any one woman make? There are times even when one is tempted to have a good laugh at her expense.

As I said, it has been some years since the manuscript that serves as the bedrock for this book fell into my hands, and nothing I can write will ever properly reproduce the shudder that went through me when, on 13 May 1987, I began to peruse the contents of a brown envelope that had been handed to me. At the time I was working for the London antiquarian bookseller, Bertram Rota, a firm of some considerable repute. We were preparing for a change of premises, which necessitated going through the contents of cupboards and, in some instances, giving them an airing for the first time in decades. My colleague asked me to decide whether or not the contents of the envelope should be chucked because when moving from a bigger into a smaller place chucking is very much the rule. At such moments it is as easy to incur losses as it is to make discoveries. I had been working there for almost a decade, during which time the materials in that particular cupboard had lain undisturbed for that plus what my colleague told me was at least another decade. A great deal of it had been undisturbed because it was too much of a bother to face or because there was always something more important to do. If one would like to call to the stand Destiny as our first witness, she'd swear I had not yet come to this country when the envelope was placed there. London was not even in my sights. The material had come from the stock of another bookseller, the wonderfully-named Dusty Miller and where he got it from is anybody's guess. Dusty himself had become ashes. So let's say I'd been journeying towards Charlotte's 'sad and "unvarnished tale"' for well over twenty years.

Among various papers in the envelope were a manuscript that at one point had been stitched together to make a small booklet of twenty-eight quarto pages (three of them blank) and a covering letter of sixteen octavo pages, dated 26 February, 1821, and signed "Charlotte B —", which begins: 'I fear, my dear General, your first impression on opening this packet will be that I am taking a liberty with you which an acquaintance so long suspended does not authorise.' Those were inviting words indeed. I read on. Clearly it was composed by an older woman of precarious health, who, fearing she was bound for a 'better world', was now writing to 'the person I have most loved in *this*.' I was immediately struck by the sheer breathlessness of the prose, the urgency with which an elderly woman was trying to explain to the first love of her life, who is not named, events that befell her many decades before.

As I read on, I felt there was something familiar in certain of the details she provides — the Mahratta War of 1803, the Wars of the Mysore, and mention of her 'dear General' being left with the Emperor at Delhi. I was no expert in Anglo-Indian history but why did I already know these things? It was as if mentally I had yet to catch up with what I already knew. I stopped with disbelief (or is that too weak a word?) at a sentence that read, 'The Hero of Nepaul little imagined that his early friend was on the 15th of May 1816 giving a Ball in celebration of the anniversary of his treaty after the reduction of Malown, to some of the prettiest women in Paris.' This would not have been, to an outsider's eyes, the most exciting of observations but the effect it made on me was absolutely electrifying. I realised that the man to whom Charlotte was writing was my great-great-great grandfather on my mother's side. There is a single point in the manuscript that confirmed absolutely the recipient's identity where she addresses him by name, accidentally, and then she runs her pen over it several times. When I raised the page to the light I could make out the scrawled-through letters that spelled my ancestor's name. Maybe she did not want him wholly erased. Only recently I had been gathering materials towards a biography of him. It was as if the post had arrived over a century and a half late.

Sir David Ochterlony, conqueror of Nepal, and, for me, much more intriguingly, one of the 'glorious sahibs' who had gone native and of whom legend has it that he would take his thirteen Indian wives on the backs of thirteen elephants for evening strolls through Delhi, this was the man to whom she was writing in her crisp Anglican tone. Sadly the book I had hoped to write never materialised. A military study would have been relatively easy to write, a social one just about possible, but in both instances my subject would have remained a silhouette against an immensely colourful background. There were occasional glints of his character here and there, but I had been hamstrung by the failure to find anything approaching a personal archive or collection of letters that would make him come alive on the page. Some years later, William Dalrymple began to write a book about him but he, too, was unable to discover much about the man himself. Such material as he gathered was absorbed into the larger historical picture that became his *White Mughals* (2002). Ochterlony remains one of the most fascinating figures to have never been accorded a full biography because invested in his person is the so-called 'twilight' period in Anglo-Indian history when there was a genuine movement between, and absorption of, cultures. We are speaking here of the closing decades of the eighteenth century and the first couple of the nineteenth. The bitterness of his story is that he lived long enough to have moved from one set of social mores, when marrying Indian women, which is to say more than one, was not only acceptable but positively encouraged, to another set of social mores, signalled by the arrival of English women in India, when a life previously led in multiple marital bliss was now deemed beyond the pale. As such Ochterlony would become one of history's casualties, a figure of lost times, and he died a broken man, in Meerut, in 1825. All this requires saying because it underlies the many ironies that lie in Charlotte's letter to him. 'I am quite a stranger, sir, to your present circumstances,' she writes. Indeed she was. She could not have grasped the extent to which her old love had changed since he left England forever in 1777 in order to make a new life for himself in India. One can only guess what she would have made of his harem when for her he had remained throughout her life 'the first object' of her affections. She might have loved the uniform but not his Mughal robes.

The mishaps that Charlotte suffered in her youth were, if one follows a gothic line, visited upon the manuscript she wrote. I took it home in order that I might begin to make a transcription but soon I discovered the occasional problem with Charlotte's hand. I took it back into work and presented it to my colleague, John Byrne, who in his capacity as cataloguer of archives had a skilled eye. He took the manuscript home for the weekend. The following Monday he came into work with a long face, several bruises and a black eye. The previous Friday evening he had been mugged on a street in Pimlico and his briefcase containing the manuscript was taken. As sorry as I was to observe him in such a battered state, I was sorrier still to have lost a manuscript without which a good story would now be reduced to mere hearsay. I had not even taken the precaution to make a photocopy of the manuscript. Also, I had only just begun work on it and with so many questions unanswered and with no proof of those questions ever having existed in the first place I found myself mourning for what might have been. A week later, my colleague got a phone call from the police, advising him that the briefcase was found in a puddle on a housing estate. When he made enquiries as to its contents he was told that everything was ruined or else had been torn to pieces. The thief must have been disappointed in his findings. The bag was retrieved and indeed it was as described by the police except for a copy of a newspaper into which had been carefully folded Charlotte's manuscript. It was wet but in a single piece, and such was the quality of the handmade paper and the iron-based ink that once the sheets were dried out there was hardly any damage at all.

So began what was almost a year's work for me. If, as a couple of people thought at the time, these were the feverish ramblings of a fantasist who had probably read one too many novels for her own good – for reading was then considered to give women the vapours – then her story would greatly decrease in value. Clearly she had an elegant turn of phrase, but perhaps, at times, just a little too elegant to believe. Very well read, she could impart her deeper feelings by quoting the occasional line of poetry, for example Thomas Gray's 'On some fond breast the parting soul relies' or, when she wanted a story to move along, she could write in a manner that worryingly brings to mind Samuel Richardson. The smoother the line, the more reason there is for doubt. Still, there's something in my nature that responds to what I feel is true, and my gut feeling was that her story of rape and adduction was, despite its bodice-ripping flavour, genuine. A hunch is never enough, however, and what I had to do now was to prove it. What helped me was that she had taken considerable care to disguise names and places and yet in doing so had unwittingly provided just as many clues. As I have written elsewhere, the events she describes are dramatic enough to survive her own interpretation of them. Who was the heinous Mr H— who she describes as 'a Libertine half mad and half fool'? Were he to be identified then surely many details in her story would fall into place. As she was a bit of a snob she could not resist the temptation to drop a name here or there — Lord Harris, the Duke of Wellington, Mr Pitt, 'this vixen of a Queen [Caroline]' — or even a posh address. It was with respect to the latter that she let her mask slip a little. She mentions Peterborough House in Fulham as the scene of her confinement. I went to the local archives and discovered that the building, long demolished, had been the residence of Charles Mordaunt, Earl of Peterborough, and was reputed to be 'the haunt of Pope and all the wits of his day', a list that also included Addison, Swift, Locke and Bolingbroke. In April 1782, Peterborough House was sold to a wealthy timber merchant named Richard Heaviside, a name that was hard for me not to pounce on with some glee. She had given details of her earlier rape by him, at 5 Palace Yard, and of how even the servants had been in collusion with him: '… they had been employed to burn my torn and soiled cloaths and to get the blood out of the carpet.' I was to discover in the business directory of the time, yet again, 'Richard Heaviside, *timber merchant*, Palace Yard, Westminster'. So now I had him at two separate addresses, at different times. This was not enough to satisfy me. A story that was true in the main had also to be true in the small details, and gradually, over the months, I was able to identify almost all the people she names, subsidiary figures too, although I missed out on at least one whose identity will startle readers of this book. Who was that emissary of Mr H — who, by the time Charlotte recounts her story, had become a great man, 'a favourite with the King' and who brought her out of her self-imposed Welsh exile? I will not spoil the game. What the authors here have also achieved is to have brought together hitherto disparate characters into a tightly-woven community, with the usual intermingling of the good and the bad, and with most of them bearing the secrets everybody else knows.

I ended up with a coherent picture in which everyone, or *nearly* everyone, was identifiable. Such doubters as there were, were now silenced. I had only one problem to solve, which would prove to be the most difficult of all: who was Charlotte B—? I checked with the Bristol Record Office to see who lived at 7 Pritchard Street, which is where, on the writing desk given to her by Princess Elizabeth, kindly note, she wrote her testament. I was given a Mrs Rachel Biggs and not a Charlotte. It was only after a friend of mine turned up a Will in the name of Rachel *Charlotte* Williams Biggs that I fell upon my Charlotte, one Charlotte in an age of Charlottes. It was not absolute proof, of course, but enough to lead me to a series of letters in the British Library, from a Mrs R.C. Biggs to William Windham, a leading statesman and Secretary at War under William Pitt. (What endears me to him is that he would meet his end after sustaining injuries while attempting to rescue valuable books, not his own, from a burning house.) I had only one aim in mind and that was to discover whether the hand in those letters matched the one in mine. A single glance was enough.

The story might have stopped there. As I read through those letters I was intrigued to discover a wholly new facet to her character. She writes to Windham in the manner of a bluestocking, acutely aware of the issues, political and economic, of the day: 'The character of a female author, or female politician is not in my opinion calculated to create favourable impressions,' she writes, 'and it is certain that the situations I have been placed in, and the circumstances of the times only, could have tempted me to engage in pursuits of so unfeminine a nature.' Suddenly I was up against a not so familiar figure. She was not quite as helpless as I first believed. As the authors of this book demonstrate, she was, on the contrary, a skilled manipulator though not in the negative sense the word implies. Contained in the letters to Windham were pointers to what was to be another extraordinary chapter in her life. I was led to the figure of a man who had been dubbed 'a dull dog' and 'a feeble scarabaecide', John Gifford who, poor man, as editor for a London publishing firm, prepared Charlotte's anonymously-written book *A Residence in France, during the years 1792, 1793, 1794, and 1795* (Longman,

1797). Anyone with a mind for historical chronology should perk up at the dates. Charlotte, either accident-prone or merely whisked along by fate, had escaped the clutches of a firebrand only to be caught up by a whole country in flames. The authors of this book take that story to a degree I could not have imagined at the time, and so, too, they produce another surprise – they identify 'the trash' she mentions having written in her letter to Ochterlony, and which I had sought in vain because I had been looking in all the wrong places. And then they reveal much more on that rogue whose name is the very stuff of Restoration comedy.

There is yet another discovery to be made, or at least one among many, for it would be a shame if this were to be the last word on Charlotte. Maybe this book will bring out of the woodwork what I and the authors here most crave, a physical portrait of Charlotte. There has got to be one somewhere. She was too vain not to have been painted more than once. She enclosed with the manuscript to Ochterlony a miniature of herself made by a female artist living in Bristol. 'You will find, dear General,' she writes, 'that time which adds new verdure to the Laurel is fatal to the bloom of the Rose, and that while you have been gathering immortal wreaths for *your* brow, every charm has faded away from *mine*.' And later she writes, 'It will therefore (I repeat) be very pleasing to me to know you possess an object which may remind you of me when I am not more, and if as Gray says "even in our Ashes live their wonted fires" my spirit will be soothed should it be conscious that I am not entirely forgotten.' Where is that miniature? Maybe, though, it is for the reader to supply his or her own image. Maybe that is part of Charlotte's allure.

Marius Kociejowski, 2017

*Chapter One*

# Love, Loss and Abduction

### Bristol, 1820s

The eminently respectable Mrs Rachel Charlotte Williams Biggs would not have been suspected in the slightest by her neighbours in Bristol of being anything at all out of the ordinary. She lived a quiet life, often journeying to mainland Europe during the winter months in search of warmer weather before returning to spend the summer months in England. Behind the closed doors of her modest terraced home, however, it was a different matter. Few would guess at the life Charlotte (as she preferred to be known) had lived, and indeed continued to live even in her sixth decade. Now, as she sat at her writing desk – a present from Princess Elizabeth, third daughter of King George III – she was unburdening herself of her secrets to a man who she had once loved with all her heart. Charlotte spilled out her past life onto the writing paper in front of her; it was a letter destined to travel halfway around the world to an exotic destination far removed from the provincial constraints of Charlotte's Bristol home. It is from this one-sided conversation that the sad story of Charlotte's misfortunes as a young woman emerges, a drama shrouded in mystery in which she took centre stage in a role worthy of the tragic heroine of a Samuel Richardson novel.

### India, 1820s

In vibrant Mughal India, General Sir David Ochterlony of the East India Company's (EIC) army, comfortably dressed for the climate in a richly-decorated *choga* and *pagri* (long robe and turban), found a little peace and seclusion from his harem of thirteen wives. He reclined his tall frame among the cushions of his *diwan*, smoking his hookah while servants holding peacock feather *pankhas* (fans) stood behind to cool him from the heat of the day and picked up Charlotte's letter to discover the startling fate to which his youthful love had fallen prey when he had sailed away from England's shores more than four decades earlier. Ochterlony, gone native in India to the despair of the EIC, was on the verge of retirement and thinking of abandoning India and his many Muslim wives with whom he promenaded every evening atop a procession of elephants. Did Charlotte hope that he would return to wrap her, in her dotage, in his arms and give her the future she had once hoped for, a life destined to be lived out by his side?

Charlotte's pen transported her back to her formative years in Lambeth, when all her hopes and dreams for the future had still been intact.

## Lambeth, 1770s

Lambeth, on the southern shoreline of the River Thames, was, in the latter half of the eighteenth century, a thriving and bustling place. Close to the foreshore, along the pathway known as Narrow Wall, houses nestled alongside the timber yards, potteries, refinery businesses and Eleanor Coade's artificial stone factory. Various public landing places and watermen's stairs dotted the riverbank to be used at high tide to access the river craft. At the rear of Narrow Wall was Cuper's Gardens, also known as Cupid's Gardens and once a pleasure ground with a reputation for an 'erotic ambience'; its immoral reputation led to it falling into disrepair and the gardens closed in 1760, lying derelict until the land was used to build houses and a vinegar and wine distillery. To the south lay marshland and fields; to the north, across the river via Westminster Bridge, were the Houses of Parliament and an emergent metropolis.

The Williams family lived in Cuper's Gardens. Headed by John Williams and his wife Mary, the family had relocated from south Wales where, in the early 1760s, Charlotte had been born, either in or around the ancient town of Caerleon in Gwent. Charlotte received a convent education in France and spoke fluent French; she could almost pass for a native of the country and retained a lifelong affinity for all things Gallic but Lambeth was her home. It was while living there that she met a young man barely out of boyhood named David Ochterlony. He was destined for great things, not least among them the honour of being the love of Charlotte's life.[1]

When she first met the tall and good-looking young Master Ochterlony, Charlotte was about 15 years old with little more to commend her to her suitor than a pretty face and a good education, but she had a zest for life and a sophistication that was lacking in other girls. She had arrived back in Lambeth after her convent education with French mannerisms and a few of the latest Parisian fashions. Her family was not rich and John Williams had no great wealth with which to help his daughter but the late eighteenth century was a time of opportunity when men could make fortunes and climb the social ladder. Everything was to play for and the future looked bright, especially one lived by David Ochterlony's side as he followed his adventurous spirit and wanderlust.

David Ochterlony was already well-travelled. He was of dual Scottish and American heritage and had been born in Boston, Massachusetts. His widowed mother fled first to Canada and then to England with her children at the commencement of the American Revolution and since then his life had been split between his grandfather's ancestral estate in the Scottish Highlands and his stepfather Sir Isaac Heard's home in the City of London.[2]

How serious was Charlotte's relationship with David? Charlotte later mentioned an 'error' into which youthful passion had led the young couple. She also let slip that there had been a time when she had not viewed Ochterlony's actions towards her in as honourable a way as she did in her later life. Certainly, whatever the youthful 'error' had been, Charlotte was still naïve, innocent of the world and the ways of men; she had not let temptation overtake her entirely. Young as she was, Charlotte knew that her reputation was everything and she was already risking this with a clandestine courtship.[3]

In the end, it all came to nothing. David was keen to see something of the world and rejected a career by the side of his stepfather at the College of Arms in favour of one of adventure and travel in India; armed with a letter of introduction from his father's old friend Lauchlin Macleane (a doctor, political agent and a man with business interests in India), David set sail aboard the *Lord North* East Indiaman in search of employment and leaving England – and Charlotte – perhaps forever. Whatever promises he made to Charlotte, she understood that she would get no word of him for many months and so she settled down in her Lambeth home, prepared for a long wait to hear from her love again but pinning all her hopes on him not forgetting her. Was she hoping that he would send for her to follow him to India? David, more practical than Charlotte, understood better than she the need for an income before marriage could be considered. Knowing that Charlotte had no dowry to bring to a marriage and that he would not be in any position to maintain a wife and household for some years, he probably left the shores of England with little to no anticipation of a future together with Charlotte, much to her chagrin. In turning down an opportunity of remaining in London with Charlotte, he firmly turned his back on her too. Once in India, David eagerly sampled the delights that the country offered to a young man and within days of his arrival, while at a nautch dance, his pocket was picked. Along with his money he lost Macleane's letter, but all might still have been saved except for the unfortunate fact that, in the meantime, Macleane had been returning to England from India on board a ship that had been lost at sea, and he along with it. With his options drastically curtailed, Ochterlony travelled to Bengal where he joined the EIC's armed forces.[4]

In David's absence, the young and pretty Charlotte was not without male admirers. Most ardent among them was the braggart son of a wealthy Lambeth timber merchant, Richard Heaviside. He was around a decade older than Charlotte and one of a 'fast set' who congregated in lively Covent Garden. Amid the market stalls noisily selling their wares, the crowded precincts of the piazza contained plentiful taverns and coffee shops, hemmed in at either end by the two main London theatres. In the evening, the area came alive with a different clientele when fashionable visitors to the theatre rubbed shoulders with prostitutes and pimps. Here, Heaviside and his cronies enjoyed the sights and sounds of London's seedy underbelly as they paid court to the actresses, to the well-dressed and fashionable courtesans and patronized the whores who plied their trade in the area once night had fallen. For Heaviside, however, his attention was also diverted closer to home. He entertained an almost frantic passion for poor Charlotte; one that would lead to her downfall and destroy all her youthful hopes.[5]

Richard Heaviside's family was originally from Bishop Auckland in County Durham in the north of England. Heaviside's father, also named Richard, had moved south to begin an industrious and successful career as a timber merchant. His timber yard, which he ran in partnership with James Morris Esquire, Master Carpenter to his Majesty's Ordnance, was in the part of Lambeth known as Stangate and he also rented premises across Westminster Bridge in Parliament Street (a side road running along the Palace of Whitehall and leading to the Palace of Westminster), where he kept lodgings and his counting-house. His home, however, was on the street along the Lambeth foreshore known as Narrow Wall and the family were close neighbours of the Williamses. Heaviside senior lived with his mistress – and nominal housekeeper – Sarah Prudden who was mother to his namesake son. By a previous relationship, Heaviside also had an older daughter, Elizabeth.[6]

The younger Richard Heaviside plays a major part in Charlotte's story, resolutely cast as the villain of the piece. It is interesting to speculate how his childhood may have influenced the man he became. His father was wealthy and financially secure but still 'trade' and certainly not classed as a gentleman. As a young man, Richard was apprenticed to his father's timber business although, as he was not of legitimate birth, this had to be an informal rather than a formal arrangement, but he stood to inherit his father's share of the business together with his share in the leases of houses he had built in Lambeth. For all their prosperity, what the Heaviside family lacked was respectability. The younger Richard Heaviside planned to use his fortune to join the upper classes and live life as a gentleman but he was tainted with the self-knowledge that his real origins were as the illegitimate son of two parents who were 'trade'. One gets the impression from Richard's later story that he did indeed feel a stigma attached to his childhood and went through life with something of a chip on his shoulder.

In the last month of 1775, Richard Heaviside senior died. His will (undated but probably written some years earlier) left the bulk of his fortune and his share in the timber yard to his namesake son with a generous bequest to the woman who had lived with him for so many years, Sarah Prudden. Richard, still a young man, now had the means to launch himself into London society as a gentleman and to bury both his illegitimacy and his working-class roots. He also had the money to enjoy London life to the full. It was a licentious and debauched age, and he was determined to partake of it.[7]

Growing into an attractive young woman, Charlotte caught the eye of Richard Heaviside who, despite an age gap of some ten or twelve years between them, became besotted with her. He had tried to induce her to accept a trinket as a token of his love for her and she had refused, having no fondness for the preening, overbearing man that Heaviside had become. With disdainful haughtiness she looked down on Heaviside and chose to remain true to the memory of the man she hoped would write from India to claim her for his own. However, Charlotte's unobtainability only heightened her desirability and Heaviside's need to possess her.

Eighteen months had passed since David Ochterlony had sailed for India and Charlotte knew that if he had written to her that letter would by now have reached England. She needed to check the newspaper lists of ships recently docked that may have carried post from India but she had no one to ask for help in this task. Her mother was ill, and perhaps this was why Charlotte could take advantage of a little more freedom than would normally be granted to girls of her station. Indeed, in her relationship with Ochterlony she already seems to have taken advantage of such a situation, independently pursuing her own agenda. Charlotte approached Mrs Green, the wife of another Lambeth timber merchant. Mrs Green agreed to help; she told Charlotte that her husband had a friend who kept a file of the *Morning Post* newspapers and promised to take Charlotte to view them.[8]

The trusting and unsuspecting Charlotte agreed to this plan and, dressed demurely in a white gown, she went to the Greens' timber yard on the appointed day and allowed Mrs Green to lead her over the bridge across the Thames to Westminster. Mrs Green enjoyed Charlotte's company and she distracted her attention to the nearby shops, pointing out goods in their windows. Charlotte was impatient to be taken to look through the newspapers as promised but she did not object and by the time they reached their destination it was late in the day and the light was beginning to fade.

Mrs Green led Charlotte to 5 New Palace Yard in Westminster, close to the Houses of Parliament and directly across the River Thames from Lambeth via Westminster Bridge. Opposite their destination stood the north entrance to Westminster Hall and a couple of houses further down was the King's Arms Tavern. The door to the house was opened by a boy who told them that the unnamed owner of the house was away from home but that they were expected and to go upstairs. Mrs Green ushered Charlotte into an elegant and newly-furnished drawing room where a pile of the *Morning Post* newspapers sat upon a table in anticipation of their visit. Charlotte was soon engrossed in the papers, searching through them for mention of any ship that may have brought her a letter from India and hardly noticed Mrs Green leave; the older woman directed the boy to serve Charlotte some coffee and then left, saying she had a list of errands to fulfil at the haberdashers on nearby Bridge Street, located to the rear of New Palace Yard.

The coffee was set down beside her and as she sipped it Charlotte paused in her search to flick through some books on the table. Written inside one she noticed a name she recognized: Richard Heaviside! The name struck horror into Charlotte but she was in 5 New Palace Yard and she knew that Heaviside did not have rooms there. He had lodgings at Parliament Street, not far away from New Palace Yard admittedly but distant enough for her not to fear for her safety. Still, she glanced around the room, taking stock of her surroundings for the first time and, with a sinking heart, noticed that the trinket she had refused to accept the day before was placed upon the mantelpiece.

The room spun as Charlotte began to feel heavy and before she had time to collect her thoughts Richard Heaviside strode into the drawing room. Letting out a piercing scream, Charlotte ran for the door but she stumbled. She did not know it at the time but her coffee had been drugged with laudanum. Heaviside had known that she was coming, had contrived to separate her from her friends and had planned to render her vulnerable and alone in his rooms, dependent on his mercy. As Charlotte fell to the drawing room floor, she hit her head and her nose began to bleed violently. Perhaps mercifully she lost consciousness as Heaviside proved what a monster he truly was: he took full advantage of her, raping her while she was powerless to resist.

This was a girl who was a neighbour, a girl who knew and was fond of Heaviside's own mother. His passions must have been strong indeed to force him to enact such horrors on the defenceless Charlotte. Did he not care about his public reputation, should any of this become known? It seems strange that he would risk all and he must have known that he stood a grave chance of being discovered but he wanted Charlotte and she had rebuffed his advances; he was determined to make her his, one way or another. She later described Heaviside as being, prior to this attack, her 'ridicule and aversion'. The daughter of a gentleman, albeit an impoverished one, had Charlotte made fun of the jumped-up tradesman's son for wanting to pass himself off as well-to-do? Heaviside's rationale, if such it could be called, was that by ruining Charlotte he believed that he could then persuade her to stay with him as his mistress and, in this way, could mitigate the ill opinions that others would have of his deed. After all, his parents had enjoyed a very similar union.

It was some hours before Charlotte regained consciousness. Bruised, with a swollen head and a sprained ankle, she still had on her white dress, only now it was torn and covered in blood. She allowed herself to be put to bed by a female servant.

For three days Charlotte stayed in bed, concussed and not fully aware of her surroundings. In lucid moments she begged the servant to help her get home but her pleas fell on deaf ears for the servant dare not naysay her master. Heaviside, now fearful of the consequences, had not approached her until – finally – he sent word that he would return her to her father if she could leave her bed and be dressed. With the help of a servant, Charlotte quickly dressed and was helped down the stairs and into a waiting carriage.

Once again, she had been lied to. As the carriage pulled away it did not cross the river to Lambeth but instead turned in the opposite direction and travelled past St James's Park until it reached its destination: a house in St James's Place that Charlotte did not recognize. Here, though, at least Heaviside ensured that she was cared for by nurses and medical attendants. It was some days before Charlotte dared to tell the physician what had happened but this had no effect other than his instant dismissal.

With Charlotte unyielding to his advances, Heaviside – desperately trying to repair the situation – came to her room and begged forgiveness, deploring his violence. He offered to make amends but Charlotte refused to agree to his terms; Heaviside, totally irrational in his desperation, swung between acting like a madman and appearing truly penitent. Finally, he asked the worn-out Charlotte to take an oath to conceal what had happened and threatened to shoot himself otherwise. Charlotte had an escape plan forming in her head so she played for time and said that if she could have some books, needlework and threads, she would consider it. Once she had these implements she cut out letters from the books and sewed them together to create a message which she gave to the visiting apothecary, Mr Saunders of nearby St James's Street. Luckily for Charlotte, Mr Saunders was to be trusted. The letter was addressed to Mr Mark Beaufoy, a Lambeth neighbour of the Williams family and their landlord, and Mr Saunders went directly to him with Charlotte's letter.

The Beaufoys were a Quaker family headed by the elderly Mark Beaufoy and, like the Williams and Heaviside families, recent settlers into Lambeth. They acquired the lease of the derelict Cuper's Gardens pleasure grounds and began to put them to a more practical use. One of the leading industrialists of the day, Mark Beaufoy established a vinegar and 'mimicked wines' distillery with great success. Mark and his wife Elizabeth lived in one of several houses they owned in Cuper's Gardens and another was let to the Williamses. The relationship between the two families was one of trust and respect.[9]

However, it was not Mark Beaufoy who came to rescue Charlotte but a young gentleman from Putney named Benjamin Hunt Biggs. Alerted by Mark Beaufoy and Charlotte's family, he sent his carriage and housekeeper to St James's Place to collect her. From this time forward, Mr Biggs was to play a prominent role in Charlotte's life.

Charlotte returned home to her parents, wearing new clothes but deathly pale and as thin as a skeleton. Her father was shocked to see the state of his daughter and immediately ran to Heaviside, challenging him to a duel. John Williams met with Richard Heaviside for this purpose the next day, fired his pistol at the man who had abused his daughter but failed to hit him. Heaviside, conscience-stricken and certainly reluctant to compound the problem he faced, escaped without returning fire. This very act demonstrated his guilt; a gentleman who felt himself wrongly accused would not have cast away his honour and run.

*Chapter Two*

# Freemasonry, Theatres and Friends in High Places

Although this is Charlotte's story, we must take a closer look at Richard Heaviside. We have accused him of a heinous crime with just Charlotte's word to rely on and so, out of justice to him and to try to better understand both the man and his actions, we need to delve into the world he inhabited. A few well-known names also require an introduction into our tale, especially two men who lived cheek-by-jowl with Richard Heaviside and who were counted by him as friends: the architect John Nash (later the favourite of King George IV), and the playwright, actor and future politician Richard Brinsley Sheridan.

The Nash family was, like the Williamses, originally from south Wales (from Neath in Glamorganshire) and owned one of the mills that punctuated the Lambeth riverbank amid the timber yards and manufactories. They were kin to another Welsh family, the Edwards, who owned Belvedere House which abutted Cuper's Gardens. John Nash was born in Lambeth around 1752 so was a similar age to Richard Heaviside and the two boys grew up together, both emerging from the rough and tumble of their childhood among the timber yards to transform themselves into well-to-do young gentlemen. Nash was to later describe himself as a 'wild, irregular youth' and it is not hard to imagine that this description would also fit Richard Heaviside very well. The two were partners in crime. Charlotte also knew John Nash and he must have been only too aware of his dissolute friend's infatuation with their pretty young neighbour.[1]

While Nash was the companion of Heaviside's boyhood, Richard Brinsley Sheridan was an acquaintance made when he was a young man, enjoying the attractions of Covent Garden. Sheridan was living in Covent Garden at the time of his marriage in 1773 to Elizabeth Ann Linley at Marylebone in Westminster.

This was a second marriage to the same lady. The first had been contracted in France a year earlier and conducted by a Roman Catholic priest after Elizabeth had taken refuge in a convent there. Back in London Sheridan fought – and won – a duel at the Castle Tavern in Henrietta Street, Covent Garden with Captain Matthews, who Elizabeth had been fleeing when she left England to enter the convent; Matthews had called Sheridan both a liar and a scoundrel in print. (A second duel was fought later that year at Bath after Matthews refused to accept his original defeat and Sheridan was seriously wounded.)

Surely Sheridan knew Heaviside's older sister Elizabeth, who was living on Henrietta Street a year later when she married Samuel Hill who supplemented his income as a vintner with a job as a 'numberer' at the Covent Garden Theatre where Sheridan's first play would be performed? A numberer was tasked with counting the audience in the theatre (as a check against the money received at the door and the honesty of the doorkeepers), and it is entirely possible that Elizabeth appeared on the stage in some capacity. Richard Heaviside also frequented the theatre and paid court to the actresses in the 'green rooms', probably in company with his roguish friend, John Nash. It was a tight-knit clique; maybe, to Charlotte, these swaggering bucks had offered a peek into an adult world that offered excitement, glamour and just a little danger, one far removed from her modest Lambeth home. However, Heaviside's tyranny brought her face-to-face with the ugly reality of the situation.[2]

Even before his father's death, Richard Heaviside played the part of the gentleman-about-town. He had been proposed as a member of the Freemasons, probably by the surgeon Bartholomew Ruspini, a prominent member of that secretive society who was to remain a friend and something of a mentor for several years to come. Heaviside was initiated into the St Alban's Lodge which met at the Thatched House Tavern in St James's Street, Westminster where Ruspini was already a member. From the first documented case of a Freemason in England just over 100 years prior to this, the society was gaining in prominence in the mid-eighteenth century, helped by the current fashion for gentleman's clubs and societies in London at that time. To be proposed and accepted as a Freemason, Heaviside must have been recognized as more than merely a crude timber merchant's son from the Lambeth foreshore and already be established as a respected and respectable gentleman. A year later the Reverend William Dodd, known as the 'Macaroni Preacher' because of his flamboyant clothes, was also initiated into the St Alban's Lodge. Dodd was a vain but popular man, a social climber eager to seek out preferment and always living beyond his means, a failing that had already resulted in a stay in a debtors' prison.[3]

Like John Nash, Richard Heaviside was a 'wild, irregular youth'. On 7 June 1776, he baptized a daughter named Charlotte at the 'actors' church' in Covent Garden where his nephew John William Hill, the son of his sister Elizabeth, had been baptized just months earlier. The mother of this babe was named Sarah and she passed for Heaviside's wife. Heaviside had recently come into his majority and was already exhibiting something of the dual personality that would plague his coming years. He was cavorting with the theatre folk around Covent Garden and siring illegitimate children while at the same time moving among a more artistic and intellectual set through his involvement with the Freemasons. Was he the debauched rake or a refined and upstanding gentleman? With almost effortless ease, he moved from one persona to the other.

Covent Garden was notorious for prostitution, with two-thirds of London's 'bawdy houses' situated in the locale. Gradually both the original open-air fruit and vegetable market and the surrounding area fell into disrepute and, as the gentry moved away from the area, rakes, wits and playwrights moved in. During the latter half of the eighteenth century, *Harris's List of Covent-Garden Ladies (or a Man of Pleasure's Kalendar)* was published annually at the end of the year, containing 'an exact Description of the most celebrated Ladies of Pleasure who frequent Covent-garden and other Parts of this Metropolis'. Essentially it was a trade directory of the whores and courtesans to be found in London, its purpose to 'guide the desirous to the desirable' but, thanks to the editor Sam Derrick's wicked pen, it was also a 'witty chronicle of the Piazza's women…their exploits, assessments of their personalities and retellings of inside jokes, all intended to raise a laugh from Covent Garden's circle of rakes'. Alongside the ladies of pleasure, the actors and actresses who were the stars of the day appeared on the boards of the London stages nightly, luminaries such as Mary Robinson who would go on to captivate royalty, making her name as the young Prince of Wales's mistress and the actress and courtesan Sophia Baddeley together with her estranged husband Robert. Heaviside was not the only young man to have sprung from the timber yards to pay court to the actresses; it is debateable though as to whether he would have received more or less of a warm reception from Mrs Baddeley and her friend Elizabeth Steele than did a neighbouring merchant:[4]

[Sophia] was addressed by Mr. Smith, a timber-merchant, near Westminster-bridge, and could not get rid of him, without consenting to his waiting on us, in Grafton-street. He was a fashionable young man, who was frequently with us afterwards, and made strong love to Mrs. Baddeley; but, she returned it with little more than common civility.[5]

This was Richard Heaviside's world. No doubt he was one of the rakes who owned a copy of *Harris's List*, dallied with some of the girls named within and loitered in the theatre green rooms. In the same year that Heaviside's daughter was born and baptized, Sheridan, together with his father-in-law Thomas Linley and one other partner, bought a half-interest in the Drury Lane Theatre in Covent Garden when the owner David Garrick retired.[6]

On 10 June 1776, just three days after little Charlotte Heaviside's baptism, a bond was passed under the hands and seal of Simon Goodman Ewart of Crutched Friars, Esquire and Richard Brinsley Sheridan of Orchard Street, Portman Square, Esquire, by which they, their heirs, executors and administrators became bound to Richard Heaviside of Parliament Street, Esquire, for £1,400 or a yearly annuity of £100 for the life of them, in consideration of £700 paid by Richard Heaviside. It is likely that this £700 formed a small part of the capital raised by Richard Brinsley Sheridan to purchase the interest in the theatre. Heaviside drove a hard bargain, even when he was dealing with friends.[7]

Early in 1777 Bartholomew Ruspini founded a new Freemasons lodge named The Nine Muses which had a leaning towards the arts and charitable projects. He took at least two of the brethren from the St Alban's Lodge with him: the Reverend William Dodd and Richard Heaviside. This new lodge met at the same public house as that used by the St Alban's Lodge, the Thatched House Tavern in St James's Street. Did Heaviside, when he attended later meetings there, think of Charlotte who had been held captive in the house on St James's Place, just off the street where the Thatched House Tavern was located? Heaviside's initiation into The Nine Muses took place on 14 January of that year, meaning that, although he was not described as one of the founders of the society, he was most certainly an integral part of The Nine Muses lodge from the very beginning; further proof, if it is needed, of the esteem and regard in which Ruspini held him.

Dodd was not destined to be part of this new lodge for more than a few weeks and left under a cloud. Increasing levels of debt led to him forging the signature of the Earl of Chesterfield, his former pupil, on a bond for £4,200. Even though he paid back the money once he had been discovered, he found himself in the dock of the Old Bailey in February 1777, standing trial for forgery which was a capital offence. He was found guilty and despite many appeals for clemency from the public, with whom he was popular, including a petition with some 23,000 names on it (undoubtedly one of them Richard Heaviside's), Dodd was taken to the gallows at Tyburn on a rainy June morning and hanged:

> Yesterday, were executed at Tyburn the Rev. Dr. Dodd, for forgery and Joseph Harris, for a highway robbery. At nine o'clock the mournful Procession began from Newgate – First, the Marshalmen and constables – next the sheriffs in their carriages and the deputy sheriff on horseback – then a cart lined with black, in which was Harris – after which followed Dr. Dodd in a mourning coach, attended by the Rev. Mr. Villette, Ordinary of Newgate, the Rev. Mr. Dobie, of the Magdalen and a sheriff's officer.
>
> About half past ten they reached the place of execution: Harris being tied up, the coach in which was the Doctor, drew near, when he, with the clergymen, came out and walked to the steps which were set for them to ascend the cart by; the Doctor was now tied up, and after praying very fervently about twenty minutes, during which he spoke several times to his fellow-sufferer, his cap was put on, and the executioner, which was unusual, tied his hands together with a cord, besides that about his arms, and he was thereon launched into eternity… Just as he was turned off there was a universal silence; tears flowed from many eyes, but from one quarter there was almost instantly a general groan. He appeared not to suffer much in dying, though it was near two minutes before all motion ceased.
>
> Thus, perished all that was mortal of William Dodd, Doctor of Laws, heretofore Prebend of Brecon and Chaplain in Ordinary to his Majesty.
>
> After hanging an hour, their Bodies were cut down and delivered to their respective Friends.[8]

Dodd's body was rushed to an undertaker's house in Goodge Street where the surgeon John Hunter – a founder member of the Humane Society (later the Royal Humane Society) – and three other medical men were waiting. The year before his death Dodd had made a sizeable and somewhat presentiment donation to the society and now Hunter intended to repay his generosity; he believed it was possible to bring someone back to life and had conducted experiments – mainly on animals – with varying degrees of success. The four men eagerly awaited the arrival of Dodd's body but their plans were thwarted as it took longer than anticipated to deliver Dodd's corpse thanks to the huge crowd that had gathered to witness his execution. Hunter and his cohorts nevertheless tried for two hours to bring Dodd back to life before finally admitting defeat.

Whether or not he was aware of the plan to bring Dodd back to life, there can be no doubt that Richard Heaviside was affected by the sad and awful end of a friend and was struck by the way in which a reputation could be quickly ruined and a promising career ended in the degrading public spectacle of being hung as a common criminal. Although oblivious to it at the time, this was a situation he would have real cause to dread for himself in the very near future following his abduction and rape of Charlotte. Of more pressing concern to him at that time though was his own personal suffering. Heaviside's daughter, baptised in 1776, died at just over 1 year of age and was buried on 22 October 1777 in the churchyard at St Martin-in-the-Fields, Westminster. There is no further mention of her mother.

Charlotte, once back home, learned how her abduction had been accomplished and who she had to blame for her misfortune. Heaviside had paid Mrs Green fifty guineas and gifted her a watch to bring Charlotte to his room and leave her there. Mrs Green insisted that she had no idea that he would defile her (although when she was on her deathbed some years later she sent for Charlotte to beg her forgiveness, suggesting that she was indeed all too complicit in Heaviside's scheme). After making her purchases at the haberdashery, Mrs Green had returned to Heaviside's drawing room only to be told that Charlotte had left, but when John Williams sent to her to ask the whereabouts of his missing daughter she claimed that she didn't know, glibly lying that Charlotte had left her in the street. Mrs Green could have directed the search to Heaviside's very doorstep but she concealed her involvement in the plot and left Charlotte to her fate.

Heaviside did live in Parliament Street, as Charlotte had known, but was in the process of moving to New Palace Yard, hence the drawing room being newly-furnished. To one side of 5 New Palace Yard lived Mr Molineaux, MP for King's Lynn, but he only used this property when he was sitting in the House and it was almost always empty without even a servant in it. Next to Mr Molineaux's was a courtyard leading into Bridge Street, on the other side of No. 5 was an empty house and then the King's Arms Tavern. Opposite stood Westminster Hall. The situation was almost perfect for Heaviside's scheme with no immediate neighbours to hear any disturbance above the hubbub of the tavern. Almost but not quite perfect, as two boys at a pastry cook's on Bridge Street at the rear of Heaviside's house alerted their master to dreadful cries that they heard coming from the property and a coachman waiting for a fare at the hackney stand opposite the house had also heard Charlotte's screams. He had knocked at the door twice to ask if all was well and the second time had been told by the boy who answered it that a young woman inside was 'in fitts'. Aside from the kindly female servant, who was absolved of any blame, the only servants in the employ of Heaviside were the boy who had answered the door, a man and a deaf woman and all these were quickly sent away from the house, the boy and deaf woman subsequently sent into Wales to get them clear away.

It is interesting to note that Heaviside's two servants were sent, of all places, to Wales to get them out of the way. Heaviside had no connection with Wales other than through his friend John Nash. Was Nash instrumental in sending the servants to Wales, one wonders, and if so, was he aware of Charlotte's presence in his friend's rooms? Or could he have been the one who discovered the two servants and brought them back to verify Charlotte's story? For discovered they were and they confessed that they had been ordered to burn Charlotte's torn, bloodstained clothes and had cleaned the blood from the carpet. They had even been responsible for buying the laudanum and Charlotte found that she had accidentally been given a much larger dose than she should have, hence her insensibility in the ensuing days. Her medical attendants were found and questioned, as were the owners of the house in St James's Place and the female servant verified Charlotte's accusation of rape against Heaviside.

Mark Beaufoy was taking sensible steps to bring Heaviside to justice and approached a lawyer. A charge of rape, if proved, was a capital offence and Heaviside knew that if convicted he would end his life swinging on a rope at Tyburn. It was only two years since his friend the Reverend William Dodd had received his punishment on the gallows. Heaviside was now facing a similar penalty and he was afraid. The barrister and MP John Dunning, Baron Ashburton, had been engaged by Mark Beaufoy to try the case. Beaufoy was aiming high for Dunning had been involved in many famous cases, notably successfully prosecuting the bigamous Duchess of Kingston and a representative in the *Douglas Cause or Case*.[9]

Faced with a trial in a court of law Heaviside fled, aiming to get across the Channel to France and safety, but a warrant for his arrest had been issued and Mr Dunning declared that nothing could now save his life. Then Heaviside's mother, Sarah Prudden, who still lived on Narrow Wall in Lambeth, begged Charlotte to save her son's life. Sarah – respectable, grey-haired and a woman Charlotte knew and liked – knelt before her.

Although she could not condone his actions, Richard Heaviside was still her son, her only child and Sarah wept at Charlotte's feet and pleaded with her to reconsider a trial that could lead her son to the gallows. Charlotte was already afraid of the humiliating ordeal that would lay bare her woes to a packed public courtroom and Benjamin Hunt Biggs and John Williams both began to doubt the wisdom of taking the matter further, fearing that the consequence to Charlotte's peace of mind would be worse than the satisfaction of seeing justice served. Now Sarah Prudden's anguish had to be taken into consideration too. Charlotte, as a woman, lacked a legal identity in her own right and it was her father who had to instigate proceedings. Success was not a foregone conclusion either given that Charlotte, although little more than a child, was legally over the age of consent and responsibility for guarding her chastity against a man's natural urges fell to her, in the eyes of the men who would judge her. She had voluntarily entered Heaviside's home and consented to be left alone there, even though she had not known of his presence. Against Beaufoy's better judgement, it was decided to abandon the criminal charge in favour of a civil action. Heaviside sent his attorney to say that he would not defend this and he offered to make financial reparation to Charlotte in lieu of the action, a route that would keep the matter private, but Mark Beaufoy insisted on a court hearing and persuaded the others to agree and so the day appointed approached.[10]

Charlotte was terrified and distraught. As the courtroom was a public place, the world at large would hear of her sufferings, would be free to gossip and her reputation would be sullied beyond rescue. Chastity was a woman's most important virtue. As things stood, only a handful of people knew what had happened and Charlotte much preferred to keep it that way. She begged her father, Mr Biggs and Mr Beaufoy to desist, but they refused to be swayed. Finally, with less than an hour to go before the commencement of the court proceedings, one of the leading lawyers of the day persuaded her father and Mr Biggs that, as Heaviside had offered to make any reparation that her family and friends might dictate, they would be blamed by both the lawyers and by the public for subjecting Charlotte to the horror of having to voice her accusations against him. At the last minute it was settled. Heaviside would grant an annuity on Charlotte as financial recompense, he gave his word of honour as a gentleman not to see her again and in return John Williams was bound over to keep the peace with Heaviside so long as he kept his side of the bargain.

Heaviside, for his part, claimed that he never meant to keep Charlotte a prisoner but did admit that he had intended to take advantage of her while she was alone with him in his drawing room. So sure was he that Charlotte would succumb to the lure of the luxury, finery and splendour with which he could surround her, he believed that once she had realized her reputation was lost she would willingly submit to stay with him as his mistress. He planned for her to live with him, to educate her and to exhibit her to his friends. As a man of around 30 years of age and establishing himself as a gentleman, it was part and parcel of his way of life to have a beautiful young mistress, or so Heaviside thought. Her dress and jewels would be proof not only of his affection for her but also a visible outward sign of his wealth.

In ambushing Charlotte and risking her reputation, Heaviside felt sure that she would forgive him when her reward was to share in his wealth. Was he aware of her romance with David Ochterlony? Perhaps he believed that Charlotte's relationship with Ochterlony had gone further than it had and he therefore assumed that she could be induced to give herself to him also? After all, Charlotte had been given the freedom of a form of intimacy with Ochterlony and perhaps this had led to gossip. It also suggests that Charlotte, while a gentleman's daughter, was not at that time used to such luxury as Heaviside could offer, leading to the suspicion that her father may have been severely impoverished at the time. Heaviside seems to have intended to have Charlotte while making no commitment to her.

While Heaviside planned to waylay Charlotte in his house, rape may not have been part of his initial scheme. The overdose of laudanum combined with the blow to her head had been unforeseen and it is possible that he had expected her to submit to him when she realized it was impossible to extricate herself from the situation in any other way. One of the statements Heaviside made in his defence was that 'he had ever found women were to be pacified & seduced when an evil was without remedy & had calculated on neither the moral nor the physical effects which had occurred.' He may have practised a similar deception, and possibly rape, on women before, leading to speculation about the relationship between himself and the mother of his short-lived infant daughter born a couple of years earlier.

The settlement comprised deeds that Charlotte was required to sign three years later when she 'came of age' and which gave her an annuity (one would presume a substantial one) in recompense for what she had suffered. Although glad to have been spared an ordeal in the courtroom, she still felt the remedy to the situation disgraceful and that the annuity signalled her acceptance of what had happened; that she had truly been seduced rather than raped.

Some months before his attack on Charlotte, Heaviside had been nominated by the Freemasons Lodge to which he belonged, The Nine Muses, for the position of grand steward. He never took up the role. To be grand steward was a high honour in the society and one that would not be disregarded easily. Was he unable to take up the position as he had temporarily left London to escape the consequences of his actions or was the position withdrawn when it appeared that he would stand in court accused of the rape of his young neighbour? Regardless, Heaviside did emerge from the affair with the greater part of his honour still intact and his abominable behaviour unknown to the world at large. Charlotte, by comparison, believed that by signing the deeds she had acknowledged herself as being in some way complicit and willing in her misfortunes.

Charlotte retired from the world, a ruined woman with her reputation in tatters, while Heaviside stepped forward confidently once again to retake his place in society. It was a man's world, as Charlotte was all too painfully learning.

*Chapter Three*

# Debauchery at Peterborough House

In Putney, further west along the southern side of the River Thames, lived the man who was to play a key role in Charlotte's life. Benjamin Hunt Biggs was the son of Benjamin Biggs, a carpenter/undertaker, and his wife Mary. The couple had four sons but only two survived infancy: Benjamin and his younger brother, Joseph. Biggs' carpentry business brought him and his family into contact with the Lambeth timber merchants and the Heaviside family.

Both Benjamin Biggs and Richard Heaviside senior took advantage of the increased need for housing in mid-eighteenth-century London and, utilizing their carpentry and timber backgrounds, each built and then sold or rented out streets of houses, becoming wealthy and prosperous in the process. By inheriting the good fortune of these endeavours, both Benjamin Hunt Biggs and Richard Heaviside junior, although the sons of working-class men who started their careers as apprentices to tradesmen, ended their days as gentlemen, afforded the right to add the appellation 'Esquire' after their names. However, in their younger days the idea of being a 'gentleman' was a long way off.

Benjamin Biggs senior, carpenter of Putney, died in December 1766. Interestingly, in his will he bequeathed a sum of money to a kinswoman named Mary Green, just possibly the same Mrs Green who conducted Charlotte to Heaviside's rooms. The widowed Mary Biggs was left to care for her two sons, Benjamin aged 10 and Joseph aged 7. When he was 14 years old her eldest son was apprenticed to Thomas Herne, Citizen and Wheelwright of London, living in Holborn two years later when both he and his mother, who was still in Putney, were among the subscribers to a religious pamphlet. Despite the inheritance due to him under his father's will, his mother and guardians initially intended for him to follow a trade. Similarly, Richard Heaviside was also noted in his father's will to be apprentice to his timber business, although this will may have been written up to ten years before his death. Both boys then, in the first half of the 1770s, were tradesmen's sons and were or had been apprenticed and were learning their own trade.[1]

By the time Benjamin Hunt Biggs reached the age of 21 his mother was also dead and he gained full control of the inheritance left to him from the wills of both his parents. As well as gaining a small fortune, he also had the right to claim rents from several properties in Putney built and previously owned by his father, as well as ownership of an estate in Hampshire. Both Benjamin Hunt Biggs and Richard Heaviside began their adult life with a healthy bank balance bequeathed them by their skilled tradesmen fathers and the right to style themselves as gentlemen.

Joseph Biggs was only 19 years of age and therefore still considered a 'minor'; he was not concerned with working for a living, instead leading the life of a gentleman of pleasure, encouraged by his friends. No longer was either brother bound to an apprenticeship and the background in trade was left far behind. Joseph, in imitation of Richard Heaviside, was friendly with the Drury Lane Theatre actors and the pleasure-seekers of Covent Garden. With Richard Heaviside's friendship with Sheridan and his sister living in Covent Garden, both he and the two Biggs brothers were moving in the same social circles.

Towards the end of August 1778, Joseph Biggs together with his maternal cousin Francis Hunt and three other gentlemen – Robert Carpenter, comedic actor at the Drury Lane Theatre, Mr Sutton, singer in the bass chorus at the same theatre and Mr Grovesmith – took a pleasure boat out on the Thames, heading towards the estuary. Carpenter was, at the time, lodging with Sutton at Little Russell Street, a slightly dingy and downmarket narrow alleyway off Drury Lane where many of the minor actors at the theatre had rooms. Mr Sutton was the husband of a dancer who performed at both Drury Lane and Sadler's Wells theatres, the daughter of the well-known dancing-master and choreographer Monsieur Jean Baptiste Le Maire Froment who had run a dancing school from his home at Carlisle House in Lambeth, close by Narrow Wall. Robert Carpenter had started out as a gentleman's servant but had been acting on the London stage for the past four years mainly playing the role of the clown and, like Sutton, singing in the bass chorus. Just three months earlier Carpenter had appeared on stage in *The Beggar's Opera* alongside the famed Sophia Baddeley and her estranged husband Robert. Sophia had played the lead role of Polly Peachum while Robert took the role of Filch, her loyal but squeamish servant, the performance a benefit one for himself and two other actors. A decade older than Joseph Biggs and his cousin Francis, Carpenter and his two friends were taking full advantage of the fat purses of a couple of easily-impressed youngsters who were dazzled at finding themselves in company with the actors they watched on stage.

Joseph Biggs was fond of sailing and had indulged himself in having a boat built to his own specifications. It was completed and ready for its maiden voyage. The August weather was pleasingly hot after what had been a very wet July and so Joseph contacted his friends and a short trip was planned, to be spent dawdling down the Thames towards the Isle of Sheppey on the Kent coast. On the afternoon of Saturday, 29 August they stocked the boat with all they would need and sailed down river with the tide to Erith which was as far as they could go that day. Erith was then a popular place to lay anchor, providing a small port on the riverside, and they feasted and drank well, having amply provisioned the boat. Joseph Biggs awoke early the next morning to take advantage of the tide. In darkness, befuddled from the previous evening's carousing and with the dawn still some time away, he weighed anchor at 3 o'clock with the help of the waterman and set sail, his four friends still fast asleep.[2]

Everything was quiet for an hour until the boat reached Purfleet a little further down the Thames. Anchored there alongside the Royal Gunpowder Magazine garrison was the *Janus* man-of-war, a large forty-four-gun Royal Navy warship. Sailing alone and in the dark, Joseph blundered and ran afoul of the ship. The noise woke the others from their slumber and they all leaped from their beds. Robert Carpenter saw a rope belonging to the *Janus* was tangled with the mast of their own boat and, thinking quickly, called out to a sailor on watch to throw down another rope to him. The sailor did so and Carpenter took tight hold of it, shouting to his friends to do the same. Events moved too rapidly for them, however, and before they could rally to Carpenter the boat filled with water. Heavily weighted with their provisions, the boat sank quickly and directly to the bottom of the Thames and the five men were plunged into the cold water. Carpenter still had hold of the rope and he pulled himself up it, one hand over another until his head was above the water. The rear quarterdeck of the *Janus* loomed above him as he clambered up the rope, crying out all the time for help. Looking down, he saw two of his friends afloat but being carried down river with the tide. It was still dark but he knew their heads were above water and he presumed they had hold of the rope and called out to them to 'hold fast' till help could arrive. A midshipman from the *Janus* hailed a passing brig which sent out its longboat and at the same time the captain, Bonovier Glover, came on deck and roused the crew to man their own longboat. This second longboat rescued Mr Sutton and Mr Grovesmith who were both found clinging to the end of the rope but Joseph Biggs and his cousin Francis Hunt were lost, presumed drowned.

The crew on board the *Janus* took the three shaken and sodden rescued men to their gun room and gave them a drink to calm their nerves before sending them ashore in the longboat to Purfleet. Once on land they begged and borrowed some dry clothes and set out to return home with their awful news.

In this tragic way, Joseph Biggs' young life ended. On 30 August 1778 the two cousins, their bodies recovered from the Thames, were buried together in one grave in Putney churchyard, both aged just 19. It was a sad end to two promising lives and Benjamin Hunt Biggs was left very much on his own as the only surviving member of his immediate family.

Robert Carpenter was socialising with a fast set of rakes. Some seven months after the boating tragedy he found himself invited to Peterborough House, a location that would come to have great significance to Charlotte.

Charles Mordaunt, 4th Earl of Peterborough, and his countess Robinaiana owned, as one of their many properties, Peterborough House in Parson's Green, Fulham. At that time Fulham was a pleasant village outside the bustle of London complete with farms and market gardens that supplied the capital with fruit and vegetables, and Parson's Green was a hamlet within the manor of Fulham. On the opposite side of the River Thames was Putney from where the Biggs family hailed, the two locales linked by the old Putney Bridge (a toll bridge, also known as Fulham Bridge).

In the middle of March 1779, a serving maid employed by the earl and countess ran away after claiming she had been raped at Peterborough House. The earl was in the habit of visiting the mansion with his courtesan, Miss Dawson, rather than with his wife and it appeared that the Covent Garden acting fraternity were sometimes in attendance too; the earl was keeping dubious company. The maid turned to the countess who in turn contacted the authorities and named Robert Carpenter as the man responsible. It was eleven days before the rape was reported and Carpenter, a frequent visitor to the earl's house, had supped there in the interim with no suspicion falling on him. However, he was duly arrested and charged with the rape and incarcerated in the Tothill Fields Bridewell to await his trial. He spent a fortnight in the cells before being released by Sir John Fielding, chief magistrate at Bow Street and the man in charge of the 'Bow Street Runners'. While locked up no one had appeared to make good the charge against him; the serving girl had completely disappeared and could not be found to give evidence and so it was decided that the charge was groundless. Nonetheless, it was widely reported that he had been accused of the crime.[3]

Charlotte was to make accusations of her own about a rape occurring at the same mansion just a few years later. It is often said that there is no smoke without fire, and subsequent events were to paint Peterborough House as a scene of total debauchery.

At the beginning of August 1779, the 4th Earl of Peterborough died. His only legitimate son succeeded to the title but based himself in one of the other residences held by the family and a year or two later Richard Heaviside moved into Peterborough House as a tenant of the Dowager Countess of Peterborough. As the case against him in respect to Charlotte's abduction and rape had not gone to court, Heaviside's reputation was still intact and his progress towards becoming a gentleman rather than a tradesman's son seemed complete with the stately Peterborough House as his new address.

Although past its heyday, Peterborough House was a grand mansion: a large square building with a gallery around the rooftop, many large rooms and furnished with taste and fine paintings. Originally a fourteenth-century building, it had been remodelled and rebuilt in the early Stuart style. The real beauty of the house, however, had been the impressive pleasure grounds surrounding it. Some of the land had been leased to market gardeners but there remained much of the former glory of this garden, a pleasant wilderness with shady cypress trees, inset with statues and fountains. Beyond the high brick walls on three sides of the mansion, market gardens dominated down to the riverbank while the front of the mansion faced the green with its picturesque pond. It was perfectly secluded.[4]

Had Richard Heaviside been present at the parties held in Peterborough House a few years earlier? Had he even been present on the night when the maid alleged she had been raped by Carpenter? Given the way in which the lives of the respective characters overlap in the sorry tale of Charlotte's youth, it is reasonable to assume that he was at least well acquainted with the set who dined there and with the Mordaunt family who owned the mansion. Given Joseph Biggs' friendship with Robert Carpenter and the close proximity between Putney and Parson's Green, perhaps the two Biggs brothers were also no strangers to Peterborough House? It paints a picture of a debauched coterie, the *nouveau riche* of Lambeth and Putney rubbing shoulders with dissolute aristocracy and actors, all plunged into scenes reminiscent of a Hellfire Club with maids and innocent girls as their playthings. Charlotte's second torment was about to begin.

Since her near escape from a courtroom drama, Charlotte had lived a secluded life back at her father's Lambeth home. Her mother, who had been ill before Charlotte's abduction, died and so, with her father attending to other matters, Charlotte was left under the care of a woman that the family regarded as a steady servant.[5]

With hindsight Charlotte needed a better guardian and she certainly needed a trusted confidante to whom she could turn. She had been left unchaperoned with Ochterlony and then allowed to fall prey to Richard Heaviside's tyranny. Her father, who should have protected her, instead absented himself from her everyday life. Left to her own devices Charlotte resumed her studies, reading voraciously to educate herself and slowly became more composed. She steeled herself for a lonelier existence than she had hitherto hoped for; even if she looked elsewhere for a husband and forgot about Ochterlony, her chances of making a good match were now ruined. Ochterlony had behaved like a gentleman and she clung to that proof that not all men were monsters. However, realizing that he was not going to contact her and that he was forging a new life for himself in India, she accepted that her future happiness had been lost when he sailed from England and certainly well before her encounter with Heaviside.

Charlotte regained her health and, as she described it, her 'bloom'. However, her mental state stood little chance of recovery as she was again under attack from Heaviside. Notwithstanding his promise to stay away from Charlotte, he employed various people to deliver letters to her (which she did not open) and to make proposals to which she did not listen. With growing desperation Heaviside tried to entice her, promising anything he thought would be a lure. He would provide her with a house in town or, if she preferred, a villa in the country, houses which he promised he would never approach but he wanted her to leave her father's home which he believed to be unfit and unsuitable for her. Was Peterborough House with its famous garden one of the homes with which he tempted her? Knowing Charlotte's enthusiasm for learning, he offered to provide her with masters to instruct and educate her. Finally, he even offered marriage; anything to entice her away from her home.

Why was her home unfit for her? Was John Williams so poor that he was unable to maintain a household suited to his and his daughter's station in life? Heaviside certainly felt that Charlotte deserved a better standard of living (and this from an illegitimately-born tradesman's son). It was Charlotte's misfortune that Richard Heaviside was absolutely besotted with her; there was something truly special, something distinctive about Charlotte, something that marked her out as more than simply a beautiful young woman and Heaviside, while going about it in a brutal and clumsy fashion, was entranced and wanted to possess her, body, mind and soul.

Charlotte needed advice and the person in whom she chose to confide was Benjamin Hunt Biggs. She told him of Heaviside's barrage of letters and proposals to her. Biggs, almost a decade Charlotte's senior, was placed in the dual roles of friend and adult protector, even though he possibly also had a foothold in Heaviside's chaotic life. The pair decided that it would be best for Charlotte to be placed in a convent in France, to continue her education well away from the clutches of her predator, but England was at war with France and so it would take some time to make the necessary arrangements. The delay was to Heaviside's advantage and one could almost suspect Benjamin of being complicit, much as Mrs Green had been before. However, before the convent plan could be put into operation, Charlotte was once again overtaken by events.

She was at home alone apart from the household servant and, at around ten o'clock in the evening, was preparing to go to bed. The servant briefly left the house to fetch something that was lacking for the morning but no sooner had she left the house when she came running back in, crying that there was a house on fire further down the street which she believed was Mary Belson's, a woman who had been Charlotte's nurse when she was younger and someone of whom Charlotte remained fond. Stopping only to throw her cloak over her shoulders, Charlotte left the house with the servant. There was a fire but, to Charlotte, it seemed to be more distant than Mary's house and on querying this, the servant pulled Charlotte towards the river, saying that it was more visible from there. Once at the waterside, the trap that Charlotte had unwittingly allowed herself to fall into was sprung: a thick boat cloak was thrown over her head and she was pushed into a small vessel that quickly rowed away. Fighting to free herself from the heavy cloak, Charlotte untangled herself and screamed for help but by this time the boat was already past Westminster Bridge and she was beyond assistance. At that dark hour of the evening no other boats were out on that stretch of the river and Charlotte was quite alone apart from her abductors. Two brutal-looking men rowed the small boat in which she was captive, muttering under their breath about 'women running away from their husbands', while a third man, a mulatto (as Charlotte described him), attempted to reassure her that she would not be hurt but Charlotte was terrified, believing that they were going to try to murder her. Eventually the boat approached the shore and a secluded spot where a carriage was waiting. Charlotte tried to escape but the men were too powerful and she was forced out of the boat and into the carriage which quickly carried her away. After a few minutes she arrived at the back entrance to a large mansion house which she could see stood in the middle of a large and ornate garden.[6]

Charlotte had landed at Fulham near a dead-end lane that was used only by the market gardeners and led to the hamlet of Parson's Green: one end of the lane was formed by the wall of the kitchen gardens of Peterborough House. In the dark of the night as the carriage hurtled down it, this lane was deserted. A grey-haired man and his wife were waiting for her and by the light of their lanterns Charlotte could read the note they passed to her, which asked her to be calm and promised that she should suffer no molestation. Horrified though she must have been, she probably already suspected the likely outcome. She recognized Richard Heaviside's scrawl on the paper and knew that she was once more his prisoner.

Numb and in shock, her clothes wet from her struggles while her kidnappers were landing the boat, Charlotte allowed the two servants to take her to a room in the mansion. She had no other choice but to comply. Although she did not know it at the time, she was in Peterborough House. How strange that only a year or two after the alleged rape in that very house by Robert Carpenter, friend of Benjamin Hunt Biggs' brother, Charlotte should find herself, after her own earlier rape, now held captive there. Strange indeed, but perhaps, as the young men involved all seem to have been known to each other, the coincidences take on a more sinister and serious disposition?

Charlotte was taken to a richly-decorated bedroom, the walls covered in a fresco paper depicting the ancient ruins of Rome. She allowed the female servant to undress her and take away her clothes to be dried and then, worn out, Charlotte made sure the doors were securely locked and lay down on the bed where she fell into an uneasy slumber. Alas for Charlotte, Heaviside was not to keep his promise that she would not be molested.

The fresco depicting the ancient ruins of Rome contained an image of the forum, known in medieval times as the *Campo Vaccino*. At the head of the bed in Charlotte's room was an archway within the *Campo Vaccino* and cleverly concealed within this archway was a secret door, not immediately visible. In darkness and while Charlotte slept, it was through this hidden door that Heaviside entered to once again force himself upon her.

The first time Charlotte had been unconscious, but this time she was all too fully aware. Heaviside was brutal and violent, repeatedly raping her. As dawn broke she tried to escape from the bed but during a struggle she was thrown – with some force – against the corner of a chair, broke a rib and, perhaps mercifully, fell into unconsciousness.

Heaviside obtained medical attention for her more quickly this time but it took three months for Charlotte to recover from her physical injuries, the broken rib compounded by a feverish illness. The man who attended her was John Churchill who practised as both a surgeon and as an apothecary and who was the younger brother of the poet, Charles Churchill. Mr Churchill treated Charlotte kindly but he must have been a man who Heaviside knew would not betray him. At this time Churchill lived in Parliament Street, cheek-by-jowl with Heaviside who had lived in the same street and who still retained his lodgings in the nearby New Palace Yard, Westminster where Charlotte had first been abused by him.[7]

Charlotte found that the unfaithful servant who had tricked her from the safety of her father's house in Lambeth had, under Heaviside's instructions, packed most of her clothes and effects and had them sent to Peterborough House. Not only that, she had convinced Charlotte's father that his daughter had run away voluntarily to join Heaviside. How little John Williams really knew Charlotte if he was prepared to believe that she had chosen to live with Heaviside as his mistress, regardless of all that had passed before. In consequence, there was no search for her. Charlotte was simply given up as lost to her family and no one attempted to contact her.

The novelist Samuel Richardson had once lived in Parson's Green and one could be forgiven for viewing Charlotte's misfortunes in the light of one of his heroines. Much as Richardson's *Clarissa* was spirited away and held captive by the rake Lovelace, who thought that once he had ruined her she would consent to be his, Heaviside acted out the same drama but for real. Held prisoner in Peterborough House, thinking her father and friends had abandoned her as beyond redemption, it was left to John Churchill to inform Charlotte of a new development. With as much delicacy as he could muster, he gave her the most unwanted news: Charlotte was pregnant. Depressed and inconsolable, she ceased to complain, asked no more to be returned to her father's home and instead submitted to every demand Heaviside made upon her. Charlotte was now reliant on him for her every need and dare not naysay him. It was as Heaviside had planned it with the first abduction and Charlotte felt that she had no choice but to resign herself to her fate.

However, she did have some friends to help her in her new life. Sarah Prudden, Heaviside's elderly mother, was kind in her attentions to Charlotte and John Churchill took on a fatherly role, even bringing his daughters to Peterborough House to visit. He also brought one of the most respectable of the neighbouring families with him on one visit (Charlotte named them merely as Mr and Mrs S___) and they too became fond of Charlotte and visited her regularly. Heaviside, in the meantime, now he had trapped Charlotte, began to behave in a calmer and more rational manner, only coming into her presence in the company of others and leaving her alone as much as possible. Perhaps, as her belly grew with the child inside her, he found her less desirable, lost interest now that the thrill of the hunt was over and looked for his pleasures elsewhere?

Heaviside's mother and John Churchill must have known the full facts of the case and both turned the other cheek rather than help Charlotte to escape Heaviside's clutches. Sarah Prudden feared her son's temper and so acquiesced with his plans rather than oppose them. John Churchill must have been beholden to him in some way, probably financially, so poor Charlotte had no one who was willing to risk themselves to save her.

If Charlotte was visited by Churchill's daughters and by Mr and Mrs S___, then she was not outwardly presented as Heaviside's courtesan but rather, to the latter couple at least, her true status in the house must have been disguised. Perhaps, in an echo of Sarah Prudden's past existence, Charlotte was presented as a form of 'housekeeper', a dependant but distant, widowed relation in need of bed and board?

In time a daughter was born to Charlotte but she felt only pity rather than love for her child. The girl was taken away to be nursed and was only brought to Peterborough House occasionally. These visits were a distraction for Charlotte and gave her the opportunity to try to contact the outside world. She bribed the woman nursing her child to carry letters to her father and to Benjamin Hunt Biggs, hoping they would come and rescue her, but the letters were never delivered. The nurse took Charlotte's money (for her trouble and for postage) and betrayed her trust. Charlotte assumed that the letters had been delivered and was despondent when she received no reply, believing that both men had given her up and that she really and truly had no one to whom she could turn for help. She was on her own, and would now only survive on her own wits and her own initiative.

Do we believe Charlotte? Up to this point, yes. Her story, incredible though it is, was sadly not unique and has a ring of truth about it; most of the facts given by Charlotte are verifiable. However, it is now that an element of doubt begins to creep in with regard to her version of events. She bribed the nurse to carry letters but ignored the trustworthy Mr and Mrs S___, who would surely have been better couriers? Charlotte's account was written many years later and was addressed to her old love, David Ochterlony. Resigned to her fate living as Heaviside's mistress and, as she herself openly confessed, feeling hopeless about the situation, she did not try to fight or to extricate herself from her prison. Did she later feel the need to embellish her tale, to make it appear as if she had struggled more than she had, that she had actively sought to flee Heaviside's clutches? After all, what could Charlotte as a young unmarried mother have expected if she had left Peterborough House? As far as she was aware her father had disowned her, she had no money (her annuity would not be hers until she came of age), and her reputation lay in tatters. Opportunities for a woman in Charlotte's position would be non-existent and it was likely that, simply to survive, she would be forced to sell herself on the streets or in London's bawdy houses. Viewed in that light, much better the devil she knew.

In April 1782 Richard Heaviside bought Peterborough House from the Dowager Countess of Peterborough, becoming owner of the mansion and grounds rather than merely the tenant. He also rented another house close by in Parson's Green. Perhaps his other property housed his mother and his infant daughter? Intriguingly though, another person central to Charlotte's story also lived in Fulham at that time. He is not listed in the rate books as either an occupant of a property or as a landowner, but in January 1782 it was reported in the newspapers that 'Mr Biggs of Fulham and Mr Harrison of near The Mansion House were robbed on Putney Common of their watches and about £4 by two highwaymen.' Mr Robert Harrison of Mansion House Street was a lifelong friend of Benjamin Hunt Biggs and so this was Charlotte's Mr Biggs, no longer living at Putney but having moved, of all places, to the very same area in which Charlotte found herself held prisoner. He was the man who sent his carriage to rescue Charlotte from her previous captivity and was involved in the subsequent legal decisions. He was the man that Charlotte claimed she turned to shortly before she was abducted from the Lambeth foreshore, when she was alarmed by Heaviside's repeated approaches and had no one else to turn to. It was Biggs who proposed to secrete Charlotte in a foreign convent to help her escape from Heaviside's attentions and it was he that Charlotte claimed she attempted to write to in order to escape from Heaviside. If Mr Biggs knew that Charlotte was living so close by, he made no attempts to see her, or at least none that Charlotte recorded. It is yet another inconsistency in Charlotte's account.[8]

From this point on, as regards her captivity in Peterborough House we must perhaps view Charlotte's words as ones designed to present the truth as she wished it to be seen and not strictly as it was. Words designed to persuade a man she loved, who had heard (even in faraway India) that she had been seen in society upon another man's arm and lived in sin with her keeper in finery and splendour, that she had been innocent of any blame in her downfall. She wished Ochterlony to believe the reports that had reached his ears were but smoke-and-mirror illusions masking a virtuous existence and truly, who could blame Charlotte for a little deception in drawing a veil over such a dark chapter of her life? She really had been left with no choice but to live as a kept woman. Now, though, Charlotte's captivity was to have a peculiar resolution, one that would bring her version of events seriously under question.

Having run out of options, Charlotte decided to make the best of her lot and entered into an agreement with Heaviside. She had a wing of Peterborough House to herself and Heaviside agreed to keep to the other parts of the mansion and not bring visitors to see her. Charlotte had books and music and could wander in the gardens whenever she wished. Left to her own devices and accepting of her fate, life in Peterborough House took on a veneer of normality.

The respectable neighbouring family that had been introduced to Charlotte by John Churchill stopped at Peterborough House every Sunday to take her to church in their carriage and the local vicar called to see Charlotte at her home. She was not shunned because of her situation, even though she expected to be. Heaviside had a large circle of female friends and many ladies asked to be introduced to Charlotte, although whether this was because they felt sorry for her, simply wished to know her or were curious to see the young girl who had so captivated the man is open to conjecture. Charlotte, wilful and heedless of their opinion of her, often refused to see these visitors. The bars of Charlotte's cage may have been gilded ones but she was only allowed to share in life outside her prison with Heaviside's approval and consent. If he was away from home, Charlotte was sent to stay with his mother who would act as her gaoler; Heaviside was not about to allow his prize to slip away from him when his back was turned.

Richard Heaviside was listed, during 1783, as a timber merchant operating from Palace Yard and Bridge Street, Westminster but this is the last reference found for him carrying on in trade of any sort. From this date onwards he fully embraced his new identity as a gentleman. On 26 April, Heaviside was admitted to the Inner Temple to study law. Eager to present himself as the son of a gentleman and not a tradesman, he contrived his admittance papers to describe him as the 'only son of Richard Heaviside, late of Peterborough House, Middlesex, deceased'; a slight bending of the truth which made it appear that his father had owned Peterborough House rather than a Lambeth timber yard.[9]

Following his admittance to the Inner Temple, Heaviside performed the duties of a justice of the peace; a very respectable responsibility for one guilty of raping and keeping captive a young girl! The cloak of respectability that Heaviside could throw around himself shielded him from any repercussions from his deeds. In the eyes of the world he was merely a young man sowing his wild oats before marriage and, on the surface, he was the perfect gentleman, but beneath this he was leading a dissipated existence. Heaviside's passion for Charlotte was still all-consuming and her continued dislike only served to increase his desire for her. At one point, he fell so dangerously ill that it was thought he would die and he made out a will. Finally, conscience-stricken when he feared he was about to meet the ultimate judgement, he left everything he owned to Charlotte. She saw the shallow self-serving gesture for what it was and her opinion of Heaviside remained unaltered but his death would have freed her from her captivity, made her mistress of her own fortune and estate. However, it was not to be: Heaviside recovered, revoked his will and Charlotte remained his prisoner for another two years until her daughter died. She had never loved the little girl but had determined to protect her, and the infant had been her reason for staying at Peterborough House. With nothing more to hold her there, Charlotte began to plot her escape from her gilded prison.

Charlotte's friends, Mr Churchill and Mrs S___, were concerned by two visitors to Peterborough House. Colonel Kirkpatrick together with his wife were the couple, but they were deemed unsuitable company and Charlotte was urged, against Heaviside's wishes, to refuse to see them. Born in the Carolinas to a plantation owner and (reputedly) his Creole slave, Colonel James Kirkpatrick was a colonel in the EIC's army. Colonel Kirkpatrick, known as 'the Handsome', had fathered an illegitimate son named William while living in Ireland in 1754 whose mother was a Mrs Booth. The handsome colonel later married Katherine Monro in Madras and had two legitimate sons, George and James Achilles. Katherine died in India and Kirkpatrick returned to his homeland, entertaining himself on the voyage with a Mrs Perrien or Perreira, the wife of a Portuguese Jewish mercenary; a daughter was born nine months later. Subsequently he spent time in Sumatra before landing back in England in 1779, this time for good. Who exactly was the lady passing as his wife when he visited Peterborough House is not clear but Kirkpatrick was a philanderer and possibly this was the – somewhat ironic – reason for Charlotte's friends' objection to her socializing with him. Was it really Charlotte's friends who objected to these visitors though, or Charlotte herself? William Kirkpatrick, the colonel's illegitimate son, was also out in

India with the EIC and was a personal friend of David Ochterlony. Charlotte must have been aware that gossip about her would travel back to India through this channel. Indeed, one wonders if Richard Heaviside or Charlotte was the intended recipient of Colonel Kirkpatrick's visit. Could it be possible that David Ochterlony himself asked the colonel to seek out Charlotte on his behalf with a message for her, perhaps even thinking she was still living at her father's house in Cuper's Garden's, Lambeth? When Charlotte wrote to Ochterlony decades later, she specifically mentioned Kirkpatrick's visit to Peterborough House. Was she, after all that time, trying to excuse herself to Ochterlony and explain why she refused to speak to the colonel after he had tracked her down?[10]

Escape plans were beginning to form in Charlotte's head. Somewhat surprisingly, given Heaviside's ever-watchful eyes, she was permitted to go into town with Mr and Mrs S___ in their coach and to go to church with them each Sunday. Charlotte gradually moved some of her possessions, personal ones and the trinkets and jewels given to her by Heaviside, to her neighbours' house, leaving them there for safe-keeping. Mr and Mrs S___ were initially unaware of Charlotte's scheme but in time they became privy to her plans to run away as she gradually confided in them, telling them the whole sordid story. However, was everything as it seemed? Why did Mr and Mrs S___ not take the more practical course of turning to the authorities or of contacting Charlotte's friends and father on her behalf? Why encourage a young woman to perhaps place herself in even more danger and compromising situations?

Charlotte feigned an interest in appearing at the theatre and opera and to do so she needed to be dressed in fine clothes and jewels. Richard Heaviside was happy to oblige and buy her the very best for, after all, when she was seen at the theatre in her finery she was exhibiting his own wealth. He had also waited a long time for Charlotte to willingly appear with him and to play the part of his mistress in public. Finally, he could exhibit her in the way he had longed to do. Heaviside was disposed to be generous and, within a few months, Charlotte had obtained possessions of sufficient value to put the next stage of her plan into operation.

Charlotte went to her friends Mr and Mrs S___ and asked for their help. She wanted them to find her a cheap place to live for around a year or so, a place where she could be supported by a small stash of money she hoped to raise by the sale of her trinkets and finery. She knew that Heaviside would search for her and that his rage would be tremendous; she knew she would suffer if he should find her, but she also knew that if she could hide from him for at least a year, she would then be of age and able to claim her annuity. With that sum she could support herself independently without the need to be reliant on anyone, not even her father. She just needed somewhere to hide herself for a while. Her friends readily agreed to help.

A woman of fashion known to Mrs S___ was on a tour of pleasure around the country and found a small cottage for Charlotte to rent in the grounds of Lord Vernon's estate at Briton Ferry in south Wales. Luckily for Charlotte, Mrs S___ insisted on paying the first year's rent in advance as her possessions sold for a smaller sum than she had anticipated. Without this kindness, Charlotte would have been left with little to live on. 'These arrangements being made – I took the first opportunity of escaping & I was put in a stage which was to take me to Briton Ferry my destined retreat.'

With the help of these kind neighbours and their fashionable friend, Charlotte's escape seemed easy. Too easy, perhaps? She was put into a stagecoach and began her journey to freedom. Her destination, Briton Ferry, was then little more than a small hamlet in south Wales, standing at the mouth of the River Neath. Nearby was the mansion of George Venables Vernon, 2nd Baron Vernon, which he had inherited through his first wife. This isolated part of the world had other connotations for Heaviside and his friends, though, and it is this that throws Charlotte's account of her escape from Peterborough House into serious doubt.

## Chapter Four

# Neath, of all Places!

P rior to Charlotte's abduction, John Nash had married a surgeon's daughter, Jane Elizabeth Kerr, and in 1776 baptized a son at St Mary's Church in Lambeth. The following year he set up business as an architect and negotiated a contract with Sir John Rushout, Baron Northwick, to redevelop Rushout's property on the corner of Bloomsbury Square and build new houses on some undeveloped land along Great Russell Street. Rushout, who owned the land, would claim rent on the properties but John Nash had the right to sell the houses he built. Nash accepted this contract even though the time scales were tight (the building and development needed to be completed within an eighteen-month schedule) but under the terms of the contract he had to find someone to stand surety for the completion of the works as he was an unknown and unproven architect. Nash got two friends to back him: Abraham Ewings (who had been a witness at Nash's wedding) and his childhood companion, Richard Heaviside. In April 1778 John Nash took another son, Hugh, to be baptized in the Lambeth Church before, two months later, his marriage crumbled.[1]

Jane Nash had run up considerable debts, including one with a milliner for £300. Furthermore, Nash declared that he was not the father of her two sons, that they were 'spurious' sons and had been imposed upon him by his wife. Jane was sent away by her furious husband to lodge with Ann Morgan, Nash's cousin, in Aberavon near Neath in south Wales. Nash asked another cousin, Charles Charles, who was a clerk at the Mackworth coalyard in Neath, to 'take care of' Jane and Charles, it seems, took this request a little too literally and began to visit Aberavon frequently, often staying overnight at the Morgans' home. He and Jane rode out on the pretext of him showing her 'the pleasures of the country' as he had been asked to do by Nash. Within a short distance of Aberavon, travelling towards Swansea along a stretch of sandy shoreline with crashing waves, was the idyllic local beauty spot of Briton Ferry with picturesque secluded woodlands and a rocky bay from which the River Neath flowed inland. It was on that beach leading to Briton Ferry that Charles Charles and Jane Nash were spotted by the local cockle-gatherers making love among the sand dunes. The Morgans had already caught the couple in their own parlour in a similar compromising situation and giving free reign to their urges but the intimacy between Charles and Jane was kept from Nash when he visited at Christmas 1778. There followed a few weeks when Jane was allowed back to London but it was not long before she was sent back to Wales, this time to lodge in Neath with yet another cousin. Nash said it was because she had again run up debts at the milliners but there was more to it than that. It was at Neath that Jane gave birth to a healthy baby girl whom she named after herself, Jane Elizabeth, and the father most certainly was not John Nash, although she insisted that his name was given to her daughter. Charles Charles was the father and Nash did not live with Jane again after this; he began a 'criminal conversation' action against Charles Charles as a preliminary to seeking a divorce from his errant wife.[2]

Of all the places available to her, why did Charlotte choose Briton Ferry for her escape attempt? Did she really escape or was she sent to south Wales by Heaviside as a punishment for some transgression, much as Nash had banished his wife? Do not forget, when Heaviside wanted his two servants out of the way to avoid awkward questions following his first kidnap of Charlotte, he sent them into Wales. Are we meant to believe that Charlotte voluntarily banished herself to the very place where the men of her acquaintance sent their wayward womenfolk and servants, thinking it a place of safety? In truth, we have no other version extant of the incident, no one's account but Charlotte's own and so Charlotte's words must stand and we must listen to her voice.

On the face of it Briton Ferry seems like the ideal isolated spot for Charlotte to hide from Heaviside. If we give her the benefit of doubt, perhaps the fashionable friend was also a friend of Lord Vernon and that is how the cottage was found? However, Briton Ferry was a mere 2 miles away from Neath, lying on the road in between that town and Aberavon, the very area from which Heaviside's friend John Nash's family hailed and where his errant wife still lived. Charlotte knew John Nash and she must have been aware of his history. Charlotte was all but asking to be discovered in her isolated hideaway.

The Briton Ferry cottage stood a short distance away from Lord Vernon's mansion, nestled in the brow of a hill between the woodland that surrounded the estate and the river that led into a bay. It was simply but decently furnished and two Welsh girls had been hired as domestic servants. Charlotte had no choice but to live within her means, saving as much money as she could to eke out her existence. She had no luxuries, no tea, coffee or wine but instead lived on bread and milk, vegetables and fresh shellfish from the bay. She bathed in the sea and the rugged, romantic and wild scenery inspired her. Lord Vernon's mansion usually stood empty and she ranged through his woodland with no other company than a good book, relishing the isolation. Although Charlotte contrived to keep out of sight as much as she could, Briton Ferry had a steady stream of people passing through. The road was a thoroughfare to the beach at Aberavon around the headland and the river was bustling and busy, with a ferry operating from Neath to Swansea and plenty of other craft transporting goods and plying their trade along the river and out into the Irish Sea. Charlotte, a stranger to the area and obviously a gentlewoman but living alone and unchaperoned except for the two local girls employed to keep her house, could not help but attract the attention and curiosity of the local folk. However, the simple fresh food, the fresh air and daily exercise all combined to restore Charlotte to full health; her skin glowed and she felt more beautiful at this point in her life than at any other.

Ensconced in her rural idyll, Charlotte's thoughts turned to Ochterlony and her early attachment to him and she cherished the memory of those days. One of her personal belongings that she had secreted with her friends in Parson's Green was a small trunk containing Ochterlony's letters to her: this had been sent to Briton Ferry. These letters had been exchanged between them prior to Ochterlony's sailing, dating from the time when she felt secure in his affections for her and containing written proof of his love and Charlotte had treasured and preserved them ever since. Charlotte was by now aged 20 and, for the first time since Ochterlony had sailed for India, she felt happy and was totally at peace. Despite her contentment, it did not escape her that she was having to waste her youth in hiding from the world when, through no fault of her own, she had been abandoned by the one man she loved and tormented by one she did not, forcing her to retreat from sight.

Charlotte lived in Briton Ferry for more than a year, bathing in the sea twice a week in all weathers. When her money began to run out she entertained the idea of running a school, but she hated the thought of being surrounded by the local peasant children; she abhorred uncleanliness and these children were, in Charlotte's opinion, dirty young urchins. With all the haughty sensibilities of a gentlewoman, if not the accoutrements, she preferred to keep the children at arm's length. She made no friends in the area, had no one in whom she could confide and now needed to find another way to provide herself with an income so that she could remain in her peaceful haven. Charlotte could by now make an application for her annuity, having passed her 21st birthday in Briton Ferry, but she did not know how to do so without risking the discovery of her sanctuary. The only people who had helped her thus far were her friends from Parson's Green but Charlotte was already indebted to them for paying the year's rent on the cottage. She refused to accept any more charity, despite being in need of it.

One morning towards the end of June 1783, she woke to find a gloomy haze in the air, darkening the sunlight. This haze did not dissipate but continued for many days and Charlotte felt that it mirrored her anxious mood. At this point the rural idyll collapsed entirely on Charlotte; the picturesque beauty of the place in no way compensated for the fact that she was facing certain destitution. She kept a small wooden box hidden within her desk containing her fast-diminishing money but, inside that box, only a few precious coins were left. Charlotte made one last throw of the dice and turned to the only place from which she felt she could expect any help: she approached Lord Vernon's mansion. Although empty, a skeleton staff was retained to keep it maintained and ready to be opened if Lord Vernon returned and so Charlotte approached the elderly housekeeper to ask for employment. The housekeeper, a kindly woman who had been sending baskets of produce to Charlotte's cottage, quickly agreed to provide Charlotte with linen to mend for which she would receive a small payment. Charlotte's initial relief at this kindness was short-lived though as the housekeeper, thinking Charlotte would be pleased at the prospect, informed her that Lord Vernon was bringing guests to the house and the ladies of the party would doubtless provide more work for Charlotte. This was both a blessing and a curse. A party of gentlefolk would disturb Charlotte's solitude and, more importantly, they would be curious about who she was and the circumstances that had led to her isolation in Briton Ferry.

As it turned out, Charlotte need not have worried. A few days later when returning to her cottage she noticed in the distance a man walking away from it, and the two Welsh servants confessed that they had allowed him to enter when he had knocked at the door to ask if the cottage could be leased. Charlotte discovered hours later that the box containing what was left of her money had vanished...

The next day a chaise pulled up outside the cottage and Charlotte came face-to-face with the past from which she had tried so hard to escape. The occupant of the chaise was an intimate friend of Richard Heaviside and a man well-known to Charlotte herself. John Nash was in the habit of visiting his cousins in Aberavon and Neath and, while separated from her, was still legally married to and responsible for the wife he had banished to that remote corner of south Wales. Just a few years earlier, Jane Nash and Charles Charles had been caught by the cockle-gatherers on Aberavon beach making love there; is it unreasonable to suppose that the couple still perhaps travelled the short distance from Neath to that very beach, passing through Briton Ferry on their way? There were myriad ways in which Charlotte could have been discovered and it is not surprising, Briton Ferry being so close to Neath and local gossip being what it was, that on one of those visits Nash had discovered Charlotte was living close by and reported back to Richard Heaviside. Perhaps – even – if we doubt Charlotte's account of how she came to reside at Briton Ferry, Heaviside and Nash had always known exactly where she was. However it came to be, Nash now intended to take Charlotte back to her captivity, bearing letters to her from both Heaviside and Sarah Prudden containing many promises, not least that if she agreed to return plans would be discussed to put her in a convent if she could not bring herself to continue to live as Heaviside's mistress. Charlotte knew better than to believe such promises but what choice did she have? She questioned Nash as to her missing money and he denied having taken it; she was destitute and her options had run out. The gloomy skies above perfectly matched Charlotte's fears for her future.

John Nash was financially beholden to his friend Heaviside at this point in his life, his future successes and rewards still some years away. He was, in 1783, staring bankruptcy full in the face, his houses in Great Russell Square were largely empty and he was heavily in debt to many other people as well as Heaviside. Described as having a 'giddy disposition' he also, self-admittedly, led a profligate lifestyle. Around this time he inherited a small property in Carmarthen where he indulged to the full for several years in drinking, gambling and hunting with 'the most desperate sportsmen', heedless of his financial woes but all the time maintaining the character of a gentleman. 'During this time Nash never read a book, and followed nothing but his pleasures, till he became weary of such a life, and perhaps was unable to support it any longer.'[3]

Despite being cut from the same cloth as Heaviside and also his crony, Charlotte believed that Nash was not acting with malice towards her and so she reluctantly agreed to return to Peterborough House, though not in company with Nash. Returning as a form of prisoner was not her intention; if she was going to return she would at least have the appearance of doing so of her own free will. She agreed to take the stagecoach and Nash provided her with the money to pay for this.[4]

The journey back to Fulham took a few days and the skies continued to be full of the same dark foggy haze which, Charlotte learned from her travelling companions, was the residue of a volcanic eruption in Iceland that had blown south and was blanketing most of Europe. Crops were beginning to fail and the mortality rates among agricultural labourers working outdoors in the fields were increasing at an alarming rate. The world seemed to have shifted on its axis and nothing but doom and gloom were evident.[5]

Arriving back in Fulham, Charlotte was received by Heaviside's mother who had come to Peterborough House and, once she had reached the point of no return, John Nash confessed to what Charlotte already suspected: that he had indeed taken and hidden her money to oblige her to leave Wales. The money was returned to her possession. Charlotte was relieved to find that Richard Heaviside was in Kent where his mother had prudently told him to stay for a while. The two women discussed the project to place Charlotte in a convent but Sarah Prudden had another plan to which she tried to persuade Charlotte to agree. She wanted Charlotte to marry her son. Heaviside must have instigated this, must have purposely stayed away from Peterborough House to give his mother time to try to gently talk Charlotte round. Was it guilt that was now the driving force behind his proposal or was he still frantically besotted by Charlotte? These two schemes were relentlessly talked about and, to add to the pressure under which Charlotte found herself, Heaviside was unable to stay away and returned to speak for himself. He was indeed intent on a marriage to Charlotte but she insisted on being placed within the safe refuge of a convent, no matter what he did or said to persuade her otherwise.

Charlotte had no money other than the few coins that Nash returned to her and while Heaviside stalled and delayed as much as he could, she had no way of freeing herself. Totally dependent upon Heaviside once more, she had no choice but to remain under his roof where he was determined to eventually wear her down and make her submit to be his wife.

Charlotte attempted to earn a small living and to gain a modicum of independence from Heaviside by writing an article that she sent to a magazine, hoping they would use it. They did indeed include it and paid her a small sum for doing so; the first but certainly not the last time that Charlotte would see her own words in print and profit by her pen. This initial piece of writing was, she freely admitted, 'trash' but she needed the money and within the same magazine she took a chance of appealing to some old friends from her girlhood, the Miss Sibthorpes, hoping they would see her message and perhaps would be able to help her gain the place she wanted in a convent. One Miss Sibthorpe responded and Charlotte, overjoyed, replied to her. For days Charlotte waited for Miss Sibthorpe's subsequent letter but none came and nor did a letter from any of Miss Sibthorpe's sisters. Charlotte suspected that her own letter had been intercepted by Heaviside and any further hope of assistance from this source was quashed.

Charlotte's life in Peterborough House settled back into an all-too-familiar routine. The means of independence that should have been hers as she was now over 21 years of age, the annuity that had been instigated as recompense for her sufferings following that first attack and rape, still lay dormant. She did not know how to go about claiming it and Heaviside was not about to help and give her the means of evading his clutches. Her neighbours in Parson's Green, Mr and Mrs S___, still visited her, still treated her with kindness but even the family who had helped her to escape and knew her full history did nothing more to aid her. She went to church and to public amusements, often accompanied by an elderly gentleman, a respectable relation of Heaviside's. She spent her time reading, or with the masters and tutors who had been hired for her continued education and to the outside world it seemed that she was living happily in Peterborough House. However, those closest to her knew differently: she was miserably unhappy, living as a captive in a state of constant hostility.

Night was a time of terror for Charlotte. Never free from Heaviside, if she refused him entry to her room he would work up his rage until he was in a complete frenzy. Locked doors were no bar to him as he would smash them apart in his attempts to reach her; he even climbed through open windows to reach her bed. Charlotte, when she had the chance, persuaded a maid to sleep in her bedroom with her, to offer some protection and comfort. Eventually, totally worn down by her ordeal and realizing that Heaviside was never going to agree to her going to a convent, Charlotte tried to bargain. She offered to sell the annuity to him for £300 if he would only let her leave Peterborough House and not bother her again. This was a considerable sum of money but substantially less than Heaviside would be likely to pay on the annuity over the course of Charlotte's lifetime. However, it would be enough for Charlotte to establish herself in a small house or cottage somewhere and for her to make a start on rebuilding her life. In establishing this annuity, Charlotte's friends had been able to have their say and to stipulate conditions and Benjamin Hunt Biggs was responsible for a condition that put paid to this scheme. If the annuity was ever sold, it would revert to the Magdalen, a refuge for 'penitent prostitutes' that also offered reformation for victims of 'seduction'. It was founded in 1758 in London (the first such refuge in the

English-speaking world) and the Reverend William Dodd had conducted evening services to the fallen women within its walls before his own downfall. The inclusion of this clause on the annuity neatly reflects the views of – or at least the suspicions of – Charlotte's friends concerning her behaviour.

The annuity could therefore not be sold but Heaviside came up with an alternative plan. If he purchased an annuity from Charlotte, effectively each annuity cancelling out the other, then he would give her the £300 and they would trouble each other no more. The documents were drawn up and Heaviside's servants brought in to witness Charlotte's signature and see the £300 handed over to Charlotte. She was delighted and had already arranged for Mr and Mrs S___ to take her into London the next day in their carriage so she could find out how to travel to France and the safety of a convent. She ran upstairs to lock the money in her bureau before packing her belongings.

However, before she could open the bureau in her room, Heaviside ran in behind her, snatched the banknotes out of her hand and left. It all happened so quickly. Charlotte had been tricked – again – and she had signed the legal documents in the presence of witnesses of her own free will so she now had no money and no prospect of her annuity either. She ran from Peterborough House to the neighbouring one belonging to her friends; Mr and Mrs S___ marched round to Peterborough House with Charlotte and remonstrated with Heaviside but he brushed them aside and calmly told them that Charlotte was telling fibs; he had not stolen the money, he was a gentleman and a justice of the peace and could not be suspected of acting like a common criminal. Instead, he persuaded his neighbours that it was Charlotte who had been a careless, silly girl and lost the banknotes.

Charlotte was now finally, truly, totally broken. She fell into a fever and was heedless whether she lived or died. The surgeon bled her up to three times a day, weakening her further until she could not even rise from her bed. For weeks Charlotte remained ill but she was young and slowly recovered. Having lost her annuity and with it any hope for the future, she now effected a simpler escape plan, one that she should have put into action before. It was so easy that it raises yet more questions: why on earth did Charlotte not do this sooner? Sneaking away from Peterborough House, she found her way to her father's Lambeth home and threw herself on his mercy. She discovered that the letters she had tried to smuggle out of her gilded prison to both her father and to Benjamin Hunt Biggs had never been delivered, and she found out about the lies told by her old servant to her father to make him believe she had left of her own volition. Charlotte believed that they had ignored her appeals but now she understood the full scale of the deception that had been practised, not only on herself but also on her family and friends. Mark Beaufoy had died while Charlotte had been held captive but his son, also named Mark, stepped in to help; an application was made to a register office and Charlotte was placed under the protection of him and her father.

The younger Mark Beaufoy was recently married, having run away to Gretna Green with his cousin, Margaretta Beaufoy. The newlywed couple planned to travel to Switzerland and then on to Mont Blanc (Beaufoy was one of the earliest mountaineers and he planned to scale the mountain). Charlotte still wanted to be placed in a French convent and so the Beaufoys took her with them when they left and, as they passed through Arras in northern France, she was placed in the convent there as the protégée of Mrs Margaretta Beaufoy. To support herself Charlotte acted as a governess while at the convent to a young English girl, Miss Greenwood.

Richard Heaviside tried to cover his tracks. He wrote to Mark Beaufoy telling him that the trick with the annuity was merely to keep Charlotte dependent upon him, that the document she signed was, he admitted, of no validity and professed himself ready to pay the arrears on the annuity. Another player in the story was still close by: the *Morning Post* newspaper of 15 November 1785 reported Benjamin Hunt Biggs of Fulham as one of the men who applied for a Game Duty Certificate. Throughout Charlotte's entire ordeal he had lived as her close neighbour, unwilling – or unable – to help her, although he can hardly have been unaware of her fate. Just how much he was involved or knowing of the affair is debateable, but given his later prominence in her life one could be forgiven for suspecting that he was a constant presence throughout these years, even if only in the background.

Even the partial admittance of guilt to Beaufoy did not impact on Richard Heaviside's outward persona as a respectable gentleman. He was elected in November 1785 as a member of the Society for the Encouragement of Arts, Manufactures and Commerce and he remained on their board for many years. He continued, throughout his imprisonment of Charlotte, to act as a justice of the peace and he was proposed to the society by Nathaniel Conant Esquire, a fellow justice, later to become Sir Nathaniel and the chief magistrate at Bow Street. Conant, the son of a reverend, had a similar background in trade to Heaviside and had been apprenticed to a London stationer in 1759 for seven years. His endorsement of Heaviside highlights the extent to which Charlotte's tormentor could present himself to the world as a man with the full respect and friendship of his contemporaries.

Although Charlotte had left London by the end of 1784 to enter the convent at Arras, eighteen months later she was back once again in Lambeth to witness her father's second marriage. On 15 July 1786, John Williams married Sarah Reed, a widow from Frith Street in Soho. The marriage was by licence and witnessed by three people: a married couple named Christian and Thomas Leighton and Rachel Williams. Who else could Rachel Williams be but John's daughter, using her official forename rather than the middle name by which she was commonly known? Less than two years after her escape she was back in Lambeth, sitting in a pew in St Mary's Church celebrating her father's marriage with friends, family and acquaintances around her and in full view of Heaviside, should he choose to look.[6]

# Chapter Five

# Residence in France

After Charlotte had left Peterborough House for the last time, Richard Heaviside spent less time there and more at his lodgings at the Inner Temple. Peterborough House became simply his country retreat. By the late summer he had been appointed to the position of captain of a company of the Western Regiment of the Middlesex Militia (similar to the Territorial Army today, this was a regiment comprising civilians, designed to supplement the regular army in an emergency). Another gentleman who was also made captain, and adjutant too in the same militia regiment, was one Thomas Poplett, formerly an officer on half-pay and a friend of Heaviside's. In late January 1788, Poplett came to the assistance of his friend when a dispute arose between Heaviside and his fellow justice of the peace, Nicholas Forster.[1]

Forster insulted Heaviside and did so publicly. Heaviside, Forster believed, had been inattentive to a matter that concerned Forster personally and he told him so in no uncertain terms. Heaviside brooded on the affair and then retaliated by sending his friend Captain Thomas Poplett with a message: Heaviside proposed to challenge Forster to a duel if he did not receive an apology. Poplett sent a letter to the *Morning Herald* newspaper giving brief details of the misunderstanding and enclosed an account of Forster's apology, which he claimed had been personally given to him. In this apology, Forster said that he was drunk when he had insulted Heaviside, had not meant to traduce his character and intended him no injury. Richard Heaviside's reputation and public character meant a lot to him and he was prepared to go to great lengths to defend them, even to the point of challenging another man to a duel, a situation almost ironic given Charlotte's accusations against him. The matter was far from concluded. Two days later the same newspaper carried a very simple denial of Forster's apology: 'The paragraph in Saturday's paper respecting Justice Heaviside and myself, is a misrepresentation. N. FORSTER.'[2]

Captain Poplett and Richard Heaviside were not about to let the matter drop. With the apology renounced, Poplett had now been called out as either a dupe or a liar. Preferring to air their grievances in public, the argument was carried on for some days in the letters column of the *Morning Herald* until an amicable resolution was established, without recourse to duelling pistols.[3]

Later in the year Heaviside sat as a magistrate at a petty session to determine whether threats had been used in the recent Westminster election, sitting alongside his old friend Richard Brinsley Sheridan and two other gentlemen, Lord Robert Spencer, youngest son of the 2nd Duke of Marlborough (a confidante of the Prince of Wales) and the Honourable Richard FitzPatrick, Charles James Fox's boon companion.

In 1788 William Pitt the Younger was the head of government while the opposition Whig party was led by Fox. Sheridan, Spencer and FitzPatrick were Whigs and Richard Heaviside joined the Whig Club, showing where his political sympathies also lay. Lord John Townshend had beaten the Tory candidate in the Westminster election, Admiral Lord Hood, after a spectacular effort in canvassing from both parties that cost a small fortune, and Lord Hood had raised a petition into the result. Ultimately, Townshend was confirmed in his seat. A few short months after the Westminster election King George III suffered the first of his bouts of insanity, sparking a constitutional crisis and leading to talks of regency. The Prince of Wales, in opposition to his father, had placed his political allegiances firmly with his friend Charles James Fox and the Whigs were in full support of the prince being made regent.

It is clear that Heaviside had not suffered any consequence in the years immediately following his kidnap of Charlotte. He was still a Freemason and performed the duties of a justice of the peace, counting Members of Parliament and Bow Street magistrates among his acquaintances and having the privilege of sitting in judgement on others while evading justice himself. His good reputation was intact and he was prepared to go to great lengths to defend it, to preserve his good name and to demand the respect he felt his due. This was all while Charlotte worked as a governess in a French convent to make ends meet, preferring to stay in another country rather than face the people who would judge her and besmirch her reputation.

Charlotte spent some time in one of the most aristocratic convents in Paris, the Panthemont (Pentemont Abbey). Until the French Revolution the abbey was a convent for nuns as well as an educational establishment for the daughters of nobility and some apartments were reserved for ladies of good standing. Protestant students were accepted, even though it was a Catholic convent. Martha and Mary Jefferson, Thomas Jefferson's daughters, received their education there while Jefferson was the United

States Minister to France and Joséphine de Beauharnais retired to the Panthemont after she had separated from her first husband (she would later marry Napoléon Bonaparte). Jefferson enrolled his two daughters after receiving assurances that they would be exempt from religious instruction but Martha evidently bypassed that and later informed her father that she wished to convert to Catholicism to become a nun. She was swiftly removed from the school.

Charlotte's attendance at the Panthemont must have been around the same time as the Jefferson girls. In this convent, she claimed that she formed several friendships that would last for many years. One girl Charlotte named as Eugenia de Santerre, stunningly beautiful and with two sisters, one older and one younger than she, but with a father whose fortune was inadequate to provide for his three daughters. Charlotte recorded Eugenia's removal from the convent.[4]

In 1788, when she was just 16 years of age, Eugenia caught the eye of a man many years older than her: an aristocrat named Monsieur de St Evremond who proposed to take her from the convent and marry her, even though she had no dowry. With all parties agreeing to the plan, Eugenia was whisked from the convent to become Madame de St Evremond. Her husband lived a dissipated life, however, and within less than a year of marriage he had tired of his wife, returned her to her father and absconded to Italy.[5]

In the same year, another friend of Charlotte's from the Panthemont was forced into a similar marriage. This girl, Adelaide, had been orphaned at an early age and left in the care of her older brother who placed her in the convent with the intention that she would take the veil and become a nun. The brother wanted nothing to do with her and, when it became clear that she had no vocation for a religious life, she was permitted to stay on there as a pensioner, having nowhere else to go.

Adelaide's release from the convent was also through marriage to a much older man, a marquis who was bad-tempered and of an age to be her father rather than her husband. With echoes of Heaviside's infatuation with Charlotte, the marquis was a rich man who had become obsessed with the beautiful young orphan. The marriage lasted less than three years: the old marquis died and left his wife a wealthy young widow. Charlotte referred to Adelaide as La Marquise and, cryptically, Madame de F___, both of which were her married titles.[6]

Although these two French girls kept their reputations intact their situation does, in some ways, mirror that of Charlotte. They all had fathers unable to provide and care for them or no parents at all and were taken, either by matrimony or by force, by men who were determined to possess them. While such arrangements were common, Charlotte felt a kinship with these girls as all three came, via different routes, to their own type of independence.

During 1789 Charlotte spent some time in Orléans with her friend Eugenia de St Evremond. With Monsieur de St Evremond still in Italy, Eugenia formed an attachment to a young man in her circle of acquaintance, a distant relative, and the two became lovers. This was to have disastrous consequences.

Back in England, Richard Heaviside had finally moved on. Behaving with absolute propriety, he married a lady from Devon, Miss Ann Spicer of Mount Wear near Exeter. Miss Spicer's family were wealthy Exeter merchants, in possession of a large mansion and a fortune to suit. In the same year as his marriage Heaviside bought the manor and lordship of Sandhurst in Berkshire plus 2 acres of land there and commissioned the building of a fine house to be named Sandhurst Lodge. In time he bought more of the surrounding land, adding to his estate, and a year after his marriage he moved out of Peterborough House for good, leaving it standing empty and falling into disrepair.[7]

Did Charlotte know of her tormentor's marriage? It is a distinct possibility that news of it reached her in France for, in the springtime of 1790, she returned home, crossing the Channel and landing at Dover. With a new Mrs Heaviside on the scene, she now felt safe enough from his passions to return to London and spent two years living quietly there while the men she had known in her youth occupied themselves with matters other than herself. Heaviside lived the affluent life of a country gentleman in Berkshire and John Nash had been disappointed in his attempts to divorce his errant wife. He was instead concentrating on his fledgling architecture business, albeit with little financial success in those early years.

Early in 1792 Charlotte travelled back to France, in company with someone else from her past: Benjamin Hunt Biggs. The two later passed for man and wife but the proof of an official union remains elusive. Indeed, what evidence is available points in the other direction: to a marriage that was in name only and purely for convenience. It is clear what Charlotte would gain from such an arrangement. In an age when women had few rights and were generally seen as the property of either a father or a husband, she would gain independence but without the control of a husband. She could exert an element of freedom in her day-to-day activities that would otherwise have been denied her, under the guise of a married lady. Additionally, Charlotte was 'ruined goods' when it came to the marriage market and would be unlikely to make a good match with neither her virginity nor a fortune to recommend her, even if she found another man to whom she wanted to give herself. Still in love with Ochterlony, even though it was a hopeless situation, and scarred from her connection with Heaviside, Charlotte was not predisposed to give herself mind, body and soul to another man. Regarding Benjamin Hunt Biggs, the benefits are less clear. Did he feel pity for Charlotte and perhaps guilt for not helping her sooner and so agreed to let her use his name and pass for his wife? Perhaps – possibly – Biggs' sexual inclination was towards men and not women. In a period during which this was a criminal offence – buggery carried the death sentence and although this was rarely carried out, a man's reputation would be ruined if 'outed' as homosexual – his marriage to Charlotte may have proved a useful cover. Benjamin was certainly secretive, not even letting his few remaining relations know that he was travelling to France. He simply disappeared from London and from their lives.

Had Charlotte and Benjamin known it, they were entering France at entirely the wrong time and would find themselves trapped there – and imprisoned – during the turbulent years to follow. France was about to undergo a revolution.

Charlotte's account of her adventures in France during the revolutionary years comes from her own hand. Once safely back in England she published her account, purportedly written in secret and safely hidden from sight while she was imprisoned in a series of institutions. How much can we rely on Charlotte's words, though?[8]

Charlotte's published memoir, *A Residence in France during the Years 1792, 1793, 1794 and 1795*, was written in the first person and in a series of detailed letters to a supposed 'brother'. Few people were mentioned by their real names; instead just the first letter of their surname was used and Benjamin Hunt Biggs, who was by her side, was not mentioned by his own name. While Charlotte placed herself at the centre of the action, often in company with her old convent acquaintance Adelaide, La Marquise, an English couple was on the periphery of the action, named only as Mr and Mrs D___. Mr D___ was presented as bad-tempered, irritable and a little ineffectual and it was Mrs D___'s illness that prevented Charlotte from returning home to safety. All four were imprisoned: Mr and Mrs D___ were held in Arras and Charlotte and her titled friend arrested in the fortified town of Péronne before being taken to prisons in both Arras and Amiens.

Charlotte's old school friend, styled as a marchioness following her marriage and also described as Madame de F___, had been left a wealthy young widow on the death of her much older husband. For the first time in her life she was enjoying the liberty of independence but for all too brief a time. Her brother, a count who had placed her in the Panthemont convent where Charlotte claimed to have met her, had initially embraced the revolution and the cause of the people. The massacres of September 1792 soon changed his allegiance, though, when he narrowly escaped with his life. The count chose to emigrate immediately. La Marquise remained in Paris and amused herself with aristocratic pursuits: she painted, translated Italian romances, petted her dogs and taught her flock of a dozen canary birds to sing in accompaniment to a harp. Her two favourite canaries could be told apart from the rest, their curious topknots and rings around their necks marking them out. However, this pampered life ended a year later when, as the sister of an émigré, she came under suspicion and was arrested.

Charlotte's version of events differs from the truth, however. A Mr and Mrs Biggs were held in the Providence *maison d'arrêt* (a form of prison) at Amiens from September 1793 to August 1794. Between those dates, Charlotte put herself in the pages of her book squarely by the side of the marquise, held first at Arras then at the *Bicêtre* in Amiens and, from December 1793, in the Providence at the same place. In Charlotte's account, the unfortunate English couple, Mr and Mrs D___, are held at Arras for the duration. Biggs is not a common name and Charlotte could not be in two places at once. Our belief is that Mr and Mrs D___ were in fact Mr and Mrs B___, otherwise Biggs, and that Charlotte's memoir was not altogether what it seemed. Could the truth of her experience be of a more mundane and less exciting turn of events and so she embellished her account? Or did she appropriate the experiences of someone else, presenting them as her own?[9]

Similar accusations have been levelled at another lady who published her own account of those years, the infamous courtesan Grace Dalrymple Elliott. In turn the lover of the Earl of Cholmondeley, the Duke of Orléans (Philippe Égalité) and the Prince of Wales (whose child she bore before returning to France and the arms of her French duke), Grace, like Charlotte, found herself trapped in France and at the mercy of the revolutionaries. Mrs Elliott wrote her *Journal of My Life During the French Revolution* in 1802 and supposedly it was written while she lived at her elderly aunt's house in Twickenham and at the instigation of King George III's doctor, to entertain his royal patient. It was published posthumously three decades after Grace's death and remains a fascinating resource. In the main it is accurate and detailed, even though Grace is sometimes vague about dates and names, but towards the end the journal descends into falsehoods: Grace is placed in prisons with well-known people and it can be proved impossible that she was there at that time. However, the original of the journal has been lost and the inaccuracies that creep in appear to stem not from Grace's own pen but from the over-enthusiastic editing of the publisher Richard Bentley, added, no doubt, to boost sales. Charlotte's account was published during her lifetime and with her own consent; if she embellished her account then she must therefore take the full blame for any inconsistencies.[10]

Charlotte's friend, La Marquise, prematurely aged and worn down by her imprisonment, died in Paris in June 1795 after her release. Charlotte claimed to be in Paris with her at the time. Just over two weeks later Charlotte and Benjamin Hunt Biggs returned to England aboard an American ship, *The Young Eagle*. Did Charlotte also bring back her friend's memoirs to be subtly doctored, the real presence of herself and her supposed husband left disguised in their pages almost as a private joke with the initial of their first name changed to one that sounds very similar and the place of their incarceration changed from Amiens to Arras?[11]

With this knowledge, Charlotte's memoir presents a dilemma. We have no reason to disbelieve the facts as presented, merely that Charlotte herself was probably not a first-hand witness to each and every incident recounted but it is likely that her own experiences did mirror those she claimed for her own, and she certainly was an eye-witness to the horrors of the time and spent time incarcerated and terrified for her very life. She may also have interwoven her own experiences into the narrative and it then becomes imperative to try to establish what may be her own account and which parts have been appropriated. We have found ourselves in the same situation before when trying to unravel and prove Charlotte's account of her kidnap and rape at the hands of Richard Heaviside. Regardless of any of this, *A Residence in France* remains a good account of France during the revolution, of the attitudes and norms of the day, of the terror and hardship faced both inside and outside the prisons and as a witness to the tragic events that befell the French royal family. We therefore give Charlotte's account of her adventures.

It was in Soissons while staying with an aristocrat that Charlotte learned that Marie Antoinette, the unfortunate queen of France, was to stand trial. Charlotte was wary of her host for the evening, an aristocrat like her friend La Marquise but one who had warmly embraced the principles of the revolution despite the advice of his family; Charlotte had been warned to be careful what she said. Although a count, this gentleman's household had replaced their plate with pewter and the supper comprised simple fare in keeping with his newly-adopted ideals but it became clear to Charlotte during the conversation that he feared the republican government was becoming too radical and the good he had thought they would do was in danger of being lost. Despite supporting the cause and with both his sons distinguishing themselves in the republican army, he had not been safe from domiciliary visits to his home and he was all too worried that his rank would be of greater significance than his principles.

That evening Charlotte browsed through the count's newspapers and was shocked to read that Marie Antoinette had been transferred to La Conciergerie, a former medieval royal palace that stood alongside the Palais de Justice. Now it was used as a prison and had a reputation, in 1793, as the 'antechamber for the guillotine'. Marie Antoinette, or the Widow Capet as she was officially known following the execution of her husband Louis XVI earlier that year, was gravely ill. Suffering from tuberculosis and possibly also uterine cancer, following the death of her husband she ceased to take exercise or to eat. Haemorrhaging (indicative of the cancer) and with her hair turned snowy-white, Marie Antoinette had the appearance of a woman much older than her 37 years. She entered La Conciergerie as 'Prisoner no. 280' to await her appearance in front of the Revolutionary Tribunal that would ultimately decide her fate. On the same day her son, the nominal king of France but known simply as Louis Capet who had been torn from his mother's side, was sent a toy guillotine.[12]

In August 1793, the French passed a law requiring all English people living in the country to produce two witnesses who could attest to their *civisme* (citizenship). After this they would be awarded a 'ticket of hospitality' which they had to wear, pinned to their clothing, as a protection. Those who could not produce two witnesses would be arrested. Charlotte was not unduly worried; she knew that she could produce many witnesses and was confident that most English people resident in France could do the same. However, days later the mood changed.

Sir Samuel Hood, admiral of the navy and commander-in-chief of the Mediterranean fleet, had joined forces with the Spanish fleet to come to the aid of the royalists holding the port of Toulon against the revolutionaries. He was the same Lord Hood who had stood for the Tory Party and been defeated in the 1788 Westminster election and had petitioned the result, with Richard Heaviside sitting on the heavily Whig-influenced ensuing petty sessions in judgement. The royalists invited Hood, who was blockading the fort, to occupy the town. The occupation was not long-lived; the revolutionary forces (which included a young Captain Napoléon Bonaparte) besieged the town and forced the British and Spanish fleets to withdraw but not before

Hood had given an order to burn the fifty-eight ships of the French fleet in the harbour. In retaliation, orders were given to arrest every English person in France who had not been resident in the country before 1789, that they should be imprisoned and held as hostages, answerable with their lives for the conduct of their countrymen and of the Toulonese.

Charlotte and Mr Biggs were among those arrested and were taken to the *maison d'arrêt* at Amiens; official records show that the couple arrived there on 7 September 1793 and so it is at this point that we can be certain that Charlotte was no longer actually by the side of her friend La Marquise, even though she places herself there for a while longer in *A Residence in France*.[13]

In Péronne, La Marquise was also in trouble. A few evenings passed before the town bell began to ring followed by the sound of cannons, both of which announced the arrival of André Dumont, a member of the National Convention and head of the department of the Somme and the man who had jurisdiction of Péronne. Dumont had voted for the death of Louis XVI a year earlier and was known as a man to be feared. A former clerk to an attorney at Abbeville, he found his chosen profession to be insubstantial for his mode of living and embraced the revolution and the chance to become the representative of the people for his area. This elevation in his status brought with it the financial rewards he craved; he left his former house at Oisemont a little south of Abbeville, which had been little more than a barn and, by the end of 1793, purchased a large mansion formerly owned by an émigré. He also now routinely travelled in a coach and four. Dumont arrived in Péronne to find that, contrary to orders, no one had been arrested. The mayor and his officials excused themselves, saying that they had no one to accuse as 'the town was in the utmost tranquillity and the people were so well disposed, that all violence was unnecessary.' Dumont furiously ranted that he knew 5,000 aristocrats were in Péronne and if at least 500 of them were not brought to him before morning he would declare the town to be in a state of rebellion. The panicked town officials sent out parties to arrest people, more keen to secure enough prisoners than to discriminate against who should or should not be singled out.

Consequently, a party of the National Guard accompanied by a town official was despatched to the house of La Marquise to escort her through the crowded but strangely silent streets to a church where she would be examined. Charlotte put herself by her friend's side in this ordeal, writing herself into her present and subsequent misfortunes when really she was undergoing a similar experience in Amiens. It is, however, worth documenting as Charlotte's own experience would have been very similar.

Charlotte's friend was among the last of the inhabitants to be examined and the church was nearly empty. Dumont himself had been on the verge of departing. He did not have to delay long; upon hearing that La Marquise was the sister of an émigré he decreed that she should be taken to another church to be held there overnight before she was taken to Arras as a prisoner. The church in which La Marquise was to pass the night was in darkness, some of the guards were drunk and the air hung thick with tobacco smoke. With approximately 150 prisoners crammed inside as well as the guards, it was unbearably hot and stuffy and this only added to the terror. La Marquise was mindful of the 'September Massacres' in Paris a year earlier, in which prisoners in a similar situation to herself had been killed.

The next morning the loyal servants of the prisoners entered with breakfast, many offering to stay with their masters and mistresses and accompany them to Arras. The day dragged on and it was not until six o'clock in the evening that a detachment of dragoons brought some small covered wagons to the church for the journey. La Marquise's maid brought news that men had searched the house, sealed it and appointed a guard to remain there at a daily cost that she must bear.

The wagons were uncomfortable, the horses tired and the roads bad. It started to rain and the coverings on the wagons did little to shield the miserable prisoners huddled beneath. After spending more than six hours travelling in the darkness they had only reached the town of Bapaume a mere 15 miles from Péronne, so the officer in charge called a halt and crowded everyone into the local church where they spent an uncomfortable night in their damp clothes. The journey began again in the early hours and Arras was reached by late morning. The streets were quiet and the prisoners only attracted interest from a group of Dutch refugee soldiers who shouted 'To the guillotine! To the guillotine!' as the wagons trundled by.

The house of detention to which they were taken had been the private home of an émigré, a large house but now crowded with unhappy and unfortunate souls. At first there was no room for the new prisoners and they had to wait in the courtyard, cold and tired, until space had been made by 'dislodging and compressing the other inhabitants'.

Charlotte was not present in this Arras prison, but her account in *Residence* might indeed have some truth as it concerned her own captivity. Charlotte claimed that she, La Marquise and their two maids were shown to a corner of a garret, a dirty room without a ceiling that would have been cold were it not for the scores of people, men and women, crowded within. These people, once *gens comme il faut* (people of fashion), had been there for a while in appalling conditions and Charlotte, with her habitual hatred of dirty people, although weary could not sleep until she had tried to do away with some of the filth and offensive odours. She delved into her baggage to find her *vinaigre des quatre voleurs* (four thieves' vinegar) and a perfume made of essence of roses. 'Four thieves' vinegar' was a strong white vinegar infused with herbs and spices that had been a popular protection from the plague, the name derived from a legend that a group of thieves – from either Marseille or Toulouse – were caught stealing from the dead and dying. In return for leniency, the thieves revealed their secret recipe for a potion that afforded them protection from catching the plague. Charlotte set to work sprinkling this around her and burning her perfume to freshen the air. It would have had little benefit in protecting her from disease but was a way of Charlotte asserting some authority on her situation and regaining a modicum of control over her new environment. It upset some of her neighbours but Charlotte ignored them, spread her mattresses on the floor and separated her corner from the rest of the room with a makeshift curtain. There were men in the room and Charlotte wanted some privacy. By morning she had the beginnings of a violent fever and for three weeks remained on her mattress in the corner of the garret, miserable and delirious. Slowly, Charlotte recovered her health and strength.

The truth was that Charlotte had Benjamin Hunt Biggs by her side and not La Marquise, but otherwise this could well be an accurate depiction of her first experience of life inside a French prison. She had mentioned a strong dislike of the local, dirty children in Briton Ferry where she had recoiled from the idea of teaching the urchins and her fastidious nature would have been equally repulsed by a stinking and overcrowded garret. It is easy to imagine her upsetting the other prisoners with her insistence on sprinkling her perfume around her corner and she was ever prone to being a little sickly (probably she was being entirely honest when she described Mrs D___ as something of an invalid).

Around 300 men, women and children now resided in the *maison d'arrêt* at Arras. Among this throng were aristocrats, the relatives of émigrés, priests, nuns, farmers, shopkeepers and merchants. Some had been accused – falsely or otherwise – of concealing provisions or creating a monopoly, others for not attending the constitutional mass at their church, while some simply had the misfortune to be in the wrong place at the wrong time. Victoire, 21 years old and a pretty *couturiere* or seamstress who had stitched shirts and linen for the girls in the Panthemont at Paris, had left to help her brother in his shop at St Omer, a town on the road between Arras and Calais. There she had repulsed the advances of a local townsman. By way of revenge, the spurned man reported Victoire to the authorities, claiming that she had not attended the constitutional mass, and she was arrested, put into a cart and transported to the prison. The man who had caused her incarceration appeared daily at the prison gates, promising to get her released if she would only grant him sexual favours. If friends – or enemies – wished to speak to a prisoner they could do so at the gate in the presence of the guards and while parcels and letters could pass to and from the building, all were examined. The servants who had accompanied their masters and mistresses were not held as prisoners themselves but even so were not allowed to go into the town, a rule that forced many people to rely on the keeper of the prison for their every want and he made them pay handsomely for the privilege.

This was the period known to history as the 'Reign of Terror', when the revolution descended into months of increased and radical violence. Jean-Marie Collot d'Herbois, a former actor and playwright but now a member of the Committee of Public Safety, proposed separating the prisoners and putting them into buildings that had been mined with gunpowder and at the first sign of an insurrection the buildings could be blown up. At any other time, Charlotte would have relied on the common decency of her fellow man and been certain that such a plan would never be put into operation. Now, however, she was not so sure. Many servants left their masters and mistresses to fend for themselves; to stay and serve the employers to whom they were loyal was one thing, but to stay and risk being blown to smithereens was an entirely different matter. Charlotte noticed that more of the female servants bravely chose to stay than their male counterparts; there was more loyalty, trust and friendship between a mistress and her personal maid as well as a bond through their sex, regardless of their different social status.

The man who was deputy commissioner of the revolutionary tribunals in Arras – tribunals in which there were no appeals to the sentence handed down – was Joseph Le Bon; Charlotte described him as immoral and bloodthirsty. He directed the juries to find as he wished, saving the unfortunate prisoner or condemning them to death as his whims directed. Le Bon was a former priest and mayor of Arras and his abuse of power would lead to his own demise upon the guillotine but, late in 1793, he was a man whose very name struck terror into the hearts of the prisoners. One story told about him concerned two beautiful young girls in Arras, both under 20 years of age, who were practising on their pianofortes on the morning that news of the surrender of Valenciennes reached their city; Le Bon was walking past their window and happened to hear them. The two girls were playing the revolutionary air

*Ça Ira* but Le Bon was incensed and had them arrested and condemned to the guillotine. The mere act of playing the piano, he asserted, on the day that news of a republican defeat reached the city was proof of their treachery. He accused them of playing *Ça Ira* 'for the Austrian army…they desired the Austrian advance and the capture of other French fortresses. Why did they not, if they were true patriots, play *Le Réveil du Peuple?*'[14]

Charlotte's friend Eugenia de St Evremond was also a prisoner along with her sisters. Her father had been taken to Paris where he was executed after a letter from a female relation who had emigrated was found in his possession and her husband, himself an émigré, returned in disguise from Italy but was recognized and arrested. He too was guillotined. Eugenia's lover heard of her misfortune but before he could get leave from the army he was mortally wounded in a skirmish and died. One of his last acts had been to write to his father asking him to protect Eugenia, but the old man had also been rounded up and taken to the guillotine. Eugenia was grief-stricken.

The aristocratic La Marquise was bereft at losing her liberty and bored without her traditional pursuits. Her earlier life had been spent, in the main, at the Panthemont, followed by three years married to a bad-tempered husband. After just a short period of freedom she now found herself a prisoner and despaired of ever enjoying her independence again. Charlotte was in a similar position. She had spent three years as a prisoner in Peterborough House before escaping to reside in a convent. After a brief spell of enjoying her freedom and liberty she now, once again, had to learn to live without these.

On 14 October 1793 Marie Antoinette was taken to stand trial, accused of incest, treason and conspiracy (although the charge of incest – a trumped-up allegation that she had sexually abused her own son – was dropped before the jury retired to find their verdict). She was found guilty, the verdict decided upon by the Committee of Public Safety in the early hours of 16 October. From then on things moved quickly. Back in her cell at La Conciergerie, Marie Antoinette wrote a letter to her sister-in-law Madame Élisabeth leaving instructions for her children and imploring Madame Élisabeth to look after them if they managed to reunite in the future. She ended the letter by writing: 'Farewell, my good and loving sister; may this letter reach you safely! Think always of me, I embrace you with all my heart, as well as my poor dear children: my God! How dreadful it is to leave them forever! Farewell! Farewell!' The letter was never delivered but was preserved by the tyrant of the revolution, Maximilien Robespierre.[15]

At around 7 o'clock in the morning, Marie Antoinette's maid cut her hair and she dressed in a white cotton gown with a black petticoat and a white mob cap threaded with a black ribbon (the only other clothes she had besides the black dress she had worn to her trial, which she was told not to wear to her execution). A gentleman who had witnessed Marie Antoinette pass by him on her way to the guillotine told Charlotte that the former queen's cotton dress was short like a bedgown and, like her cap, was discoloured by smoke. In his opinion, her whole appearance was designed to degrade her in the eyes of the people.

Prior to leaving La Conciergerie, Marie Antoinette's hands were tied behind her back by the executioner. Louis XVI had been allowed to keep his hands unbound until he reached the Place de la Révolution and had travelled there in a carriage, both small marks of respect towards him and the position he had held. Marie Antoinette received no such compassion and, with her hands bound behind her, she was made to travel in an open cart, no distinction made between her and any common criminal. The crowd shouted abuse at her but the former queen remained calm and dignified, sitting straight-backed in the cart. The only time she showed emotion was when she caught sight of the Tuileries palace and was wracked with memories of her children and her past life. It was noon when Marie Antoinette reached the guillotine and fifteen minutes later she was dead, her head severed from her body.[16]

Inside Charlotte's prison, Marie Antoinette's demise was a taboo subject, partly due to fear that spies were present disguised as fellow prisoners who would report back to the authorities. Most kept their heads down and their mouths closed and tried to pass without attracting any undue interest. Charlotte despaired of release from her captivity. For La Marquise, a ray of hope shone that at least she may be able to gain a transfer to a less crowded prison. Her confidential servant, a man named Fleury, travelled from Péronne to visit his mistress with some promising news. Fleury had learned that a former acquaintance, a man who had worked with the tailor used by La Marquise's husband before his death, had changed professions and become a privy counsellor to the deputy commissioner of the tribunals, the dreaded Joseph Le Bon. The former tailor had promised Fleury that he would use his influence with Le Bon to get La Marquise transferred to Amiens.

Fleury was lucky in his visit to the Arras *maison d'arrêt* as the guard on duty at the gate allowed him to enter a few paces into the yard and speak privately to La Marquise. He told his mistress that the former tailor's republican principles had been shaken by news of her imprisonment and his patriotic zeal had also been reduced by the loss of his 'superb English boots'. The previous night an order had gone out to everyone in Arras requisitioning boots as the cavalry needed them. The former tailor – who knew nothing of the order – was staying at an inn and had put his boots outside his door to be cleaned. His annoyance at finding himself bootless upon waking in the morning made him all the more sympathetic to La Marquise's plight.

A few days later Fleury brought good news. He had managed to get an order – signed by Joseph Le Bon – for La Marquise and her maid to be transferred to Amiens under the supervision of two members of the National Guard, providing she paid for the expense of the journey. In Amiens prisoners were treated less harshly and, more importantly, no revolutionary tribunal had yet been established there which took away the shadow of the guillotine. It was at Amiens, at the Providence convent, that Mr and Mrs Biggs were held. Charlotte, in her published account, still placed herself at La Marquise's side, travelling with her to Amiens, the town where she had really been held all along.

The journey took two days in gloomy November weather but eventually, after night had fallen, La Marquise arrived in Amiens and presented herself at the town hall. André Dumont, the man who had ordered La Marquise's arrest at Péronne, was present. An enmity had arisen between Dumont and Joseph Le Bon and once he heard that La Marquise and her maid had travelled from Arras he flew into a temper and threatened to send them straight back, believing it was Le Bon himself who had planned to send them to Amiens. Massaging his ego and implying respect for his authority, it was suggested that, having initially been arrested by Dumont, she wished to stay in a place where he had jurisdiction. He relented and agreed that she should remain, for the time being, in Amiens and ordered her taken to the Bicêtre.

The very name Bicêtre struck terror into the heart of La Marquise. The Bicêtre in Paris was notorious as a lunatic asylum; it was where the Marquis de Sade, famed for his sexual liberality, was later held. Fearing that the place of the same name in Amiens was a similar institution, La Marquise recoiled in horror. Despite her terror, she was escorted out into the dark and dreary night.

The Bicêtre at Amiens was a huge and sprawling building originally built as the common gaol and workhouse of the province and a quarter of a mile from the town, located in the Saint Roch area of Amiens. The building was damp and unhealthy, not least because the water was bad. Guards were placed at every road to the building and no contact was allowed with the outside world except by letter and all letters, incoming and outgoing, were scrutinized by at least three people before they were delivered. There was no garden or grounds in which the miserable prisoners could take any exercise; instead they had to content themselves with walking along the damp passageways or congregating in a small yard only 30 feet square, if they could stand the smell of the dank little area.

La Marquise entered the Bicêtre by a cavernous kitchen and her pocket-books were searched for papers or letters, while the guards rummaged in her trunks and baggage in case knives or firearms had been secreted within. Satisfied that she did not pose a threat, she was escorted to a draughty, elevated barn, 70 feet long and with the rain falling through the roof where it was missing tiles. This barn was occupied by sixty old, sick and wretched priests and there was scant room left. As well as prisoners of the revolution, the Bicêtre at Amiens housed common criminals and lunatics, although not an asylum like the Bicêtre in Paris, but despite this, La Marquise's fears gradually receded. Indeed, over the ensuing days the knowledge that she was, for the present, safe from the guillotine gave her some peace of mind.

Conditions in La Marquise's old *maison d'arrêt* at Arras had significantly worsened. The agents working for Le Bon stole the prisoners' belongings, food and provisions and separated husbands from wives and parents from children. Moreover, they treated the elderly with savage barbarity and forced themselves onto the young women who were held there. Similar scenes were played out in prisons across the country and Amiens felt safe in comparison. Among her fellow prisoners was a man who, four months previously, had been in charge of the Army of the North. General Le Veneur had taken command following the arrest for treason of another general, Adam Phillipe, Comte de Custine who had failed to aid the besieged town of Condé-sur-l'Escaut (a town on the border with Belgium) in their struggle against the Austrian forces. The Comte de Custine, known affectionately by his troops as '*général moustache*' due to his wonderful whiskers, had been taken to Paris to stand trial.

Command of the Army of the North had therefore devolved upon General Alexis-Paul-Michel Tanneguy Le Veneur de Tillières. General Le Veneur was only in command for a month; he felt it incumbent upon himself to send a letter to Paris in defence of one of the charges laid against *général moustache*, that of having sent out some countersigns. It had been Le Veneur who had received the list of countersigns upon taking command and it had been he who had sent them out. This admission made no difference to the fate of Custine who was found guilty of treason and taken to the guillotine in Paris. Instead, Le Veneur's letter drew suspicion upon himself and he was relieved of his command and arrested, held in various dungeons and prisons before eventually being deposited in the Bicêtre at Amiens.[17]

A kindly gentleman, concerned for his wife and children in Paris, General Le Veneur often walked around the small prison yard with La Marquise. His aide-de-camp had been arrested with him together with another officer, a friend who was suspended from duties and living in Amiens. This friend had called on Dumont to ask that General Le Veneur's servant might be permitted to go in and out of the prison while carrying out the general's instructions and errands. After enjoying a breakfast with his guest, Dumont turned to the officer and told him, very civilly, that as he was so concerned with his friend then he would send him to keep company with the general. Consequently, after finishing breakfast the unfortunate friend was despatched as a prisoner to the Bicêtre.

Winter was now upon the prisoners, making their situation even more unbearable. La Marquise was still housed in the elevated barn where the wind howled through the gaps in the roof and doors and there was nowhere to light a fire for warmth. The prisoners huddled in their cloaks with blankets wrapped around themselves and had scant provisions. The water was tainted and bread was scarce and gave little nourishment. Added to the physical ills was the mental anguish of not knowing their destiny, not knowing how long they were to be confined or even if there was a yet worse fate in store for them. One night the prisoners were woken from their slumbers by the sound of tramping feet and heard their door being unlocked. As it creaked open, an unpleasant, threatening man entered, carrying a lantern and followed by two soldiers with drawn swords and a large dog. This little company walked slowly down the barn, looking at each bed in turn, before eventually reaching the end where La Marquise and her maid lay in abject terror. Remembering the September massacres, they feared the soldiers were going to start cutting about them with their swords. Instead, after silently staring at the women they turned and left the room. With no explanation for this nocturnal visit, the ladies could only conclude that it was designed to scare and alarm the prisoners and increase their torment.

At this point in her memoir, Charlotte mentioned that the English couple, Mr and Mrs D___ who, we suspect, were really Charlotte and Benjamin Hunt Biggs, had been away from home when Toulon was taken by Admiral Hood and the order went out to arrest all the English who had not been in France since before 1789. Charlotte claimed that they had been taken up and imprisoned at Arras but Mr and Mrs Biggs had, in reality, been held in the Providence at Amiens since 7 September 1793. Charlotte's published memoirs and real life were – at last – about to collide as La Marquise was moved to the actual prison in which the Biggs' resided.

A few days into the month of December, La Marquise was given the news that she and her maid were to be transferred once again. Remaining in Amiens, they were to be taken from the Bicêtre and placed instead into the Providence *maison d'arrêt*, a former convent. The faithful Fleury was waiting outside when La Marquise was marched to the Providence. He had contacted every one of La Marquise's friends who might have been able to help but none were willing to risk their own liberty or necks. Beginning to despair, he accidentally bumped into a girl who had worked as a housemaid for La Marquise and discovered that she had become one of Dumont's mistresses. Thus he obtained the patronage he sought, not from one of La Marquise's noble friends but from one of her servants who still remembered her fondly and with kindness. Could it be a possibility that it might have been now, in December 1793 and in the former Providence convent, that Charlotte first made the acquaintance of La Marquise rather than as a young woman in the Panthemont convent?

The Providence was crowded with prisoners but it was a spacious building in a decent state of repair and it was possible to secure a small and private cell, although any attendant servants had to sleep outside in the corridor. There was a large garden in which to walk, the drinking water was good and the prisoners could deliver letters and messages personally to their friends if a guard was present. All in all, it was a much more comfortable lodging than many other prisons. Still, the days passed slowly and Charlotte's main concern was keeping herself occupied. La Marquise knitted and drew landscapes on the back of cards but Charlotte preferred to read. She had first borrowed books from among her fellow prisoners but soon got through the small quantity available and so a correspondence was quickly established with a local bookseller, an old man who blithely sent in works on chemistry and fortifications for Charlotte to read instead of the poetry and memoirs she wished for, but she was grateful all the same.

It was not only those of aristocratic birth who fell under the suspicion of the revolutionaries. Charlotte noted that the persecution of merchants and clergymen had increased. Even the guards at the Providence could not escape the perils of suspicion. An old man had been a prisoner in the Providence for some time and his son worked as a guard there. The son had petitioned Dumont on behalf of his father and in return, at the end of the day when he was preparing to go home, was faced with his wife and children under armed escort and the whole family was soon held in custody. Nobody was safe as Dumont continued to run the district in accordance with his own rules. A fellow inmate at the Providence was Madame de Witt, a Fleming belonging to an ancient Dutch family. As an old lady, more than 70 years of age and accused of nothing more than being charitable and religious, she was imprisoned, while a fellow Flemish lady who had lived for some time in Amiens, a young pretty woman who by the law should also have been incarcerated as a foreigner, still enjoyed her liberty and appeared daily on the arm of Dumont. He was the maker, the interpreter and the executor of the laws and able to exempt those he chose. Although he was married, Dumont enjoyed the attractions of a pretty face, especially one whose owner also held high rank. If it was known that he was visiting a *maison d'arrêt* there was inevitably a commotion among the younger females who used whatever arts were available to improve their appearance before waiting in the yard to present a petition to him asking for clemency and mercy. Dumont refused to accept a petition from any woman who was old or ugly – and was rendered furious if a man dared to do so – but he did sometimes, just occasionally, allow the smiles and tears of a well-born and attractive woman to sway his judgement in return for payment in kind from the fair penitent. Charlotte and La Marquise, both now having passed the first flush of youth and having had their fill of such men in their previous lives, looked on the activity occasioned by his visits to the Providence with bemusement and did not bother to debase themselves.

When an order was made in the spring of 1794 to arrest all the families of nobility in the area and to prevent them from communicating with the outside world, the prisons were soon so full that no more inmates could be squeezed in. Two large buildings in Amiens were appointed to receive male prisoners and, at the same time, it was decided to adopt a more severe regimen, separating husbands from wives and splitting families apart. Ostensibly this was to preserve good morals but, in reality, it merely added to the misery already faced by the poor prisoners. Charlotte's spurious English friends Mr and Mrs D___ were suffering hardship and Mrs D___ had become so ill that she had been taken to a hospital; they both had their belongings stolen including a small supply of necessary items and were struggling financially. If, as we assume, Mrs D___ was Charlotte in disguise, does this mean that she was taken to an Amiens hospital, possibly made ill by a nervous complaint when she was cruelly separated from Benjamin Hunt Biggs? La Marquise was also taken ill and moved to the hospital.

At the beginning of June, André Dumont was recalled to Paris. Fearful that he had not been severe enough in his management of his department, he ordered that the prisons in Amiens be more strictly guarded. Although Dumont had been a tyrant and a monster, Charlotte lamented his departure when she learned who was to replace him: none other than Joseph Le Bon, the man who had been head of the prisons at Arras. The cruelties he imposed there had marked him out for elevation and rewards and his jurisdiction had been increased to cover the department in which Charlotte resided. Stories had reached her ears that he had ordered executions at Arras to take place in a small square rather than the larger town square so Le Bon, his wife and friends could watch from the balcony of the theatre, enjoying the spectacle as the musicians played along in accompaniment to the butchery of the guillotine. Some friends of Charlotte's happened to be passing one such execution in open carts on their way to prison; Dumont ordered the carts to halt and the passengers to watch the guillotine fall. They were obliged to cry '*Vive la Republique*' each time the blade dropped. By now many people known to Charlotte had fallen victim to the guillotine, some of them her personal friends, and her fate once again lay at the mercy of this dreaded man.

The author of *A Residence in France* now fell silent for some weeks, afraid of the imminent arrival of Le Bon until, in mid-August, emboldened by recent developments in the world outside the prison walls, she was once again bold enough to take up her pen.

Maximilien Robespierre, who had sent so many to have their heads severed from their bodies, had himself fallen victim to the guillotine on 28 July 1794. Charged with tyranny and dictatorship, he and five of his colleagues – including his brother Augustin – gathered at the Hôtel de Ville (city hall) in Paris. Declared outlaws, a decree which meant they could – without a trial – summarily be put to death within twenty-four hours, Robespierre and his friends despaired and tried to cheat the guillotine. Georges Couthon, a politician, lawyer and member of the Committee of Public Safety who was confined to a wheelchair due to paralysis of his legs (his doctors blamed meningitis but he himself blamed his sexual activities as a youth), threw himself down a staircase and was found at the bottom, still alive but in agony. François Hanriot, a low-born street orator who had risen during the revolution to be commandant general of the Parisian National Guard had arrived with his troops to release his friends but instead found himself trapped with them when counter-troops arrived. He fell from a side window and was discovered, unconscious, in an open sewer. Augustin

Robespierre escaped through an upstairs window to evade capture but plummeted onto the steps of the Hôtel de Ville when he slipped from a ledge. Maximilien Robespierre attempted suicide; he shot himself in the head but only managed to shatter his lower jaw, while his comrade, Philippe Lebas, replicated the act but with more success. Only Louis Antoine de Saint-Just, the youngest of the deputies elected to the National Convention in 1792, was left able to walk from the building.

The next day the five men who had not managed to end their lives in the Hôtel de Ville were taken to the guillotine in open carts with other prisoners condemned to death. Everyone wanted to see the dreaded tyrant Robespierre on his last journey and the Parisian streets were crowded along the route to the Place de la Révolution. Maximilien Robespierre met his end amid screams of pain as the dirty bandage holding his shattered jaw together was wrenched from his head prior to his execution. Couthon too died in agony; due to his paralysis it took fifteen minutes to arrange him on the board of the guillotine and his screams equalled those of Robespierre. Augustin Robespierre was likewise carried to the guillotine, already half-dead. Saint-Just went calmly to his death, while Hanriot was only half-conscious and had to be dragged to the scaffold.[18]

Robespierre's death marked the beginning of the end as far as Charlotte's captivity was concerned. She would not have to wait too much longer now to regain her freedom and liberty.

## Chapter Six

# Return to England

The infamous eighteenth-century courtesan Grace Dalrymple Elliott was Charlotte's contemporary in France and, like Charlotte, Grace later wrote down her account of that period as it related to her own experiences and adventures. Grace's *Journal of My Life During the French Revolution* had started off recording her experiences in France with some accuracy. The proven inaccuracies crept in towards the end of her account and, we suspect, were added by her publisher to increase interest and sales. Charlotte's *A Residence in France during the years 1792–1795* conversely begins with an embellished account of her adventures but towards the end begins to chime with the true facts, an exact opposite of Grace's journal. When Charlotte related that she was released from her prison and allowed home to Amiens, she was indeed partially telling the truth as letters were received in England from Mr and Mrs Biggs, pleading for help in returning to England. The letters were directed to Charlotte's father and sent to his new home at Theakston near Bedale in North Yorkshire.[1]

While Charlotte was absent in France, John Williams and his new wife Sarah relocated from busy and bustling Lambeth to the remoteness of Theakston, little more than a hamlet situated amid the (mainly agricultural) rolling countryside to be found at the foot of the Yorkshire Dales. The nearest church was St Lambert's in the village of Burneston half a mile away, and Bedale, a small market town that had undergone a great deal of improvement in the late eighteenth century and was known for its millinery and shoe-making businesses, lay 3 miles to the north-west. John's house was recently built and provided 'every convenience and accommodation for a genteel small family' with the additional benefit of a coach house and stabling for eight horses, a large dovecote and a walled garden lined with fruit trees. It was a world away from noisy Lambeth and its riverside industries.[2]

Charlotte's account in *A Residence in France* was only partially true, however, as she was not in Amiens any more but instead was living at Abbeville some 30 miles away, for it was there that she wrote to her father on 20 September 1794 asking for his help in getting passports for herself and Benjamin Hunt Biggs. The couple were, she wrote, tolerably well considering their unhappy situation but Charlotte wanted more than anything to come home. John

Williams approached Mr Hardey, a man who had influence with Thomas Brudenell-Bruce, 1st Earl of Ailesbury (whose family were North Yorkshire landowners), asking for his or the earl's assistance in obtaining passports for his daughter and her husband. John Williams, in the letter he wrote to Mr Hardey, referred to the couple as Mr and Mrs Biggs; did John Williams believe that the pair were married? He also mentioned that any letter or passport should be addressed to:

> la Citoyenne Biggs Abbeville department de la France Abbeville
> Department de la France
> Inclosed [sic] as under
> Messrs Nicholas and Nicolas Priors – Banquiers a Basle Suisse.[3]

It appears that Charlotte and Benjamin held an account with a Swiss banking house and wished their correspondence to be directed to them. Their movements are shrouded in mystery, secrecy and a certain amount of subterfuge. Exactly one week later an advert was placed in the *London Gazette* newspaper:

> Mr. Benjamin Biggs, late of Putney in the County of Surry [sic], Gentleman.
>     Whereas the said Benjamin Biggs has for several Years past been absent from his Relations and Friends; Notice is hereby given, that if any Person can give Information to Mr. Parker, of Greville-Street, Hatton-Garden, where the said Mr. Biggs now is, or, if dead, where he was buried, they shall be handsomely rewarded for their Trouble.[4]

Benjamin Hunt Biggs was certainly in France, in Abbeville with Charlotte who was passing to the world at large as his wife. In 1792, before he left for France, Benjamin had taken out a Sun Fire Office insurance policy on 17 Old Broad Street in the City of London, a property he jointly occupied with a stockbroker named Joseph Blizard (who owned property in Barnes, Wandsworth and in Putney alongside houses owned by Benjamin). Blizard acted for Benjamin and had probably been entrusted to handle his affairs while he was overseas (he had also witnessed the will of Mary Biggs, Benjamin's mother, years earlier). Was it Blizard who had put the enquiry regarding Benjamin's whereabouts in the newspapers, asking for information? On 16 May 1795, the 3rd Duke of Portland (as the Home Secretary and on behalf of King George III) licensed Joseph Blizard to remit a payment to 'B.H. Biggs in Abbeville, France'. The money was invaluable and was needed by the Biggses to pay for their passage home.[5]

Throughout the remainder of 1794 and into the following year Charlotte, in *A Residence in France*, places herself resolutely in Amiens despite the actual evidence that she was now in Abbeville. She claims to have travelled to Péronne to see her friend La Marquise, made another trip to visit Madame Eugenia de St Evremond and her two sisters and journeyed to Basse Ville, Arras to fetch Mr and Mrs D___ back to Amiens. Her guard was finally withdrawn and she gives a couple of personal details. She received post from England and had obviously been informed of the death of someone close to her as she wished to wear mourning but felt unable to as it would draw unwanted attention to herself. Charlotte also mentioned that an American friend of her brother had passed through Amiens and delivered two parcels containing finery. A brother? Charlotte had no brother. This more than anything else points to the letters having been written by her friend La Marquise whose brother had left France as an émigré.

Charlotte's friend died at the beginning of June 1795 in Paris. With La Marquise conveniently out of the way, is it possible that Charlotte appropriated that lady's adventures, falsely putting herself alongside the marquise as a narrator and then publishing the account as her own work? It is a distinct possibility that this is indeed the case for the few documented glimpses of Charlotte during these years disprove her version of events as it relates to herself. However, *A Residence in France* is too detailed, too accurate in its representation to be merely a work of fiction and if Charlotte did not directly experience all the events recorded within its pages, then someone close to her surely did.

By the end of the month Benjamin Hunt Biggs and Charlotte were at Le Havre, seeking a ship upon which they could cross the Channel and return home. With the money remitted to them by Blizard and their new passports they found a berth but, upon reaching Dover, Charlotte was detained and her papers, which were suspected to be seditious, were searched. After a few worrying hours she was permitted to pass through the port. Finally, Charlotte was safe.[6]

One of the first priorities for Charlotte and Benjamin upon their return to England was to find somewhere to live. They took possession of Farrington House, a fine old mansion house complete with a stable, garden and 2-acre orchard in the village of Farrington Gurney, Somerset. It was not too far from Bath and was a property owned by the Mogg family who leased the estate of Farrington from the Duchy of Cornwall. Five years before the Biggs' arrival, the Reverend John Collinson wrote that the village

> contains about ninety houses, and four hundred and sixty inhabitants. The country here is closely wooded, and more on a level than most of the adjacent parishes. There is a coal-work here, belonging to Mr Mogg, of High Littleton, who owns the greatest part of the parish, and has two good houses therein.[7]

From the late nineteenth century and long after the Biggs' tenure there, the house became known as The Parsonage as it was used for precisely that purpose although never owned by the church, but in 1795 it was simply the smaller of two manor houses in the village. It stands at the corner of Main Street which was once, as its name suggests, the principal village street and Rush Hill, then the turnpike road from Bristol (13 miles away) to Wells via Shepton Mallet but now the busy A37. The city of Bath lay just over 10 miles distant and Wells 8 miles away. Built of dressed red sandstone in the late seventeenth century, probably in the 1680s, the mansion has a U-shaped façade (it was re-orientated around 1715 by the addition of two wings to the west-facing elevation, giving the building a new and more imposing 'front', and adding a new staircase) and comprises two storeys. The whole appearance is redolent of a French château and maybe the Biggses, after their long – if forced – residence in France, found the appearance of their new home familiar and somewhat reassuring. Charlotte, despite her imprisonment during the revolutionary years, ever remained a committed Francophile.[8]

Now that his ordeal was over, Benjamin Hunt Biggs was content to live in quiet obscurity, his inheritance and the rents from the properties in Putney built by his father providing a handsome income. Charlotte, however, was cut from a different cloth. The late summer months of 1795 were exceptionally hot and dry but Charlotte had no time to enjoy the countryside around her new home. She set to trying to get the bundle of letters that she had brought back from France published anonymously and approached the well-known publisher John Stockdale, a man who Charlotte knew to be in favour with the government of the day. Although he had a reputation as a prolific publisher, Stockdale flatly turned down Charlotte's manuscript. His answer was 'impolite and repulsive' and he rejected Charlotte's manuscript with disdain as it was anonymous.[9]

Why would Charlotte wish for anonymity in the publication of her work? It may have been because, as in the opinion of the contemporaneous Scottish author Elizabeth Hamilton, 'prejudice against the known opinions, or even the *sex*, of a writer may unwittingly bias the reader's mind.' Conversely, Helen Maria Williams, a writer who was also caught up in the turmoil in France, brooked no such female reserve and published her accounts under her own name. With these two examples before her, Charlotte's choice most probably was borne of a third option. She had an ulterior motive for remaining anonymous: if Charlotte had appropriated another lady's memoirs then she had every reason to want her name kept off the title page, lest she be found out. There had been a flurry of memoirs released in 1795 from people caught up in the drama in France, Helen Maria Williams' among them. If Charlotte was to stand any chance of being published then she needed a 'dramatic' account but one that smacked of authenticity. She had spent her captivity in a small provincial prison where she was not subjected to excessive hardship and so her own account would suffer among the competition and appear tame. With her own first-hand experiences meshed with those of her aristocratic friend, however, she had a memoir to publish that might capture public interest.[10]

Although she was irked by Stockdale's comments, Charlotte still hoped that another publisher would look more favourably upon her manuscript and rather ambitiously dedicated it to Edmund Burke, MP. Burke, who was a vehement opponent of the principles behind the French republic, had formerly been the Whig minister for Malton, the very area in which Charlotte's father lived. Had John Williams supported and voted for Burke, one wonders? Burke aligned himself with Pitt's government due to his stance on the French Revolution which was in accord with Charlotte's views and sympathies but at odds with that taken by Charles James Fox, the leader of the Whig Party.[11]

## DEDICATION
## TO THE
## RIGHT HON. EDMUND BURKE

SIR,

It is with extreme diffidence that I offer the following pages to Your notice; yet as they describe circumstances which more than justify Your own prophetic reflections, and are submitted to the public eye from no other motive than a love of truth and my country, I may, perhaps, be excused for presuming them to be not altogether unworthy of such a distinction.

While Your puny opponents, if opponents they may be called, are either sunk into oblivion, or remembered only as associated with the degrading cause they attempted to support, every true friend of mankind, anticipating the judgment of posterity, views, with esteem and veneration, the unvarying Moralist, the profound politician, the indefatigable Servant of the Public, and the warm Promoter of his country's happiness.

To this universal testimony of the great and good, permit me, Sir, to join my humble tribute; being, with the utmost respect,

SIR,

Your obedient Servant,

THE AUTHOR.

SEPTEMBER 12, 1796

Determined to see her manuscript in print, complete with the dedication to Edmund Burke, Charlotte turned instead to John Gifford.

Gifford had been born John Richards Green and inherited a considerable estate from his grandparents while still young which, perhaps predictably, he ran through quickly. Escaping to France to avoid the clutches of his creditors, at the age of 23 he changed his name to John Gifford. Sometime later he returned to England and found success as an historian and political writer; his *History of France* marked him out as an anti-revolutionary and he began collaborating with Pitt's government on a series of publications both anti-Jacobin and favourable to the ministry. In 1796 he became the editor of the *True Briton* newspaper and it was by this means that Charlotte initially made his acquaintance.

After the rude rejection of her manuscript by Stockdale, she began to correspond with the newspapers to get her voice heard. The *True Briton* printed several of her letters and Charlotte at last approached the editor (whose name, she said, she did not know at that time) to ask for his help in getting her book published. Gifford agreed at once and offered to counter its anonymity by warranting 'its authenticity by the sanction of his name'. He put the manuscript into the hands of Thomas Norton Longman, a respected publishing house located on Paternoster Row in the City of London and Charlotte's book found its way into the world, titled *A Residence in France*

*during the years 1792, 1793, 1794, and 1795; described in a series of letters from
an English Lady: with general and incidental remarks on the French character
and manners.* Gifford's name also appeared on the title page and just below
was a quote from the French actor and playwright Pierre-Laurent Buirette
de Belloy, otherwise Dormont de Belloy, taken from his patriotic work *Le
Siège de Calais (1765): Plus je vis l'Etranger plus j'aimai ma Patrie* (The
longer I live abroad the more I love my country).[12]

Generally the reviews were extremely good but Charlotte would have
been disappointed by what the *Monthly Review* had to say. Their criticism
highlighted all too clearly the reasons why Charlotte might have 'enhanced'
her own first-hand recollections and we begin to see why, with an acute
perception in judging her readership, Charlotte may have been persuaded
to do so. In fact, she had perhaps not gone far enough and in the *Monthly
Review*'s opinion, *A Residence in France* did not stand out from the other
narratives that had been published:

> This copious and somewhat tedious correspondence describes the
> impression made, in two or three provincial towns of France, by the
> revolution which occurred at Paris, between 1792 and 1795... Few
> facts occur which are not already familiar; and few reflections are
> interspersed which are of great importance; yet the historian may
> obtain material information, and the public some amusement, from
> a perusal of the volumes.[13]

Emboldened by her debut as an author and memorialist, albeit an anonymous
one, Charlotte's second foray into print bore little relation to her first work
but did have echoes of her past life stamped throughout it. Charlotte wrote
a comedy in five acts titled *What Is She?* which was performed in 1799 at
the Theatre Royal in London's Covent Garden. The end of the prologue
revealed the anonymous author to be a female.[14]

> To night a female Scribe, less bold, appears,
> She dreads to pull the house about your ears;
> Her inexperienc'd Muse no plan durst form,
> To raise the Spectre, or direct the Storm;
> And if her pen no genuine plaudits steal,
> From ears – to eyes she offers no appeal;
> Her Muse, tho' humble, scorns extrinsic art,
> And asks her meed – from judgement to the heart.

A comedy of errors in which all the main characters were pretending to be someone other than who they really were, it was Mrs Eugenia Derville, one of the two female leads, who invoked the ghost of Charlotte's past life. Set in north Wales, Mrs Derville was living alone in a Caernarfonshire village inciting suspicion and gossip from her neighbours as to her true station in life, much as Charlotte had spent the year in Briton Ferry in south Wales hoping to escape attention and unwarranted curiosity. In the second act two other characters, Mrs Gurnet and Lady Zephyrine Mutable, are discussing Mrs Derville:

> *Mrs Gurnet*: Well now I think there's something most romantically interesting in a young woman's living in a farm here by herself, and nobody to know who she is, or whence she came. I'm sure there's some mystery.
>
> *Lady Zephyrine*: 'Tis vulgar to be curious – and I really know no more, than that she is very young, very pretty, and very prudent, and doesn't seem accustomed to the state she is in.

Throughout the play, Mrs Derville hints at a sorry episode in her past. It is revealed to be an unfortunate marriage, contracted when she was very young, and Charlotte has obviously drawn upon the memory of her treatment at the hands of Richard Heaviside in her narrative. It also hints that perhaps she had been more accepting of her plight than she later suggested:

> *Mrs Derville (gaily)*: Oh! my history, Madam, is the history of everybody; and for that reason, nobody wou'd read it (*ironically*). 'Tis so common for men to be base, and women weak, that the vices of one sex, and the follies of the other, are subjects for jests and bon-mots rather than history.

A further piece of dialogue between Mrs Derville and her admirer Mr Belford (who is really Lord Orton), speaks directly about Ochterlony straight from Charlotte's own impassioned heart and about her degradation at the hands of her tormentor. It is indeed Charlotte's own history, used as a narrative for the back-story and emotions of her fictional character:

> *Mrs Derville (with an accent of depression)*: But where [to] find such a lover, such sincerity? Where is the man that has not to reproach

himself with the misery of woman? Is there a female who has not, some time in her life, been the victim of her sensibility? – (*becomes impassioned as she proceeds, and ends almost in tears*) – Yet, you wonder that we become false, dissipated coquettes, and sometimes worse. Warm, enthusiastic, we fancy life a path strewed with roses. We expect to find nothing but happiness and integrity. At an age when our hearts are tender, and our reason weak, we make the choice which is to fix our destiny for ever – and she who, perhaps, might have lived in the bosom of peace and virtue, had she been fortunate in her first affections, irritated and degraded by the conduct of a seducer, devotes herself to all the vices which his example has taught her – and thus revenges her own wretchedness wherever her charms procure her dupes, or victims.

*Belford (alarm'd)*: Oh, misery! Is it possible you can have been exposed to these horrors...

*Mrs Derville (with dignity)*: No Sir; I have nothing to reproach myself with. 'Tis this consoling idea of my own innocence, which has supported, and still supports me under my misfortunes. (*feelingly*) Yet, the deceit, neglect, ingratitude, I have experienced – Oh Sir! You know not what I have suffer'd.

Mrs Derville's forename, Eugenia, conjures up shades of Charlotte's friend from her days in the French convent, the unfortunate Eugenia de Santerre who married Monsieur de St Evremond, both she and Charlotte's friend Adelaide, La Marquise, serve as the inspiration for another episode in Mrs Derville's fictional youth. Both Adelaide and Eugenia were released from their French convent via their respective marriages and neither marriage lasted beyond a few years. Eugenia's husband proved to be a dissipated man who soon abandoned his young wife and Adelaide was married off to an elderly man. A few extracts from the end of *What Is She?* in which Eugenia Derville reveals her past and the cause of her misanthropy and distrust of men serve to illustrate how much Charlotte drew upon her friends' histories as well as on her own (the last extract below may also reference Charlotte's time spent by Richard Heaviside's side and her wish to reinvent herself following her ordeal):

*Mrs Derville*: Alas! Sir, I can scarcely tell – If possible, where I shall be no longer liable to the persecution of man.

*Mrs Derville*: I have already confessed, Sir, that my birth was elevated, my fortune large. At an early age, I was deprived of my parents, and left to the guardianship of an uncle, whose bigotry and avarice suggested to him the design of burying the claimant of a fortune, to which he was next kin, in a convent. Aware of his design – averse to a cloister and irritated by persecution, I accepted of the assistance of a young Englishman, whom chance threw in my way, and escaped from the convent where I was placed.

*Mrs Derville*: My deliverer, I found, was poor; and, e'er I had time to consult my heart, with all the enthusiasm of gratitude at sixteen, I gave him my hand.

*Mrs Derville*: My fortune dissipated, alone, unprotected, awakened to a sense of my early imprudence, and weaned from an attachment which I had in a thoughtless moment rendered a duty, I now felt all the horrors of my situation. My heart wounded by injuries, my spirit embittered by ingratitude, I beheld the world with disgust, mankind with horror, and at nineteen I fancied myself a misanthropist. With the scattered remains of my fortune I retired, under a borrow'd name, to a convent; but the disappointed avarice of my guardian pursued me to my retreat, and obliged me to escape from Florence to Leghorn [Livorno]. Public events again removed me to England; and by the assistance of an English servant I at length settled in my present situation.

Had Charlotte also been rescued from her French convent by a young Englishman, only with a better outcome? It is a possibility that Charlotte's supposed marriage to Benjamin Hunt Biggs was also secretly referenced in her narrative. Charlotte had no fortune for Benjamin to dissipate; instead he was the one with the means to support the pair of them, but he did offer a 'borrowed' name to Charlotte and the opportunity to escape her past and be considered a respectable married lady, an opportunity seized upon willingly by Charlotte. On the other hand, could the man whom Eugenia Derville married when only 16 years of age represent Richard Heaviside? Did he offer an escape from John Williams' plans for his daughter? Perhaps, after Charlotte's first abduction, her father had intended returning her to the convent where she had received her education against her wishes and so, in a moment of madness, Charlotte rewrote her own future with disastrous consequences and returned to Heaviside more willingly than she admitted, only to long for the refuge of the cloisters when the ugly reality of her situation became all too clear?

After it had been performed on the stage, the comedy was printed and offered for sale by the same publishing house used by Charlotte for her former work, Longman of Paternoster Row. She dedicated *What Is She?* to Thomas Harris, the stage manager at the theatre where it had been performed. Harris, predictably given his line of work, was well acquainted with Richard Heaviside's old companion Richard Brinsley Sheridan and with all the references to her former life, to her sufferings at the hands of Heaviside, Charlotte was perhaps sailing very close to the wind. Did Heaviside know of the play, even attend the performance, one wonders, and, if so, did he alone guess the identity of the anonymous female author?

Heaviside was now well married to his Devonshire heiress with whom he had a son and was leading the respectable life of a country gentleman, still occupied in serving (with irony given his past) as a justice of the peace, and perhaps this was Charlotte's way of exacting some revenge. She was reminding him of his crimes, letting him know that she had the power, if she so wished, to unmask him to the world at large. Who knows, it may be that Heaviside was induced to additional financial recompense to Charlotte to secure her secrecy and to keep his past buried. Would anyone really blame Charlotte if she had taken this course, given how Heaviside had blighted her life?[15]

Richard Heaviside's mother, Sarah Prudden, had died in August 1798 at her home on Lambeth's Narrow Wall. Charlotte had been fond of Sarah Prudden and, whatever her opinion of her son, had not wanted to hurt the old lady who had treated her with kindness. Is it relevant that *What Is She?* appeared on the London stage just months after Sarah's death? Had Charlotte been biding her time and waiting for the opportune moment to unleash it at a time when she no longer had to worry that it would cause renewed anguish to Sarah Prudden and when it would be a double blow to Heaviside to strike him in this way when he was still grieving for his mother?[16]

The play was performed at the Theatre Royal in Covent Garden for six nights between 27 April and 2 May 1799 to generally positive acclaim and the printed copy ran to several editions. *The Critical Review, Or, Annals of Literature* said of it that it was 'a comedy more interesting in perusal than many modern pieces, not possessing sufficient merit to last beyond one season, yet with no faults so prominent as to deserve particular censure.' The *Monthly Review* held a similar opinion:

The chief merit of this piece consists in its ridicule on fashionable follies. Absurdities, like those which the author attacks, can only be preserved to memory at the expence of much wit, like carcases embalmed in the most precious spices: but when they are exposed in their own jargon, as in this play, we laugh at them one moment, and almost disbelieve them the next. – This piece, in the Green-Room phrase, is well *cast* for the stage; and, while the modish style of some of the characters remains intelligible, it will bear a perusal.[17]

*What Is She?* then moved out to the provinces. It was performed at the theatre in Canterbury on 1 June 1799 at a benefit performance for the actress Mrs Baker. Having dipped her toes into the waters of the wider world with this brief, if anonymous, venture into literary and theatrical circles, Charlotte began to reinvent herself. She craved travel, recognition and adventure in her life while all the time presenting herself as a misanthropic and unprepossessing married lady. She was anything but that.[18]

## Chapter Seven

# A Female Politician

In the early days of the new century, on 2 March 1800, Charlotte sat down at the desk in her London lodgings, picked up her pen and ventured to write to the Whig MP William Windham, offering him a few 'hints' as to how the government should proceed on matters relating to trade, referring both to country folk working in agriculture and mercantile townspeople. As a woman, Charlotte could never even dream of holding political office but, after reinventing herself as a writer, she now had a new ambition: to be a female politician as far as she was able as a woman in early nineteenth-century England. Her confidence in her own abilities was astounding, as was her blind belief that the statesmen she wrote to would deign to listen and take note of her.

When Charlotte wrote to him, Windham held the position of Secretary at War in Pitt's government and, like the other men that Charlotte chose to ally herself with, was anti-Jacobin and in favour of the restoration of the Bourbon monarchy in France. Windham had been great friends with Charles James Fox and had initially followed his friend in supporting the French Revolution; he had been in Paris in 1789 and 1791. However, his latter visit changed his mind and he now strongly opposed it, with his views echoing those of another of his close acquaintances, Edmund Burke. Eton and Oxford-educated and supremely intelligent, Windham suffered bouts of anxiety at public speaking and thought himself 'a little of two characters and good in neither: a politician among scholars and a scholar among politicians.' He had been a bachelor – and something of a rake – into his late 40s before marrying in 1798.

The return address given by Charlotte on her letter was 141 Fleet Street, premises occupied by Faulkner and Radley's British Wine Manufactory who, like Mark Beaufoy's Lambeth distillery, made raisin wine, a coincidence that harks back to Charlotte's childhood when the Beaufoys had been such good friends to her family. Charlotte was using this address to receive and hold her mail while lodging elsewhere.[1]

Charlotte, as was her wont, managed to mask her forwardness behind a veil of false modesty. Forward enough to brazenly offer her 'hints' to

Windham and to 'respectfully request' that he would suggest them to the prime minister no less but, knowing that her gender would hold her back, she modestly asked Windham to adopt her words and to present them to Pitt as his own. Truly, Charlotte was born in the wrong body. One can all too easily imagine her frustration at being denied the opportunity to stand forth and present her views and opinions on a cause about which she felt strongly. It is also noteworthy that the letter to Windham came from Charlotte and not her 'husband' Benjamin Hunt Biggs. If Charlotte needed a male mouthpiece, Benjamin would have been the ideal candidate and, known as a gentleman, could have readily spoken at meetings and corresponded with the influential men of the day on a more equal basis than Charlotte could ever hope to do. Did Charlotte not fully trust Mr Biggs, or did she feel that he was lacking the drive to promote her work? Did Benjamin even know what she was up to? He always remained a shadowy character in Charlotte's life, occasionally mentioned only in relation to his ill health, there merely to provide an illusion of respectability and to allow Charlotte to pass as a married lady of some independence. Charlotte's overriding desire to have her views heard by the government drove her to seek a different route rather than employing Benjamin as the vessel for her words, and how long had it taken for her to build up the courage and determination to approach Windham, one wonders? Had she approached other men beforehand and been rebuffed but was stubborn enough to continue to seek some form of approval in much the same way that she had persevered in getting her manuscript published upon her return from France? Whatever Windham's surprise may have been on receiving Charlotte's letter, his reply was encouraging enough for her to approach him once again in the summer months, this time writing to suggest to the prime minister via Windham that the price of gamekeeper licences should be increased to raise more revenue.

Charlotte wrote again at the end of November from her country home in Farrington Gurney, but this time she needed to ask a favour of Windham. She revealed that she intended to start work on a short pamphlet that she proposed to call *A Maximum; or, the Rise and Progress of Famine, addressed to the British People*.

The French *maximum* had been imposed by the Convention in 1793, designed to protect the common people from starvation as prices of commodities rose. As Vergnaud, an Orléans merchant and pamphleteer who defended rioters protesting in 1789 said, 'the people ought to have the certainty that the price of bread will never rise beyond their wages.' All well and good, but wages also had a *maximum* applied to them and when prices once more began to rise, the same producers and merchants who were keen to evade the *maximum* on the goods they sold were equally determined to see the *maximum* strictly adhered to as it concerned the wages they paid. Thus, this system that was designed to prevent starvation prices ultimately enabled employers to pay less than a living wage and defeated its own object. Charlotte had initially embraced the principle but now had her eyes open and was determined to speak against it. She recalled a conversation while in prison in which a member of the Convention told her that he treated farmers like dogs, to which Charlotte replied that she hoped the farmers would not repay this by treating the people as worse than dogs, 'for dogs are fed, and, I fear, if we go on this way, we shall be starved'. The man told Charlotte that, in his opinion, it would be as well for France if all the farmers were sent to 'peep out of the national casement' (the guillotine), and Charlotte held her tongue ere she shared a similar fate:

> This law, as foolish as it was wicked, and injurious alike to all without exception, rent asunder the bonds of society, destroyed the main-springs of agriculture, of commerce, industry and the arts; and, as had been too well foreseen, manufactures and works of all kinds consequently ran to decay.[2]

There were suggestions in 1800 to impose a *maximum* in Britain to reduce the price of corn and other provisions and Charlotte had managed to get the ear of a 'Gentleman of the House of Commons' who was known to Windham and whose words would be listened to with respect by the British public. She had proffered her views to this gentleman on the French *maximum* based on her first-hand experience. With casual understatement, Charlotte just matter-of-factly dropped this information into her letter to Windham. Who had Charlotte contacted and exactly who did she know, to be able to enter freely into discussions with eminent government ministers? Moreover, this specific minister had been so impressed with Charlotte's persuasive argument against the *maximum* that he wrote to her, asking her to repeat her words in a pamphlet, 'calculated for the understanding of the lower classes of people, particularly the manufacturers.' Who could this man have been?

A clue can be found within the ministers who spoke in the House of Commons on 26 November 1800 regarding the high price of provisions at that time, some for and some against implementing a *maximum*. William Wilberforce, the independent MP for Yorkshire and well-known as a slavery abolitionist, was one who spoke against such a measure. He referenced a letter he had recently received from an 'honourable gentleman' who had been in France when the *maximum* had been imposed there. It was Wilberforce whom Charlotte had contacted; he was her mouthpiece in the House of Commons to get her staunch viewpoint across to the other ministers, her words given more legitimacy by confounding her sex:

> [Wilberforce] then adverted to an argument made use of by an hon. Gentleman to him, relative to a *maximum*, a measure which he could not but look on with abhorrence, and which he deprecated in the strongest terms, as pregnant with the most mischievous consequences. In this country, the measure had always, when resorted to, been fatal in its effects; and he had received a letter very lately, from a gentleman who happened to be in France when a *maximum* was there resorted to, and he assured him, that from the moment it took place, the very opposite effects were produced by it, which it was intended to remedy.[3]

She may have been anonymous and presented as a man rather than a woman, but Charlotte's ambition had been realized; her opinion had been heard by the ministers sitting in parliament and by all those who read of the debates in the newspapers, helping to influence the views of others. It is quite an incredible achievement for someone of Charlotte's status, a middle-class woman on the outside of the political elite. Although it was not unknown or uncommon for women to influence politics (for example, Georgiana, Duchess of Devonshire had famously canvassed for the Whig Party back in 1778), they were usually wives or relatives of the 'inner circle' of Westminster ministers. Charlotte broke through that and – in a most unfeminine manner – forced herself upon the notice of those ministers she felt were sympathetic to her aims.

Attempting to win Windham's approval, for she needed to ask him a favour, Charlotte unmasked herself as the author of *A Residence in France*. Assuring Windham that she was not publishing *A Maximum* for either fame or profit but merely at the instigation of William Wilberforce and to help the government, she was forced to admit that, while she was willing to bear the initial costs of the publication, she had an outstanding debt with her publisher. To get her new manuscript through the printing press she hinted to Windham that he might help her by advancing some money. Charlotte referred Windham to Lord Ailesbury (whose influence had been sought to help her father obtain passports just over five years earlier) if he needed a second opinion regarding her trustworthiness.

Why approach Windham for help in paying off this debt and not Wilberforce, if it was Wilberforce who had suggested that she write *A Maximum*? Had Wilberforce rebuffed an earlier request for cash in hand and she was now, in some way, playing one man off against the other? As ever, Charlotte's dealings with influential men remain enigmatic.

Windham replied to Charlotte's letter almost straight away, politely pointing out that while he wished to serve her, he had doubts that it was within his power to do so. Charlotte was nonetheless flattered by his marked attention and boldly requested yet another favour, notwithstanding the dubious success of her last. Charlotte wanted to secure financial aid for her father and it was in this letter that she described how John Gifford had taken an interest in her manuscript after Stockdale had rudely rebutted her submission to him. She eagerly displayed to Windham her anti-revolutionary fervour:

> It was impossible for any thinking person to witness (as I have done) the effects of the French Revolution, without feeling a deep & animated hatred against the principles which produced it, & in endeavouring to inspire others with the sentiments I had imbibed myself I have neglected no duty, & have only devoted those hours to my country, which I am liberty to devote to amusement.[4]

Charlotte then set out her request: 'The person for whom I solicit is a Mr John Williams between 60 & 70 years of age – living on a very small income at Theakstone near Bedale in Yorkshire…' She did not mention that this man was her father, although she did admit to Windham that he had a 'claim on her'. Perhaps her father's reduced circumstances were the spur to Charlotte beginning the next chapter of her adventurous life or maybe he just proved the excuse she needed to legitimately ask for help and for a species of employment by the government. John Williams was suffering from gout and because of this, as well as his age, he was incapable of active work. There had recently been an unfortunate circumstance – which Charlotte obliquely referred to only as a sudden reduction in his means of subsistence – and he was financially embarrassed, unable to allow himself any of the comforts necessary to a man of his years. Charlotte confessed to Windham that it looked odd that she, so perfectly independent and wanting for nothing, could not help someone who had a claim on her, and so it did. Charlotte, a woman in a man's world and denied the chance to earn her own living other than what she could make as an author, was not shy of trying to claim recompense where she could in return (as she saw it) for her help in promoting an anti-revolutionary propagandist stance in support of the monarchy and ministry of the day. While she stopped short of blatantly asking for an income for herself, she was more than happy to ask for her debts to be settled or for her father to be given assistance instead.

Charlotte ended her letter to Windham by letting him know her forwarding addresses; she would be in London for a week before travelling to North Yorkshire in mid-December where she planned to stay until 6 January 1801 (to celebrate Christmas and the New Year with her father and stepmother in their remote home, although she did not state this to Windham) and asked that any letters should be directed to the Post Office in Bedale.[5]

It was to be the start of a long correspondence between the two. Windham did reply to Charlotte and suggested that she should call on him in London, while offering his praise on *A Residence in France*. Upon her return to the capital, Charlotte quickly wrote to Windham in the hope of taking up his invitation; she would be in the city for just over another week. Did Charlotte manage to meet her correspondent face-to-face? Sadly, she has not recorded the event but, if Windham had indeed extended such an invitation to her, we do not doubt for a second that Charlotte would have made sure she availed herself of the opportunity. An indication that the meeting did indeed go ahead is to be found in the publication of Charlotte's pamphlet, *A Maximum; or, The Rise and Progress of Famine, addressed to the British People* in April 1801. The debts with her printers had obviously been settled satisfactorily (although her request for financial aid for her father appears to have fallen on deaf ears), and the pamphlet appeared in two versions: a cheap one selling at 6d (or 4s 6d per dozen for general distribution) and a more expensive edition priced at 1s 6d. She dedicated the pamphlet to a gentleman named John Reeves who would come to be a great friend to her in the future. Reeves was a barrister, writer, anti-radical and anti-revolutionary: his views chimed in accordance with Charlotte's own and he had published several political pamphlets including one that had seen him prosecuted for libel (he was acquitted of the charge). At the time Charlotte dedicated her own pamphlet to him, Reeves had been appointed the king's printer, possibly by way of recompense for his tribulations. It was the newspaper advertisements for *A Maximum* which, while still withholding Charlotte's name (and even her gender) revealed her to be the author of the comedic play *What Is She?* when both it and *A Residence in France* were listed as 'other works' by the same author. The advert also included a couple of lines from *Hamlet* by William Shakespeare: 'Rather bear those ills we have, Than fly to others that we know not of.'[6]

Why remain anonymous? Both of Charlotte's previous works had been successful; *A Residence in France* had been well received and her play had generally positive reviews. Charlotte professed to feel herself at a disadvantage as a female author and modestly craved anonymity because of this but her dealings with the first men of the day illustrate a woman who was not at all afraid to push herself forward and acknowledge her literary endeavours. Even though she claimed she had remained anonymous in her authorship of *A Residence in France* to protect her friends still living there and at the mercy of the republic, we suspect that she had, in fact, withheld her name as she had appropriated at least an element of the memoirs of another lady. As such, if she wished to trade on her past success with her first literary venture, she was forced to also remain anonymous in her future works or risk discovery.

By the time *A Maximum* appeared in print, William Windham was no longer Secretary at War and was out of office, having resigned alongside Prime Minister William Pitt in an act of protest over the veto by King George III on the matter of Catholic emancipation. The Act of Union had united the Kingdom of Great Britain with the Kingdom of Ireland and it was hoped by many including Windham that Catholic emancipation would duly follow. Although staunch to his principles, Windham was worried by the prospect of a new ministry supporting peace talks with the French Republic. The letters between Charlotte and himself in the summer of 1801 centred on these very concerns.

Charlotte had returned to Farrington Gurney and wrote to express her alarm over the journalist William Cobbett inciting a storm against the Catholics in his newspaper the *Porcupine Gazette*, before reminding Windham that she was available for any work in a literary propagandist vein for which he felt she could be useful. Windham did indeed have a job for her.[7]

A gentleman (not named) was composing a pamphlet concerning the French Republic and Windham asked Charlotte to cast her eye over the manuscript. It was possibly written in French and, with Charlotte's perfect understanding of the language, Windham wanted her to read through and make sure it was what he expected and possibly even to translate it. Charlotte was delighted and wrote back with alacrity accepting the commission, offering to work for free if the gentleman in question was not wealthy enough to pay for her services but only on the express condition that the pamphlet did not recommend peace with the republic. Keen to preserve her privacy, Charlotte asked that any parcel (presumably containing the gentleman's manuscript) be directed to C.A. Vallory, Esquire and left at the White Lion Inn which was located in the market place at Bath, assuring Windham that it would reach her safely. Did Mr Vallory really exist or would Benjamin Hunt Biggs be sent in disguise to collect the parcel? She ended her letter with a measure of just how far her friendship with Windham had progressed; he had promised to procure autographs of Edmund Burke, Lord Nelson and William Pitt for her and, as he had not yet sent them, Charlotte was not shy about reminding him.[8]

William Pitt had been replaced as prime minister by Henry Addington, Viscount Sidmouth, and under him a treaty for peace with France had been discussed. When the agreement was finally signed on 25 March 1802 in the French city of Amiens, Charlotte, with a small income now at her disposal, had the means to travel. She was soon, once more, resident in France. The botanist and explorer Sir Joseph Banks was also resident in the city and Charlotte attempted to be admitted to his presence, wishing to be introduced to the *savants* (distinguished scholars, particularly scientists) of Paris and claiming to have a letter from Banks but she could not produce it and was turned away. Once again, we are left wondering; did Charlotte really have a letter from the great man or was she simply seizing an opportunity and trying to make her own way and her own luck?[9]

The fragile peace between Britain and France lasted little more than a year and on the resumption of hostilities in May 1803, Charlotte beat a hasty retreat to the safety of England. On 22 May Napoléon Bonaparte ordered that all British men between the ages of 18 and 60 in both France and Italy should be arrested; if Benjamin Hunt Biggs had accompanied Charlotte to France then he was very fortunate to not find himself once more a prisoner. However, Charlotte does not mention that her 'husband' had travelled to France with her during the peace and perhaps Charlotte was increasingly living a separate life from him, albeit with the security of his name and her status as a married woman. It would appear, from her later reminiscences, that by the latter half of 1803 when she had returned to England, she had become somewhat smitten by a handsome young Frenchman and counter-revolutionary who held staunch royalist sympathies. Jean-Baptiste Coster (known as St Victor) was a few years younger than Charlotte. Deserting the French forces, he had joined the émigré armies, returning secretly to Paris and fighting in the *Chouannerie* revolt (he was present at the battles of Juvigné and Piré); Louis XVIII, the exiled younger brother of the ill-fated

Louis XVI who had lost his head in 1793, appointed St Victor a colonel in the Vitré division of the counter-revolutionary *Armée Catholique et Royale de Bretagne* (Catholic and Royal Army of Britain). Arrested and sentenced to five years in gaol, St Victor contrived to escape and, with a comrade, Joseph-Geneviève de Puisaye, Comte de Puisaye (a minor aristocrat and, like St Victor, a counter-revolutionary who had commanded the *Chouans*), he fled to London and then made for Canada.

The British government had been funding de Puisaye for some time, backing his attempts to overthrow the French Republic and allowing him residence in England in between; de Puisaye and his fellow émigrés, now including St Victor, received funding from public bodies and from private charities but once this had run its course a plan was put into action with help from William Windham to found a French military colony in Upper Canada. They left, St Victor among them, during the summer months of 1798 and arrived in Canada towards the end of the year where they were granted land and created a new settlement, naming it Windham in honour of William Windham. However, St Victor did not settle in Canada and, criss-crossing the Atlantic Ocean and returning to London during 1800, he became embroiled in a daring plot to end Napoléon Bonaparte's life.

The Austrian composer Joseph Haydn's masterpiece *Creation* was premièring at the Paris Opera (the Théâtre de la République et des Arts on the Rue de la Loi) on Christmas Eve and Napoléon and his wife Joséphine were to attend. Warned that an attempt on his life was imminent, Napoléon brushed aside the rumours and his party left after dinner to make their way to the opera in two carriages, Napoléon in the first and Joséphine in the second together with her daughter Hortense, Napoléon's heavily pregnant sister Caroline (the wife of General Joachim Murat) and General Rapp, her husband's aide-de-camp. At the last minute, Rapp decided to rearrange the new shawl from Constantinople that Joséphine was wearing into the Egyptian fashion (Rapp had served with Napoléon in Egypt) and Napoléon departed ahead in his carriage.

Upon entering the Rue Saint-Nicaise, Napoléon's coach was blocked by a horse and cart and his coachman turned into another street. As he did so the cart exploded, rocking Napoléon's coach and throwing the women in the second coach, which had almost caught up, onto the floor. Joséphine's carriage suffered more damage than her husband's and was covered with broken glass from the windows but, other than the shock and some cuts, the entire party was unharmed. Not so the poor people who had unsuspectingly been nearby the cart; it was reported that as many as twelve civilians were killed and thirty more injured, with damage to the surrounding houses. One of the dead was a 15-year-old girl who had been asked to hold the horse harnessed to the booby-trapped cart and had unwittingly done so; she was found in a gutter on the Rue Saint-Nicaise, her clothes and both her arms torn from her body by the blast. Shaken, Napoléon and Joséphine appeared at the opera while the hunt for the perpetrators commenced. Originally it was suspected that Jacobins were behind the attack but soon it became clear that royalist *Chouan* counter-revolutionaries were responsible. It became known as the Plot of the Rue Saint-Nicaise, and also as the plot of the 'Infernal Machine' and St Victor, now back in Paris, had been one of the *Chouans* involved in its planning.

Did Charlotte meet with St Victor when she was in France during the Peace of Amiens or did she make his acquaintance when she returned to England following the recommencement of hostilities? Charlotte's address upon her return to London is interesting. Her father had, around the year 1796, purchased two houses on Frith Street in London's Soho district, nos. 48 and 49, and it was from one of these that a hurried and undated letter from Charlotte to Windham was penned, written in the third person and a different hand. She was due to depart London, presumably to travel back to Farrington Gurney in Somerset, and wrote to Windham regarding a portrait of Napoléon Bonaparte (an accident had happened to the one she had planned to send to Windham and she had hoped to get a replacement but, as there was no chance of that, she apologized for having to send the damaged one).

Alone, there is nothing remarkable in Charlotte writing from this address. It appears that she was simply lodging temporarily and rent-free in an apartment in one of the two adjoining houses that her father had acquired. However, less than a decade later Charlotte would allow a French spy who had fled to London to lodge in one of these properties. Knowing this, and knowing that St Victor was in London in the latter half of 1803, was Charlotte then in the habit of making over lodgings to French émigrés? Did St Victor reside for a time in Frith Street while he was intriguing in London with his compatriots? If indeed Charlotte was telling the truth about falling in love with this handsome Gallic counter-revolutionary – and she later confessed in writing to Ochterlony that St Victor had reminded her of him and that he had been the only man since Ochterlony that she had been in danger of loving until the guillotine saved her from temptation – then she was indeed involved up to her neck in plots and conspiracies in the early 1800s. It is also an admission that her 'marriage' to Mr Biggs was a mere marriage of convenience and not one born out of love, at least not on Charlotte's part. As ever, Charlotte tantalizes with a glimpse of the passionate and brave woman that lay beneath her carefully-cultivated, respectable, almost nondescript demeanour before she once again draws down the veil and shields that side of her character from view.

The guillotine was indeed destined to save Charlotte from the temptation of her emotions: St Victor was once again involved in a plot to end Napoléon's life. In London, he met with Jean-Charles Pichegru and Georges Cadoudal. Pichegru had been born to a peasant family but had risen to be commander-in-chief of the French Army of the Rhine before resigning after taking part in a plot to return the Bourbon monarchy to the throne of France. Cadoudal was a *Chouannerie* leader and had been involved in the Rue Saint-Nicaise plot and was therefore well known to St Victor. From August 1803 to January 1804, four secret landings – made with the knowledge of British intelligence – were carried out by Captain John Wesley Wright of HMS *Vincejo* at Biville, depositing Pichegru, Cadoudal, St Victor and many other *Chouan* conspirators onto French soil, leaving them to make their way by means of safe houses to Paris to await further instructions. The grand scheme came to nothing; they were betrayed and the authorities were all too fully aware of their plot. The men were quickly rounded up. Pichegru took his own life in gaol and Cadoudal and St Victor were among nineteen men sentenced to death; all but Cadoudal appealed the sentence:

> Coster St Victor did not pretend to have any affection for the new Government of France, but denied that he had been guilty of any dishonourable act against it. He had not, he said, been concerned in any conspiracy; and indeed the means of the pretended conspirators to subvert a powerful government, were so weak as to refute the charge. He closed by saying, 'Magistrates, my life is in your hands; I declare, before you, that I am innocent. You are going to judge me; but remember that God will judge you.'[10]

Subsequently, six or seven of those sentenced to die were reprieved but St Victor was not among them; he was transferred to the Bicêtre to await his fate. In company with Cadoudal, he kept his appointment with the guillotine on 25 June 1804 and, by all accounts, met his end bravely. Thus, Charlotte was saved from loving another man as fervently as she had once loved Ochterlony.[11]

While Charlotte had been following the arrest, trial and subsequent execution of St Victor and his *Chouan* brothers-in-arms in the newspapers, secretly hoping for his reprieve, Benjamin Hunt Biggs was suffering from ill health; his illness would continue for at least eighteen months. Charlotte retreated from view for this period, perhaps in mourning for her brave young Frenchman as much as preoccupied with her husband's illness. Her literary endeavours in a political and propagandist vein were put on hold, as were her advisory letters to the government via William Windham. The last work she had been involved in was William Cobbett's *Important Considerations for the People of this Kingdom*, published in July 1803, which Charlotte read and contributed to before its publication. This propagandist tract, telling how the French treated the labouring class with 'direst malignity [and] sharpest bayonet' was backed by the government and released anonymously to be sent, under the royal seal, to the officiating minister of every parish in the land for them to read to their congregations from the pulpit. Charlotte met with Cobbett during her involvement with his pamphlet, introduced to him by William Windham and sworn to secrecy as to the identity of the writer. Only Charlotte, certain government ministers and Cobbett himself knew the truth, but it was a secret that Charlotte would later divulge to discredit Cobbett who she grew to hate.[12]

Cobbett, the son of a humble farm labourer, was 'a bluff, beer-drinking, beef-eating patriot whose ideal was a rural England peopled by sturdy yeomen', but as he progressed his views became more radical and he used his pen and his intellect to fight for a cause in which he believed. At the time that Charlotte met Cobbett their views of the French revolution were in agreement but the two grew poles apart in their stance. Cobbett, in Charlotte's eyes, became an enemy to the principles she held dear.[13]

In the autumn of 1806, when Charlotte wrote to her friend William Windham, Benjamin Hunt Biggs had been 'lingering above 18 months and is now in so deplorable a state that my only hope of him surviving the winter is taking him to a milder climate.' With this in mind, she asked if Windham could, if the articles for peace were signed, provide passports for both herself and Mr Biggs for France. Charlotte's intention was to land at either Dieppe or Cherbourg and travel to southern France for the duration of the winter.[14]

A peace treaty with France was indeed being discussed at the time that Charlotte wrote, although by this date most knew it was an improbable situation. William Pitt had resumed his position as prime minister in 1804 but his second tenure was all too brief as he died in January 1806, leading to the formation of the short-lived 'Ministry of All the Talents' comprising politicians from all parties and led by William Wyndham Grenville, 1st Baron Grenville (who was cousin to William Windham). In this ministry,

Windham was named as Secretary of State for War and the Colonies and Charles James Fox was appointed Foreign Secretary. Fox had met Napoléon Bonaparte and was on good terms with Talleyrand – his French ministerial counterpart – and was of the belief that he would be able to negotiate a peace settlement with France. This belief, he soon found out, was ill-conceived and with France trying to split the alliance between Britain and Russia the negotiations continued half-heartedly. James Maitland, 8th Earl of Lauderdale and supposed supporter of the revolution, was despatched to France in early August to assist the Earl of Yarmouth in bringing the peace talks to a conclusion. By the end of the month only Lauderdale remained in Paris and at the start of hostilities between France and Prussia he left for London, thereby ending the talk of peace. Charles James Fox died in office during September, never seeing the outcome of his scheme.[15]

Charlotte was, therefore, not in full possession of the facts as to the state of the negotiations for peace when she wrote and Windham was unable to help in procuring the necessary passports. She would have to face the winter in colder climes and trust that this would not have too detrimental an effect on Benjamin's deplorable state of health. In her letter, Charlotte also asked Windham for help for a friend of hers who was an officer in the militia (Charlotte gave no clues to his identity other than saying he was the son of a clergyman). She hoped to find him employment of some kind.

Charlotte had been in the habit of spending the Christmas holidays in the north with her father, so she was probably by John Williams' side when he died at his Theakston home on Christmas Eve 1807. He was buried four days later in the churchyard of St Lambert in the neighbouring village of Burneston. His last couple of years had been spent quietly, in part due to the debilitating gout from which he suffered. Earlier that year he had been one of only four people from Theakston who voted in the Yorkshire Poll. John Williams cast his two votes for the Tory candidate Henry Lascelles (later 2nd Earl of Harewood) and the slave trade abolitionist William Wilberforce who stood as an independent and who had been his daughter's mouthpiece in parliament a few years earlier.[16]

The *York Herald* newspaper announced John's death in its edition of 2 January 1808. The notice was probably written and inserted by Charlotte: 'On the 24th ult. At Theakstone, near Bedale, aged 71, John Williams, Esq.: a gentleman well known, of strict honour, a poor man's friend and whose death will be much lamented by those who had the pleasure of his acquaintance.'

Charlotte was still in Yorkshire a month later when she proved her father's last will and testament at York on 2 February 1808. John's will had been written in October 1804 just over three years before his death. His second wife, Sarah, received only a third of his household furniture and linen, a silver teapot and one silver butter boat or cream pot. A relative named as the Reverend James Williams, son of the late James Williams of Chepstow, Monmouth, was bequeathed John's diamond ring and a pair of stone knee buckles, set in gold and silver. Charlotte inherited everything else. She got

> all that fee simple and inheritance of [John William's] estate being and lying in Frith Street, Soho…known by the numbers 48, 49 with a piece or parcel ground behind no. 47 in said street annexed to no. 48 & 49…also all my estate situate being and lying at Theakstone [*sic*]… consisting of house, garden and two fields with all and every appurtenance therein belonging and now in my own possession together with all and every of my personal effects, goods & chattels.

The other two-thirds of John's furniture and linen also came to Charlotte's share and she was named sole executrix of the will. Hopefully Sarah Williams was otherwise provided for as she appears to have lost even the roof over her head! Far away from her London friends and family, she was dependent upon the goodwill and charity of her stepdaughter.[17]

Charlotte's name, as written in the will and the document attached to it when she proved it as executrix, is interesting and one of the clues that she was not really the married lady she appeared to be. John Williams referred to Charlotte in his will as 'my daughter Rachel C. Biggs by my former wife' (using her actual forename as it was an official document rather than the name she was known by). The clerk who recorded the information when Charlotte proved the will made a mistake and added an extra initial into her name, which was crossed out: 'Rachel C W̶ Biggs'. In no letter does Charlotte ever sign herself as Mrs Williams Biggs – she is always simply R.C. Biggs or Mrs Biggs – nor did her father refer to her as such. Did a careless clerk begin to write Williams as that was John's surname or had Charlotte given her name as Rachel Charlotte Williams Biggs knowing that, as she was proving and signing a legal document, she was not truly Mrs Biggs and then recanting on this when she realized that it did not match the information her father had given? She perpetuated this ambiguity when, shortly after her father's death – and before his will had been proved and she had officially inherited his estate (which she declared was worth less than £200) – she wrote her own will. For the first time in her life, she knew that she now had assets of her own besides the small annuities she possessed.

The very act of her writing her will tells us much about her marriage to Benjamin Hunt Biggs. Specifically, it helps to confirm our suspicions that the two were not legally married at all as she tellingly refers to herself in this legal document as Rachel Charlotte Williams Biggs, suggesting that the inclusion of the rogue initial when she had proved her father's will had been Charlotte's rather than a clerk's doing.

It was unusual at that time for a married woman to make a will unless she owned property in her own right as, by law, her possessions belonged to her husband. We see many wills left by spinsters and widows but fewer made by married women. Nowhere in her father's will was there any mention of the properties at Frith Street, Soho or the Theakston property being given free from her husband's control, a clause often inserted to give the woman who had inherited some rights over her inheritance. In fact, John Williams did not mention Mr Biggs at all in his will, which again seems unusual. Under the terms of Charlotte's inheritance, if she was indeed legally married to Benjamin, then he owned the properties and not Charlotte, as a husband was entitled to his wife's assets. Furthermore, the inclusion of both surnames under which she was known during her life leads us to suspect that she was, in effect, covering all options. If she was not legally married then no such person as Rachel Charlotte Biggs existed and so her former surname of Williams was given too, to avoid confusion after her death. Finally, Charlotte gave no indication of her marital status. It is common to see this given on wills, for example, 'I, Mary Smith, spinster' or 'I, Mary Smith, widow of...', or even 'I, Mary Smith, wife of...'. Charlotte's will provided no indication as to whether she was spinster, wife or widow. She was simply Rachel Charlotte Williams Biggs of Farrington Gurney in Somerset, an independent lady in an age when this was not the norm. It reinforces our belief that she adopted Benjamin's surname to provide her with an air of respectability or to give her a 'cover story' so that she could travel freely as a respectable married woman without attracting interest.

Charlotte's will was succinct and immensely frustrating. She named no further family members, merely leaving everything to Benjamin Hunt Biggs. Again, we would normally expect a relationship to be given in respect of a bequest but Charlotte gives no such information. Benjamin Hunt Biggs is not specifically named as her husband and this is yet more circumstantial evidence that he was not Charlotte's legal spouse. After all, the lawyer drawing up the will would surely question why a wife needed to will her property to her husband when he would inherit and own it by right in the event of her death? The will reads as follows: 'I give, devise and bequeath unto Benjamin Hunt Biggs Esquire of Farrington Gurney aforesaid all my Real Estate whatsoever and wherever to have and to hold to the said Benjamin Hunt Biggs Esquire his heirs and assigns forever.'[18]

Mr Biggs was also left all Charlotte's personal property and nominated as her executor. Charlotte did not mention specific properties and was perhaps unaware of exactly what she had been left under the terms of her father's will when she wrote her own on 13 January 1808 (she did not prove her father's will until 2 February, just under three weeks later). John Williams, upon his death, appears to have made no provision for keeping a roof over the head of his wife and perhaps Sarah Williams initially assumed that the Theakston property would belong to her and her alone as only three weeks after her husband's death and before his will had been proved, the *York Herald* newspaper carried an advertisement for the sale of the house (which was held freehold and not leasehold) and of the furniture. Any interested party was asked to apply to the owner, Mrs Williams. The advertisement gives us a description of the house and allows us to glimpse the situation in which Charlotte's father was living at the end of his life:

> ... a modern-built house with two parlours in front, 18ftx13, two kitchens and china closet, larders, etc., with every convenience and accommodation for a genteel small family, four good bed-chambers and four smaller ones for servants, two staircases, a garret the length of the house which might be converted into servants rooms if required, a coach house with stabling for eight horses, a large dove-cote, well stocked, an excellent walled garden lined with choice fruit trees in full bearing, two rich meadow fields (about 5 acres) with a good cow-house and pump. The furniture and fixtures are very good and may be had at a fair valuation. Further particulars apply to Mrs Williams, the owner, who resides in the house.[19]

The same advertisement appeared in the *York Herald* a week later but, after the will was proved, Mrs Sarah Williams was left in no doubt as to who owned the house she called home and two-thirds of the furniture and fixings within. Possibly Charlotte allowed Sarah to continue living in the house until she had time to find another home, but no sale would take place.

## Chapter Eight

# The Royal Jubilee

Now that Charlotte had a little income from the rents of the property she had inherited as well as from her annuities, she could exercise more independence. She moved from her manor house at Farrington Gurney in Somerset to a large and comfortable house in the tiny hamlet of Boughspring, 3 miles outside Chepstow on the border of Gloucestershire in south-west England and Monmouthshire in south Wales. It is not clear whether Charlotte lived there on her own or with Benjamin Hunt Biggs but it was certainly very commodious if she was living there with only a handful of servants for company. Benjamin remains elusive, still suffering ill health and living in a form of gentlemanly retirement, never venturing too far from home when in England and frequently travelling abroad on a kind of extended Grand Tour, seeking warmer climes to improve his constitution and perhaps even enjoying the company of fellow male travellers in relative anonymity.

Boughspring was, until the early nineteenth century, known as Boughwells (or Bowels) Green, and that is how Charlotte referred to her new home. By 1815 the hamlet consisted of around ten cottages and a property known as Caine's Hill House that dated from the late 1600s. The area is bounded by the Anglo-Saxon earthwork known as Offa's Dyke to the west and to the east by the River Severn, of which Charlotte had a picturesque view. As well as being close to Chepstow, Boughspring was just a short distance from Tidenham and Charlotte had friends and family in both locations. Her father had mentioned a Reverend James Williams, son of the late James Williams of Chepstow, in his will and at Tidenham House was a related Williams family. When Charlotte moved to Boughspring, Tidenham House was owned by the widowed Harriett Maria Williams née Lowder, something of a bluestocking who would no doubt have got on famously with Charlotte (in her will dated 1829, Harriett Maria left specific bequests for, among other things, a complete set of Hannah More's works, her telescope and a microscope). Thomas Williams, Harriett Maria's husband who died in 1806, had been the brother of the Reverend James Williams. Indeed, the relationship was even closer as Harriett Maria was first cousin to her husband through her mother, Sarah Lowder née Williams. As well as Tidenham House, Harriett Maria owned several properties in the surrounding area, one a large and comfortable property known as Boughwells Green House. This was the house that Charlotte now occupied for a couple of very significant years. A slightly later newspaper advertisement gives details of the house:[1]

> BOUGHWELLS GREEN HOUSE; containing two Parlours, five Bedchambers, Servants' Rooms, Kitchens, and other convenient Offices; Coach-House and Stabling, Gardens, and with or without a few Acres of LAND adjoining.
>   The above Premises are delightfully situated about half a mile from the Turnpike-Road, where coaches pass daily; 3 miles from Chepstow, 18 from Bristol 30 from Bath, and 26 from Gloucester.

It was while living in this remote location that Charlotte conceived the idea of instigating a national jubilee celebration for King George III. It was a preposterous project for one middle-aged lady to undertake almost entirely on her own, but Charlotte was rarely daunted by the scale of her ambitions and had an almost blind faith in her abilities. Luckily for her, this blind faith coupled with her persuasive personality usually carried her schemes through to fruition and the jubilee was to be no exception.

King George III was 71 years of age and had reigned longer than any British monarch since Edward III some four centuries earlier. It was a momentous occasion but technically, as was pointed out at the time, 25 October 1809 marked the beginning of the fiftieth year of King George III's reign – he ascended to the throne upon the death of his grandfather on that day in 1760 – and so the jubilee of 1809 celebrated his forty-nine years on the throne. Whether Charlotte intentionally or unintentionally miscalculated her dates, she had a very good reason for wishing to celebrate a year early during 1809, and not just because of the age and failing health of King George III who was going blind and had suffered several bouts of mental illness since 1788. Charlotte's main concern was the constitutional crisis that had recently engulfed the monarchy. As a lifelong royalist, Charlotte was not about to stand back when she could do something to address the situation.

King George III's second son, Frederick, Duke of York was, in 1809, commander-in-chief of the British army (the children's nursery rhyme *The Grand Old Duke of York* is commonly thought to be about him). Married in

1791 to Princess Frederica Charlotte of Prussia, the couple soon found they were not suited and lived separate lives. The Duke of York found solace in the arms of a well-known London courtesan, Mrs Mary Anne Clarke.

Mary Anne, a tradesman's daughter born in 1776 and blessed with both brains and beauty, managed to establish herself in her chosen profession of courtesan well enough to attract the eye of this royal scapegrace. He provided her with a fine house in which she lived as his mistress for some years but when in time he began to neglect her and left her short of money, she exacted her revenge upon him, sparking a national scandal in the process. Mrs Clarke had a pamphlet and copies of the Duke of York's love letters to her printed ready to be distributed, resulting in a down payment of £7,000 and a pension of £400 a year in return for the copies and her silence (although the canny Mrs Clarke, unknown to the Crown, kept one copy of the duke's letters at her bankers just in case she ever needed more leverage). There was yet more scandal to come. Between 1 February and 20 March 1809, she gave evidence before the House of Commons after it transpired that Mary Anne had been accepting payments in return for adding names to the Duke of York's patronage lists for military commissions and ecclesiastical preferments; he would sign these lists without reading them but the allegation was that he had known what was going on and was complicit in his mistress's mercenary dealings. Although the authorities tried to hush the story or have it declared a Jacobite plot, charges were brought against the Duke of York by Colonel Gwyllym Lloyd Wardle for misuse of military patronage. One disgruntled army officer, Major Denis Hogan, published an *Appeal to the Public* in which he alleged that he had been passed over for promotion because of his refusal to meet the demands of Mrs Clarke. William Cobbett, typically, fanned the flames of the scandal and decried the cover-up: 'Oh! the damned thieves! A Jacobinical conspiracy. Damned hell-fire thieves. The Duke must go.'[2]

The charges were found to be 'unproven'; a less than satisfactory outcome that left the Duke of York unable to convince anyone of his innocence and so he resigned his position. There was great public interest in the case and it reflected badly, not only on the Duke of York but also on his wider family whose popularity with certain factions in the country had waned considerably. Cobbett used his newspaper, the *Political Register*, to attack politicians who had colluded to try to sweep the whole affair under the carpet. The scandal also breathed life into a campaign for parliamentary reform.[3]

Interestingly, one further episode in the drama had a connection to a gentleman who may have been known to Charlotte from her youth. The *Morning Chronicle* newspaper of 12 April 1809 reported on evidence taken before the Committee on East India Patronage, concerned with the same matter but this time implicating King George III's youngest surviving son, Prince Adolphus, Duke of Cambridge. A gentleman named John Fuller who wanted to procure a writership in the EIC for a young friend had approached a man who told him one could be bought for £3,000 and asked for £150 for his trouble in setting this up. On paying the £150, Fuller was given a letter to a Mrs Cottin at Hampton Court Palace with instructions on how to pay the £3,000: Mrs Cottin wanted £500, with the remaining £2,500 to go to an unnamed lady, plainly Mary Anne Clarke although John Fuller stated many times he did not know who she was.

Mrs Cottin introduced John Fuller to a resident of the palace, a gentleman who was also a deputy lieutenant for the county of Middlesex. This gentleman was to take the £2,500 on behalf of the lady who could procure the writership and his name had already cropped up in Charlotte's past in connection with her former captor, Richard Heaviside. This gentleman was none other than the Captain Poplett who acted for Heaviside in his altercation with Justice Forster in February 1788. Neither Poplett nor Mrs Cottin was asked to give evidence but John Fuller took the stand and explained how the operation worked. He was asked the following:

Did he [Poplett] mention in whose patronage the appointment was?

That she [Mary Anne Clarke] had very considerable influence with the Duke of Cambridge, who he assured me and I believe it most sincerely, was perfectly unacquainted with the object of her application; that the Duke had expressed a very great regard for her; and of course the young gentleman, whose name I mentioned, she told him was a friend of hers and the Duke in consequence wrote her a note, that he would do everything he could to get her wishes complied with; I saw the note from the Duke of Cambridge to this lady, but the superscription was carefully taken off, that I should not know who it was.

States generally the contents of it. – That he had received her application and that he should certainly make a point of endeavouring to accommodate her friend, whose character she spoke so highly of; that if he should fail in one quarter, he would endeavour to procure the patronage of the Queen; but he did not think he should be able to accomplish the object this year, though it was very probable he might in that that was coming.[1]

In the event, the £2,500 was returned to John Fuller as, on this occasion, the object could not be achieved. Thomas Poplett escaped any further suggestions of complicity as he died later that year and was buried on 16 September 1809 at Fetcham in Surrey.[5]

Against this backdrop, Charlotte sought to portray the royal family in a totally different light, one that highlighted King George III as a monarch much loved by his people. In collusion with that old family friend, the Earl of Ailesbury, Charlotte initially thought to suggest a royal tour of the country. Charlotte must have been on good terms indeed with Lord Ailesbury to be able to suggest such a scheme and ask for his advice and help. When Ailesbury told her the king was too ill for such a jaunt, Charlotte instead came up with the idea of a national celebration across the king's dominions. Writing to George Legge, 3rd Earl of Dartmouth shortly before the jubilee, she gave her reasoning: 'If the idea of a Jubilee or general festival could be successfully suggested it might unite a spirit of loyal enthusiasm well calculated to counteract the pernicious efforts of Mr Wardle & his partizans.' It seems astounding that a middle-aged lady, living in retirement in a small Welsh hamlet, could be the instigator of such a grand project but Charlotte was, quite clearly, no ordinary matron. As well as utilizing the friends she had in high places, she wrote nearly 1,000 letters (no mean feat in itself), sending them to all the county corporations and large manufacturers in the country, to the local and national newspapers and to anyone who she thought could help the project. She researched the characteristics of each town so she could tailor her letters to suit and each letter was slightly different, to attempt to deter people from thinking they sprang from the same pen. They were all sent anonymously:[6]

> It is respectfully suggested, that, on the 26th of October, (which happens on a Thursday) his Majesty enters on the 50th year of his reign; that so remarkable an epoch has not occurred in England since the reign of Edward the Third, and only twice within twelve hundred years; that it is, therefore, proposed, as a mark of personal attachment to his Majesty, and totally unconnected with parties or politics, to celebrate the day by a national jubilee, or festival, throughout the United Kingdom. Such a fete must necessarily be subservient to local circumstances, but where these do not interfere, reviews and public breakfasts in the morning, and balls and illuminations in the evening, are recommended. As a festival on so expensive a scale will require an early subscription and much previous arrangement, it is hoped this communication will not be deemed premature.[7]

Although Charlotte's initial letters suggested 26 October, the date for the jubilee was proposed as the 25th, the day upon which George III had been crowned. Charlotte wanted to project this as a scheme that appealed nationally and sprang from many different areas and people. She was later to record the dates she made trips to post her various letters, attempting to belatedly receive financial recompense for the expense she had been put to in hiring horses for her travels to the Post Office. In June Charlotte made two return journeys from her home in Boughspring to Bristol, in July two more return journeys to Bristol and two to Bath, in August three return journeys to Bristol and finally, in early September, the return journey to Bristol yet again. She had despatched most of the letters by 13 July with the remainder sent by the beginning of August and then began to send further anonymous letters to both the national and provincial newspapers, hoping to motivate each town or city to try to outdo the planned festivities of their neighbours by promoting the plans of their rivals. To suggest that plans were further advanced or of a more ambitious standing in each town or city's neighbours was an interesting tactic and very similar to one that was later employed by an infamous government agent provocateur known as Oliver the spy (William Oliver, alias W.J. Richards and Mr Hollis). More interesting still, the politician John Hiley Addington (brother of the former Prime Minister Lord Sidmouth) was, some years hence, in contact with both Charlotte and Oliver the spy. Were these tactics ones that had been suggested to Charlotte or had government spymasters learned from her?

In 1817, eight years after Charlotte had organized the jubilee celebrations, Oliver, a tradesman who had been imprisoned for debt and who had friends sympathetic to the radical cause, was recruited by the government to infiltrate the rebel and radical societies in the midland and northern counties of England. Over the course of the year he met with radicals in each area and, as well as recording names and details to report back to the Home Office, he took the opportunity to encourage each area to play its part by informing them of their neighbouring towns' plans or their neighbours' opinions. In Nottingham, for instance, while praising the delegates on their progress, he told them that places in Yorkshire had not expected them 'to go off'. In this way, he set a competitive edge between each district and encouraged each to try to match or outdo the others, mirroring Charlotte's method of gaining compliance to her plans. However, Oliver schemed for a much darker end than Charlotte's patriotic efforts. He was eventually unmasked and accused of inciting the Pentrich uprising in June 1817 which sent a number of men to their deaths and saw others sentenced to transportation for their part in the rebellion. While Lord Sidmouth resolutely claimed that Oliver had been employed 'to avert imminent danger', the Whiggish Earl Grey thought the spy, 'the foulest of traitors, and the most atrocious of criminals.' John Hiley Addington had been complicit throughout: he personally introduced Oliver to General John Byng, the commander of the northern troops, a meeting that allowed Oliver to conveniently 'escape' when a meeting at Thornhill Lees near Dewsbury in West Yorkshire was surrounded by Byng's men.[8]

Charlotte went further with her own plans: she wrote several letters opposing the jubilee, or elements of it, to invoke angry loyalist responses to the contrary and stimulate debate and public interest. However, the scheme worked against her to a degree: various newspapers printed her letters and people began to suspect that they were dealing with a 'circular' that was marginally altered before being sent on to the next town. This suggested to the radicals a loyalist conspiracy. In truth, as Charlotte later admitted, she wrote each letter individually, making sure that no two were identical. A loyalist conspiracy it might have been, but it was a conspiracy consisting of one lady with only a modicum of help.[9]

Charlotte employed a few trusted men to help her in her endeavours. The Earl of Ailesbury was obviously privy to her plans from the beginning and, perhaps at his instigation, Charlotte approached John Reeves – the man to whom she had dedicated her pamphlet on the French *maximum* – for help in putting the letters into the post. Reeves was the superintendent of the Alien Office, a Home Office department created in 1793. The Alien Office ostensibly oversaw the arrival of 'aliens' into Britain, primarily refugees from the French Revolution who needed asylum and those who were suspected of being revolutionaries who should be prevented from entering or should be watched closely. By 1809 the office's remit had devolved into one of national security and intelligence-gathering, 'the administrative office for the first comprehensive British secret service in the modern sense', and Charlotte would, in time, assist Reeves in his endeavours. Perhaps she had already been involved, in light of her 'love' for the counter-revolutionary Coster St Victor? For now, however, she merely wanted his help in making the jubilee a success. Charlotte addressed her packets to Lord Hawksley (Reeve's superior at the Home Office) when she posted her bundles of letters from Bristol and Bath – posting from Bath rather than Chepstow attracted less attention to her copious correspondence – and Reeves then intercepted them and put them into the London post without franking them, to retain the anonymity of the sender. At first Reeves treated Charlotte's plan with a little gentle teasing, promising her that he would recommend her to a diplomatic function if she succeeded in getting everyone to co-operate, but nevertheless, to oblige her, he posted the letters. A kerfuffle in the newspapers confirmed Charlotte's tactics: at a meeting of the Court of Common Council in the City of London, it was suggested by one Robert Waithman, an Alderman, Welsh linen-draper and radical, that the Lord Mayor of the Court had, some time ago, written letters to 'Corporate Bodies to support the measures of Ministers'. James Black, the Lord Provost of Glasgow, responded to this with a copy of the anonymous letter that Charlotte had sent to him, stating that it had been posted in London with a postmark of 12 August and London postage had been charged. The letter proved to have only minimal differences from those received by other corporations and towns and there was little doubt left in the minds of the radicals that there was a concerted effort by someone or some organization behind the planning of the jubilee.[10]

Charlotte wrote to George Legge, 3rd Earl of Dartmouth less than two weeks before the jubilee. In this letter she confessed that it was she who had originally suggested and promoted the celebration but asked for Lord Dartmouth's discretion in not publicly naming her. She wanted Dartmouth to grant her a 'trifling favour' which is possibly revealed in a later letter written by Charlotte in 1812 to Nicholas Vansittart, then Chancellor of the Exchequer. Lord Dartmouth, Charlotte claimed to Vansittart, had offered to recompense her financially in some way but, as she stood in no need and had not promoted the jubilee for any profit to herself, she merely asked him for one small gift. She wished for some plants and seeds from the royal gardens. Charlotte continued her letter to Dartmouth by claiming a 'literary reputation' for herself, but avowed that she had never availed herself of it. William Windham might have thought otherwise![11]

In this undertaking, which was a very arduous one for a female of delicate health & retired habits, I had no assistant or confidant, nor had I any view to remuneration or personal advantage; I was at the time actuated solely by a desire of gratifying his Majesty & of being useful to his government – particular circumstances have since made me wish to obtain a trifling favour, which I believe I shall more successfully solicit from your Lordship, than from any member of administration, for the service I have performed will perhaps not be deemed a political one however useful & well

Lambeth, looking across the River Thames and Westminster Bridge to Westminster Abbey and the Houses of Parliament. Above, from a Lambeth timber yard and below, from the King's Arms Stairs on Narrow Wall.

Richard Heaviside was the son of a tradesman; newly wealthy, he dressed in the latest fashions and frequented the theatres. He had lodgings in New Palace Yard opposite Westminster Hall (*below*) where Charlotte was drugged, raped and held prisoner. No. 5 can be seen on the right-hand side, just beyond the bow windows of the King's Arms Tavern.

When she was abducted for the second time, Charlotte was forced into a boat and rowed down the Thames to Parson's Green, Fulham where she was landed by a secluded lane (*below*).

Charlotte spent a year living in the seclusion of Briton Ferry (*above*). When she eventually escaped Heaviside's clutches, she travelled to France. Below, the Panthemont in Paris, where Charlotte claimed to have spent time.

Above, Amiens as Charlotte would have known it before the revolution (*above*). For almost a year, Charlotte and Benjamin Hunt Biggs were held as prisoners (*below*) in the Providence at Amiens.

Charlotte was a captive when she heard the news of Marie Antoinette's execution (*above*). After their release, the Biggses lived at Abbeville (*below*) from where they wrote to England requesting passports.

Front and rear views of Charlotte and Benjamin Hunt Biggs' fine manor house at Farrington Gurney, Somerset.

Charlotte's play *What Is She?* was performed in 1799 at the Covent Garden Theatre (*above*). At around the same time, Charlotte began to correspond with William Windham MP (*left*).

In 1800 William Wilberforce MP (*right*) stood up in the House of Commons (*above*) and mentioned Charlotte's letter to him decrying the French *maximum*. He asked her to write a pamphlet on the subject; it is our first glimpse of Charlotte as a 'female politician'.

Coster St Victor (*above left*), the only other man Charlotte was in danger of loving. He was involved in the plot of the 'Infernal Machine' (*below*), hoping to assassinate Napoléon Bonaparte (*above right*).

(*Above*) The countryside near Boughspring which was Charlotte's home when she organized the Jubilee for King George III (*below right*). The three eldest princesses (*below left*) came to know Charlotte through her endeavours.

George the III aged 72. 1810.
REIGN'D - 50 - Years. A ROYAL JUBILEE.
Taken at Windsor by R Dighton. Spring Gardens

Charlotte allowed the French spy, Jean Sarrazin (*left*), to live in her property at Frith Street, Soho.

(*Below*) In the summer of 1815, Charlotte witnessed the *Champ de Mai* at Paris, an assembly to modify the constitution of the Napoléonic empire.

arlotte corresponded
gularly with John Reeves
(*above left*) and Sir James
and Burges (*above right*).
er letters were written
om one of her most prized
ossessions, the writing desk
e received from Princess
izabeth (pictured (*right*) at
r own desk) after the royal
bilee of 1809.

In 1821 Charlotte and her goddaughter travelled to London to view the coronation of George IV, hoping to get seats at Westminster Hall to view the royal banquet (*above*). (*Left*) Sir Nicholas Vansittart, Baron Bexley, in his coronation robes.

In her later years, Charlotte moved to Bristol. In 1814 she was staying on Sion Row, the upper row of houses (*above*), as seen from the River Severn. Meanwhile, General Sir David Ochterlony (*below*) had gone native in India, to the despair of the East India Company.

General Sir David Ochterlony.

timed. It is rather therefore to Lord Dartmouth than to the Lord Chamberlain I now take the liberty of applying.[12]

Lord Dartmouth held the position of Lord Chamberlain, the most senior official role in the royal household and, at that date, a political role. He served under the 'Ministry of All the Talents', as he had served under Pitt the Younger. It was a favour relating to the royal family that Charlotte requested and one she wished to keep on an unofficial and private basis rather than as an official request. Charlotte later came to the notice of the princesses Augusta and Elizabeth, the second and third daughters of King George III and possibly she used Dartmouth as an intermediary to broker an introduction for her, using her loyal support of their father as the means. Time and time again Charlotte surprises us; she determined upon what she wanted, be it the national celebration of a jubilee or the attention of the princesses, and single-mindedly set out to achieve her aims, with considerable success.

The jubilee did achieve all that Charlotte wanted it to and it ran to her requirements to a surprising degree. As she wrote to Lord Dartmouth, she was initially intimidated by the 'improbability that an obscure individual should be able to bring all the towns in the United Kingdoms to concur in one project'. She was also concerned that Dartmouth should keep her identity a secret, both out of consideration for her own privacy and from a fear that 'ridicule should not attach to the approaching celebration, by its being known to have originated with one of my sex.' Charlotte wanted the event to seem as though it had stemmed from the general goodwill of the loyal populace, almost as though the idea had simultaneously sprung into the minds of people the length and breadth of the country. However, the instigator was Charlotte, writing from her home on the Welsh Borders and enlisting the help of only a few trusted men to achieve her aim.[13]

Once Charlotte's idea began to be adopted, a loyalist fervour took over but this was tempered by radical involvement in the jubilee celebrations which Charlotte almost certainly had not predicted and did not want. Britain was changing and the jubilee was an example of the process the country was going through. Radicals suggested that King George III's fifty-year reign was nothing to celebrate, citing the higher price of food, the loss of America and increased taxes among other things as evidence.[14]

At Charlotte's anonymous suggestion, feasts were planned together with special church services and illuminations in the evening (so many candles were sold that the tallow chandlers were suspected of involvement with rumours that they had stocked up in advance). Josiah Wedgwood, the English potter, was approached and he entered into the scheme by making a commemorative breakfast service that he intended to present to the Princess Elizabeth and similarly Matthew Boulton's Soho mint in Birmingham agreed to strike commemorative jubilee medals.[15]

These were among Charlotte's plans but other schemes both loyalist and radical in nature took hold alongside them. Subscriptions were raised and charitable institutions benefited (in Taunton it was agreed to fund a much-needed county hospital in honour of the king's jubilee and at Newcastle a school for poor children). Other philanthropic proposals included the release of debtors from prison. Messrs W. Burridge and Sons, a mercantile firm from Portsmouth, distributed threepence to each French prisoner on board the prison ships in the harbour there and sixpence to each Danish prisoner. Even though this was 'in consequence of the humanity shewn by Marshal Mortier to the British sick and wounded, after the battle of Talavera', where the allied forces had suffered a defeat that seemed likely to derail the jubilee festivities (it was thought immoral to celebrate in the wake of so many deaths and injuries), Charlotte would have disapproved of this act of charity towards revolutionaries being aligned to her grand loyalist project. She tried to bend the radical slant to her own preference, sending yet another round of letters signed from 'An Englishman' to regional newspapers (all just slightly different and again, tailored to their intended readers) in September, suggesting that the 'lower orders' be charitably provided with a meal of roast beef and strong beer with which to toast the king. (The French had referred to the British as *rosbifs* from the eighteenth century because of the popularity of this way of cooking beef, a tradition that endures, on both sides, to this very day.)[16]

A further letter, the writer simply signing as PENTECOSTOS (the Christian Pentecost falls fifty days after Easter Day and so this was a pseudonym referencing the commencement of the king's fiftieth year upon the throne) would also seem to stem from Charlotte's pen. She was clearly worried that, in areas with a high concentration of poor inhabitants, donations would not stretch to both charitable efforts to relieve their distress and still allow for the jubilant celebrations she wished to see on the day. Charlotte, resigned now to the hijacking of her plans by radical elements, still wanted a visible and tangible show of loyalty in every town and city. She ended her letter with a rousing plea clearly designed to instil patriotic pride into the breast of the reader.

## TO THE GOOD PEOPLE OF ENGLAND.

You have agreed that some peculiar notice shall be taken of the commencement of the 50th year of his Majesty's reign: but some differences of opinion have existed, as to the best method of celebrating the event.

The more general opinion, however, at present, seems to be, that, in addition to public Prayers and Thanksgiving, some *charitable donation* should be made to the Poor. But in some towns, the proportion of poor is so great, that the subscription of individuals would produce only a very small relief to each poor person. In short, I fear, that in many populous manufacturing towns, where the proportion of poor to rich is as several hundreds to one, it will be impossible to relieve *all*: and very great is the difficulty of selecting the proper objects.

I therefore beg leave to suggest (*for places where the Poor are too numerous to be included universally*) a method of selection, which will include as many of them as it is probable can be relieved by individual subscription; and also convey a proper compliment to our beloved King:- namely, the giving of a good dinner, or some pecuniary relief, – (or perhaps, both) *to every poor person who is of, or above, his Majesty's age*: and, in places where sufficient money can be raised, to extend the gift *to every one whose age is equal to the number of years which his Majesty shall have reigned*...

Let all parties embrace this happy opportunity of *uniting Loyalty and Charity*: and let it be known, for the honour of Englishmen, that, on this memorable day, there was not, throughout the realm, one individual, of the age of our venerable Monarch, who did not partake of the Roast Beef of Old England, – some Strong Beer to drink his Majesty's health, – and, at least on this occasion, Reason to bless his Reign.

My dear fellow subjects.

May God save the King!

October 9, 1809                    PENTECOSTOS[17]

In the end, Charlotte would have been pleased by the way in which the country celebrated. Even in the areas where the radicals held sway, private individuals still illuminated their own windows, partook of a good feast and raised a glass to the king. Chepstow, the nearest town to Charlotte's own home, celebrated the jubilee in style; although we have no way of knowing if Charlotte joined in with their festivities, she would have been bursting with secret pride at the event. She would certainly have been able to hear the celebrations from her home in Boughspring!

We cannot help taking notice of the manner in which the Jubilee was celebrated in this truly loyal town. A spirited subscription was set on foot, and in a few hours upwards of 80l. were collected, which was expended in bread and meat for the poor belonging to that parish, and the overplus laid out in blankets, which were distributed amongst the most indigent in the neighbourhood. The morning was ushered in with ringing of bells, firing of cannon, and other demonstrations of joy. The inhabitants, accompanied by the gentlemen of the Chepstow Volunteer Cavalry in their full uniform, proceeded to church, where a most excellent and appropriate discourse was delivered by the Rev. Charles Morgan... After church the cavalry mounted their horses, and went to the field of exercise, and on their return, fired three volleys in the centre of the town, in a very soldier-like stile [*sic*]. The principal gentlemen in the town and neighbourhood were invited to dinner by the Cavalry, and on the company sitting down to partake of Old English Cheer, at the Beaufort Arms Inn, fifty guns were fired by the ships in the port. In the course of the evening, many loyal songs and toasts were given; and when it grew dark, the company were very agreeably surprised by a transparency representing our most gracious Sovereign at full length, dressed in his coronation robes: over him was the Crown, and on either side the letters G.R. in variegated lamps: the whole had a very good effect. As soon as the picture was displayed, a royal salute of twenty-one guns was fired from some cannon planted on a neighbouring hill adjoining the town, and a collection of fireworks were set off. We are happy to hear that no accident happened; everything was well regulated, and the evening passed off with the most perfect hilarity.[18]

The Reverend Charles Henry Morgan would, four years later, marry Frances Williams of Tidenham House, the stepdaughter of Harriett Maria Williams who owned Boughwell's Green House where Charlotte lived. Interestingly, Charlotte claimed to have provided the sketches for transparencies to be used 'in London, Edinburgh, Dublin, Windsor and many other places', so the one shown in Chepstow was probably of her design. Even if she did not join in the celebrations but merely observed the efforts of her hard work from afar, Charlotte did gain two rewards at the time. The Earl of Ailesbury sent her a 'magnificent present of game & fruit on the jubilee day' and Lord Dartmouth forwarded a remarkable present and one that perfectly befitted Charlotte's efforts bearing in mind the number of letters she wrote to instigate the event; an elegant writing desk with an enclosed inscription. Charlotte suspected that the latter came from the princesses Augusta and Elizabeth in gratitude for the service Charlotte had shown to their family. The desk would remain one of Charlotte's most treasured possessions for the remainder of her life. Further rewards would come later.[19]

*Chapter Nine*

# A New Life in Bristol

Charlotte remained at Boughwell's Green House on the Welsh borders for around two years following the jubilee. It was from that house that she wrote her final letter to her old friend William Windham, for the pair had indeed struck up a friendship through their correspondence. Windham had been diagnosed with a tumour in his hip and needed an operation to remove it. He told Charlotte, who was in London, almost immediately about the impending procedure and perhaps expressed his fear that he would not survive the surgeon's knife as Charlotte parcelled up a quantity of the letters he had sent to her and returned them, anxious to alleviate any worry in her friend's mind that they may be used for purposes he did not approve of after his death. Windham displayed a remarkable trust in Charlotte and sent them straight back, saying

> I feel the delicacy of the motives that has led you to return my letters, but I hope you will permit me to beg that they may still remain in your custody, so far I mean as it can at all [be] an object to keep them… I could not wish them a better depository than in your hands.[1]

Charlotte accepted 'the deposit most gratefully, & will take care they shall be carefully preserved for your future biographer.' Now, sadly, they appear to be lost to posterity despite Charlotte's best intentions.[2]

One of the last propagandist schemes that Windham and Charlotte worked on in tandem was the denouncement and silencing of William Cobbett in the newspapers during Charles Yorke's attempt to secure the exclusion of strangers from the House of Commons in the debate on the Scheldt expedition and the disastrous Walcheren campaign. During the latter half of 1809, the British had blockaded the Scheldt River as a way of closing off the port of Antwerp to the French and Dutch opposing forces. Walcheren was an island at the mouth of the river, little more than a malaria-ridden swamp, and the British forces there saw little action but fever decimated their numbers. Yorke, who had been in favour of the Scheldt expedition, made a stand in favour of the ministry in early 1810 after the campaign's failure and in opposition to the radical agitator Sir Francis Burdett; Yorke's exclusion of strangers from the House was designed to preclude the radical elements and the press from gaining ammunition from the debates with which to attack the ministry. The actor and theatre manager Richard Brinsley Sheridan, that old friend of Richard Heaviside, was one of Yorke's most vocal critics. Perhaps Sheridan's former friendship with her hated tormentor was a further spur to Charlotte's ire and she was determined to use her pen to assist the government. William Cobbett was another vociferous opponent and it was Cobbett upon whom Charlotte turned her attention; he was, at the time, held in Newgate, guilty of treasonous libel but his weekly newspaper, the *Political Register*, continued in print. Charlotte sat up for an entire night going through Cobbett's works and highlighting passages where he had previously expressed very strong but opposing views to those he now held and she wrote to the papers hoping they would print her letter to expose him as a hypocrite but none were prepared to print her words. They had, Charlotte believed, 'made a common cause with the man they pretended to reprobate'. If the papers thought the matter ended, then they did not have the measure of this woman. Charlotte sent her extracts to Windham who forwarded them to Yorke and Yorke, in turn, sent them via the Treasury to the *Morning Post* newspaper where they duly appeared:[3]

> [Cobbett's] principles at large during the latter part of the Eighteenth Century, were, that a Republic was a scoundrel, France a dunghill of de[s]potism, Sir FRANCIS BURDETT a traitor, Reforming Democrats unprincipled revolutionists, and America a licentious mobocracy where no free-born Briton could reside with honour or safety.
>
> At the beginning of the 19th Century his principles at large assumed a diametrically opposite form. The Republican is honoured; France is held forth as a protensive Revolution; Sir FRANCIS BURDETT is changed into a Patriot, Democrats are adulated as honest Reformers; and America, once cursed, is now blessed as the only country… where injured innocence can find an asylum.[4]

William Windham was never to see Charlotte's letter traducing Cobbett in print. Neither was he to see the fruition of a project that he and Charlotte had long been planning; that as soon as it was safe enough, Charlotte would criss-cross all the regions of France to 'ascertain the exact state of the arts, manufacturing, commerce, habits, manners, religion & politics of the country'. He underwent his operation on 17 May 1810, four days after he had returned his letters to Charlotte. The tumour was removed successfully but the great statesman did not recover from the shock of the procedure and died on 4 June. Exactly a week later a handsome and charismatic Frenchman who had landed at Dover and who was accused of spying for – and being in the pay of – the British was given written permission to proceed to London and the Foreign Office. Charlotte was later to give him shelter, perhaps at the request of the government.[5]

General Jean Sarrazin, born in 1770 at Saint-Sylvestre-sur-Lot in south-western France, had been one of the highest-ranking generals in Napoléon Bonaparte's army. However, in June 1810 after deserting from both the French army and the side of his British-born wife (whom he had married in Livorno, Italy) and their child, he arrived in England, prepared to divulge information about the French army to the British government in return for lodgings and an income.[6]

Sarrazin had surprised the French with his desertion. While in command of a division at a camp in Boulogne, he and his servant hired a fishing boat to take them south along the French coast to Étaples; the two planned to fish during the journey. They set off at 6 o'clock in the morning of 11 June and after some time came across a British man-of-war that was patrolling the coastline. When he noticed this, Sarrazin told his servant that he was going to England and ordered the captain of the fishing boat to take him to the enemy ship in order that he could open talks with the British. The captain proved reluctant but Sarrazin and his servant pointed their pistols in his direction and he complied with their request. General Sarrazin was attired in his full dress uniform, which suggests that his plan had always been more than a mere fishing trip, and once aboard the British ship he and his servant were brought in to the Downs. They were lodged at Wright's Hotel and Ship Inn at Dover before being conducted to London where Sarrazin was received at the Foreign Office by Marquess Wellesley, the elder brother of Arthur, the future 1st Duke of Wellington.

It would appear that Sarrazin anticipated he would be arrested in France after falling foul of Napoléon who was displeased by the state of Boulogne and had thoroughly planned his escape before hiring the fishing boat.[7] The British were distrustful of Sarrazin and did not prove as accommodating as he expected. In fact, they appeared less than pleased at his arrival on British soil. His request for a British passport was rejected out of hand

and the Frenchman complained vociferously. The lodgings offered to him were unsuitable and the income proffered insufficient for his needs, yet he remained in London grumbling and pestering government ministers as he had nowhere else to go. During his enforced stay in London he was to prove almost as prolific a letter-writer as Charlotte herself.

Meanwhile, Charlotte had gained a new correspondent. The tall, handsome Sir James Bland Burges, Baronet was introduced to her by John Reeves and theirs was to prove a long-lasting friendship. Sir James, a playwright and poet who counted Lord Byron (to whom he was connected via marriage) among his supporters, was born in Gibraltar in 1752, the son of a civil servant and former army officer who had captured the Young Pretender, Bonnie Prince Charlie's standard at the Battle of Culloden in 1745. After previously holding some minor government positions (Burges was Under-Secretary of State at the Foreign Office between 1789 and 1795), 'in very early life he had formed a close intimacy with Mr Pitt and the late Duke of Leeds, who, being anxious to attach to their party one so highly talented, prevailed upon him to embark in political affairs.' Perhaps another important consideration for Charlotte in cultivating this acquaintance was Sir James's employment within the royal household; he served as a knight marshal to King George III, a largely ceremonial position by Sir James's time ostensibly responsible for maintaining order within the Marshalsea Court (associated with the debtors' prison) and the Palace Court, the two known jointly as the King's Court. Princess Elizabeth, with whom Charlotte had briefly corresponded at the time of the jubilee, was known to Sir James and the two exchanged verses; he composed a Spenserian allegory specifically written to illustrate drawings made by the princess. Variously described as 'an amateur in an age of professionals' and 'a thorough English gentleman', Burges received only lacklustre plaudits for his literary efforts which were generally regarded as failures.[8]

It was at a performance – without theatrical aids – of one of Sir James's dramas in June 1810 that he and Charlotte met. The drama had moved Charlotte to tears and she confessed that she did not cry easily; Sir James, flattered by Charlotte's praise, readily agreed when she asked to be permitted to correspond with him. Charlotte sent her first letter to him, marked private, via John Wilson Croker, the First Secretary to the Admiralty (responsible for the government of the Royal Navy) and an Irish author and MP who was a friend of Sir James. Perhaps Charlotte, although given permission to write, had no idea where to send her letter? Croker had spoken out against Colonel Wardle in the debacle over the abuse of the Duke of York's military patronage which had led to Charlotte instigating the jubilee celebrations; he was a man that Charlotte would be sure to trust and she more than likely already had Croker's ear.[9]

Shortly after she had posted her letter to Sir James, Charlotte set off for Oxford under the guardianship of her friend, John Reeves. Oxford was crowded, not a room to be had, for all the great and the good had converged on the city to witness the inauguration of William Wyndham Grenville, 1st Baron Grenville, as chancellor of the university. Carriages from London to Oxford were fully booked for days beforehand and people who had left it too late were reduced to travelling up into the Midlands in the hope of securing a seat in a coach destined for Oxford. Grenville had formerly served as both prime minister and foreign secretary and was a man greatly admired by Charlotte. He was also William Windham's cousin. She was immensely lucky to enjoy the patronage of Reeves who had secured rooms for them both and a place at the ceremony for Charlotte.

On the day, 300 ladies, 'many…of the first distinction' and splendidly dressed, were admitted to the lower tier of the theatre where the ceremony was to take place, with many more clamouring outside for admittance. It was a scrum, with ladies elbowing each other out of the way, some losing their shoes, bracelets and accoutrements in the mayhem; the doors opened at nine but crowds had been converging outside hours earlier. Charlotte must have been amid this scuffle for entrance and she succeeded in getting inside and to her seat. 'The proportion of beautiful women assembled on this occasion was immense, and the dresses were so various as to surpass the most variegated *bed of tulips*.'[10]

At 11 o'clock the procession began. Lord Grenville had recently been ill and looked pale; as the weather was so hot he dispensed with his usual wig. He wore a dark brown court suit with a black robe, richly embroidered with gold, and an academic cap with a gold tassel. Charlotte, who had seen many great men, thought he looked impressive, 'much more splendid than Bonaparte at the head of his guards'. The celebrations ran over several days. At the theatre, the Italian opera singer Madame Angelica Catalani performed, grand dinners were served in the university halls and sermons preached in the city churches. The culmination of the event was the launch of a hot-air balloon from Merton Field that featured an inscription relating to Lord Grenville's Chancellorship of Oxford University. The balloonist James Sadler and his son ascended in the car attached underneath; an Oxford man, Sadler had become the first Englishman to ascend in a hot-air balloon from the same location in 1784 and Charlotte's late friend William Windham had been one of his greatest patrons. Charlotte thoroughly enjoyed the whole experience and took time out from the celebrations to visit the chambers in the Tower of the Five Orders at the entrance to the Bodleian Library which Sir James had particularly recommended she should seek out. She said in her next letter to him that they were 'the chief object of my enquiries at Oxford...& I assure you they were more interesting to me than all the gaieties & beauties around me, though I am willing to allow the whole scene to surpass most things I have ever beheld.'[11]

Charlotte had more than just her trip to Oxford to tell Sir James about; she also wanted to ask a favour of him. The late William Windham, during his correspondence with Charlotte, had once written a sixteen-page letter to her about the radical MP Samuel Whitbread's Bill on Public Education. In an attempt to reform the Poor Law Whitbread had proposed, among other things, a national system of education that would form part of parish relief. Under his scheme, every child would be entitled to at least two years of education and he hoped that through this modicum of knowledge, crime and poverty would be reduced. While it might now seem incredible that anyone would think otherwise, this was the eighteenth century and Windham was opposed to this bill; Charlotte had returned the letter to him in case it might prove useful to him. It was almost a foregone conclusion that Charlotte, like Windham, would take a different stance to the reforms in education proposed by Whitbread, a scion of the well-known brewing family, for he had openly expressed his admiration of Napoléon Bonaparte and wanted to adopt republican principles and reforms in Britain. He was Charlotte's antithesis. Windham felt that there was no benefit to the community at large in 'teaching the lower orders to read and write' and Charlotte had made her views clear when she had entertained the idea of opening a school for the poor children who lived near her during her enforced residence in Briton Ferry during her youth; she disliked the idea of being surrounded by dirty children and her views on the matter chimed with Windham's. In the end the bill was voted down, mainly because it ultimately proved too expensive to implement.[12]

Charlotte now wanted to reclaim Windham's letter to her and as well as asking Sir James to intercede with Windham's family on her behalf she also wrote to Mr Heneage Legge, Windham's executor. She was fortunate in having the letter returned to her together with a note from Mr Legge and one written on behalf of the widowed Mrs Windham and, as an added bonus, some of her own writing on the subject that had been found among Windham's papers. Windham had been thinking of incorporating Charlotte's words into a speech he was planning to make against Whitbread's bill or, if he made no speech, published in a pamphlet instead. It echoes Wilberforce's recital of Charlotte's letter against the French *maximum* in the Houses of Parliament years earlier and is an incredible thought that speeches made by Windham and pamphlets written by him could have incorporated Charlotte's words. Surely this was not the only time this occurred during their years of correspondence that had developed into a trusting and deep exchange of views? We are left only to wonder how often Charlotte heard her words spoken in parliament by the elite of her day and how many times she saw her words in print but ascribed to the composition of a male statesman and with no public recognition of herself. Her gain, for the time being, was the private approbation and friendship she had received from men such as William Windham, John Reeves and Sir James Bland Burges.

When Charlotte next wrote to Sir James, to thank him for his help in getting Windham's letter returned to her, she did so from an address in Chepstow where she was making an unintended stay as she had been taken ill while away from home visiting. Possibly she was staying with Reverend James Williams to whom she was related. She assured Sir James that she was on the mend and was expecting to be conveyed to her home at Boughspring the next day.[13]

Mrs Sarah Williams, John Williams' widow and Charlotte's stepmother, had moved back down to London and was living in the Holborn area when she died in August 1811. She was buried in the graveyard of St Anne's in Soho where her first husband lay. Her last will and testament had been written a year earlier and Charlotte was conspicuous by her absence within the document. Perhaps Mrs Williams thought that her stepdaughter had received her allotted share in her father's will, but the fact that Charlotte was not left a keepsake or even money for a mourning ring would suggest that relations between the two women were not exactly cordial. Instead, Sarah left a very personal ornament to the Reverend James Williams of Chepstow, the same man who had received the diamond shoe buckles in John Williams' own will. He was now bequeathed Sarah Williams' diamond ring and breast pin that contained a lock of John Williams' hair and a miniature portrait of him and was set with pearls and the initials J.W. It was a trinket that would have had great significance to Charlotte but it was Sarah's own personal property and she chose to bestow it elsewhere.[14]

Charlotte herself had links with Soho in the form of the two properties (nos. 48 and 49) on Frith Street that she had inherited from her father. By the end of 1811, General Jean Sarrazin, the French spy who was still trying to persuade the British government to grant him a financial reward for his defection, was living at 48 Frith Street when he published *The Philosopher; or, Historical and Critical Notes* that contained biographical notes on notable French military men, some thoughts on Napoléon, war and politics and Sarrazin's answer to his critics. It received a mixed reaction from the public. Sarrazin had written his manuscript in French – full of his own self-importance, he proposed to sell the original for the considerable sum of £250 – and it had been translated into English. Given his address, it is a distinct possibility that Charlotte had volunteered to rent her house to him and that she had been tasked with the translation of Sarrazin's work as a trusted government insider. Sarrazin, short of ready money, also hoped to hold a general sale of his possessions, although he drastically overestimated their worth:[15]

> General Sarrazin wishes to dispose of nine cameos, and four works in mosaic, by very capital masters, a sabre of a French general, a cross of the Legion of Honour, his portrait, painted at Rome in 1799, with another painted at Leghorn. The set price of these articles, which will only be sold together, is 3,000*l.* Should the purchaser afterwards regret his bargain, the seller engages to retake the said articles, as soon as he is paid what he has reason to expect from Government; and to return the money received, with interest, at the rate of five per cent per annum, for the time he may have had it in his possession. Apply by letter, or personally, between ten in the morning and two in the afternoon. Communications directed (post-paid) to the Author, No. 48, Frith-street, Soho-square.[16]

By the spring of 1812 Charlotte had moved from Boughwells Green House to the bustling port of Bristol, occupying 12 Pritchard Street, a terraced property in the St Paul's area of the city. She also found time to visit London, enduring the cold and damp and writing to Sir James from her lodgings in the capital. Their main topic of conversation was a girl to whom they (and possibly John Reeves too) were both to be godparents and Charlotte joked to Sir James that the Countess Leonor D'Oeynhausen had seen the child and wished to be a godparent too and thus her name must be added so the girl would be Rachel Leonora Burges Reeves Protheroe.

The Protheroes were a Bristol family who were known to Charlotte (the extended family's fortune came via their trade as West Indian merchants). Charlotte often gifted the produce – fruit and spices – to Sir James and

Mr Reeves who were grateful enough to repay the kindness by standing as godfather. The Countess D'Oeynhausen was of a much higher social status, however. Born in Portugal in 1750, she was the daughter of the Marquis of Alorna but her family's wealth and social standing had led to suspicion and disaster; her maternal grandparents were put to death and her parents imprisoned. Leonor married Count Karl August von Oeynhausen, a German officer who was serving with the Portuguese army and travelled widely, mixing in literary circles and moving among the refugee aristocrats fleeing the French Republic. She was left a widow with six children to care for when her husband died in 1793. It is rumoured that Leonor became involved in politics and espionage against Napoléon, forcing her exile from Portugal between 1803 and 1814, years that she spent first in Spain and then in England. It was while in England that she made the acquaintance of Charlotte for the two ladies had lived close by each other. In the spring of 1811 the countess and her three daughters took a property that stood midway between Lydney Park in the Forest of Dean and Chepstow, placing them almost upon Charlotte's doorstep during her tenure of Boughwells Green House.[17]

The two women had much in common. Like Charlotte, Leonor had spent many years in a form of captivity, held in a convent alongside her mother, and both Charlotte and the countess were successful in a literary vein. Among other rumours regarding Leonor's life is her involvement with French counter-revolutionaries and given Charlotte's own clandestine activities, their friendship suggests that the countess may indeed have been involved. The inclusion of John Reeves' surname in the proposed baptismal name of the goddaughter hints at a link between him and the two women; possibly, as the superintendent of the Alien Office, he fostered the budding acquaintance between them? In 1812, the year in which it was proposed that Leonor may stand as a godmother to the Protheroe girl, she semi-anonymously published Portuguese translations of Horace's *Poetics* and Alexander Pope's *Essay on Criticism*, credited simply as 'by a Portuguese woman'; in later years, she published other translations under her own name. She has repeatedly, over the years, been referred to as *varonil* (manly or man-like), a term meant as a compliment to her strength of character and it is an epithet that could equally be applied to Charlotte.

Charlotte returned to Bristol at the end of March, the dismal weather resulting in her contracting a violent fever and spending six weeks confined to her room. The christening of the Protheroe babe had to be delayed. The elusive Benjamin Hunt Biggs, almost invisible, still had some weak presence in Charlotte's life. Writing to Sir James, Charlotte told him that Mr Biggs' health was in an extremely bad way and he had been advised to travel to 'the Madeiras' for warmer weather. Benjamin, it seems, was inclined to follow his doctor's advice, leaving Charlotte in England, the independent mistress of her life and home.[18]

Independence meant standing on one's own two feet, however, and Charlotte now felt the need for some money of her own for her personal use. Although she received rent for her father's old house in Theakston (of which she had retained ownership) and her Soho properties, Charlotte still found herself short of ready cash. She was later to declare that the loss of a relation was one cause of her dwindling funds. Having few options, she decided to try to gain some backdated financial reparation from her success in organizing the jubilee. She had laid out her own money in the planning of her project, everything from ink and writing paper to the numerous journeys she made by coach to Bristol to post her packages of letters to John Reeves in London so that they could be franked and sent on to their destinations. Never one to aim low when she could aim high, Charlotte wrote to Prime Minister Spencer Perceval (who simultaneously served as the Chancellor of the Exchequer) with her request. However, her timing was terrible. Just three days after she wrote her letter, the prime minister was assassinated in the House of Commons and any hopes that Charlotte held of assistance from Perceval died with him.[19]

Ironically for Charlotte, Perceval's assassin, a Huntingdonshire man named John Bellingham, was also trying to get compensation from the government and it was his dissatisfaction with the rebuttal of his petitions that led him to take Perceval's life in revenge. Bellingham had run up debts while working for a Liverpool mercantile company based in Russia, debts he blamed on the British ambassador at St Petersburg, Granville Leveson-Gower. Once back in England he petitioned the government but with no success. On the morning of 11 May 1812, Bellingham quietly waited in the lobby of the House of Commons until the prime minister entered. Taking a pistol out from under his coat he shot Perceval at close range, fatally wounding him.

Ill fortune dogged Charlotte in the spring of 1812. Shortly after learning of Perceval's death she managed to dislocate her shoulder in an accident. She was alone in her Bristol home (Benjamin Hunt Biggs had left for Guernsey instead of Madeira in search of warmer weather as England continued wet and cold into the early summer) and Charlotte idled away too many weeks as an invalid. She corresponded with Sir James, asking for him to intercede with his friend Mr Croker, the First Secretary to the Admiralty, to find out where HMS *Swiftsure* was stationed. Charlotte had a 'young friend' on board, a midshipman named Samuel Rosser Protheroe from the Bristol Protheroe mercantile family, and she wished to write to him.

This young sailor was the son of Thomas Protheroe and Hannah Skyrme and the elder brother of the girl to whom Charlotte and Sir James were to stand as godparents; he was born in 1793 in the village of Abbots Leigh near Bristol. Samuel was around 18 years old when Charlotte wrote to Sir James and he had entered the Royal Navy the year before, serving as a first-class volunteer or 'young gentleman', one of the boys from well-to-do families who went to sea (usually aged between 9 and 19) with the intention of one day taking command of their own ship. The *Swiftsure* was a third-rate (74-gun) ship-of-the-line and had first entered service in 1804. When Charlotte wrote, the vessel was stationed in the Mediterranean but by August of that year young Samuel Rosser Protheroe had transferred, along with his captain William Stewart, to the 64-gun HMS *Stately* which was moored along the Portuguese coastline. A rise in rank came with the move; Samuel was now a midshipman. It is entirely possible that Charlotte may have been behind his promotion, pulling strings on his behalf with her influential male friends. She certainly wasn't above meddling in his career in the years to come.[20]

Charlotte still needed to persuade the government to recompense her for her sterling work in organizing the jubilee. Her approach to Mr Perceval had been made too late so now she sought to foster an interest for her cause with another high-ranking gentleman. Her choice was the new Chancellor of the Exchequer, Nicholas Vansittart.

*Chapter Ten*

# Espionage in France

Nicholas Vansittart was a Tory, allied both politically and by blood to Henry Addington, Viscount Sidmouth and a personal friend of George III's son Ernest, Duke of Cumberland, whose patronage he enjoyed. Vansittart had been employed within government under Addington's ministry but he had resigned alongside him in 1807 and then spent some time in retirement looking after his wife whose health was not good. His return to the Commons as Chancellor of the Exchequer put him under an immense amount of pressure. The continuation of the war with France had left the country deeply in debt and Vansittart had to tax heavily, a move that was obviously unpopular. However, Charlotte wisely and knowingly chose her man, and chose him extremely well. Her opening gambit to him, in a letter dated 15 September 1812 and written from her inconspicuous home on Pritchard Street in Bristol, was one of flattery, telling him that both his 'public & private character…encourages me to expect the following statement will be received with candour and indulgence.'[1]

She highlighted the jubilee, letting Vansittart know of its origins at her hands and reiterating the success of her grand scheme. She carefully dropped in the names of the Earl of Ailesbury, Lord Dartmouth and the princesses Augusta and Elizabeth to add weight to her claims and mentioned that she had petitioned Spencer Perceval prior to his death before proceeding to the thrust of her communication:

> I am aware that the secret service money is very limited…but when it is recollected, how many thousand persons were libated, cloathed [*sic*], & fed, how many charitable institutions founded, how many stakes raised, the impulse given to many manufacturers, the numbers employed, & above all the spirit of loyalty which was revived [by the jubilee], I cannot but indulge the hope, that I may be thought intitled [*sic*] to the sum I expended (now become an object to me).[2]

Charlotte cleverly took credit for the philanthropic projects that had benefited from the jubilee, even though these had not been of her instigation, as well as her loyalist endeavours. Vansittart replied to Charlotte and, true to form, once she had his ear she began to offer him advice, albeit advice couched in a very deferential tone. Apologizing for writing again so soon, she worried that Cobbett – now released from prison – would disrupt the forthcoming Westminster Election and suggested to Vansittart that he may be silenced by publishing extracts from the *Porcupine* newspaper written while Cobbett was in America which, Charlotte said, were not well known in Britain. Thus, she pointed out, Cobbett could be discredited (she helpfully included an extract at the end of her letter). It was the same tactic that Charlotte had employed before to silence Cobbett, as she did not scruple to let Vansittart know.[3]

The British conflict with America – the war of 1812 – was of concern to Charlotte, and she thought Cobbett's works could be employed as a propagandist tactic, written as they were when Cobbett had a very British bias to his writing. However, Charlotte's next letter to Vansittart, written just five days later, left the subject of Cobbett behind; she now bravely embarked on the next chapter of her life, reinventing herself once again and boldly requesting Vansittart's backing for her ambitious plans.

No longer would she be merely a political pamphleteer and female politician, advising government ministers. Now she wished to be employed as a peculiar form of female spy, travelling through France, observing the people and the country and reporting back to Vansittart in return for the money she felt was due to her following her jubilee expenditure. Perhaps, despairing of ever gaining remuneration by any other means, she felt that she had to offer something more and her scheme would kill two birds with one stone. She planned to travel to France in the spring of 1813 following a sojourn in Devon, and John Reeves had already obtained permission from the French government for Charlotte to travel; she cited continued ill health that was made worse by overwintering in England for her need to journey southwards. Whether she came by the money she needed in recompense for the jubilee or in anticipation of her covert intelligence while on her travels, it was a necessary and essential requirement.[4]

Vansittart was possibly somewhat bemused by the forthright Charlotte but nevertheless decided to make use of her services, marking the beginning of Charlotte's career as a government spy. He sent her £100 and she gratefully wrote back from Bristol to thank him. It was no ordinary letter either; Charlotte wrote it on paper that had been taken from Napoléon Bonaparte's writing desk at the Château de Saint-Cloud just outside Paris, liberally sprinkled with pink and silver sand from the same source. She noted that the paper had been made in England and that when she had visited the château a friendly guard on duty had allowed her to take her souvenirs.[5]

Saint-Cloud was a sixteenth-century palace on the banks of the River Seine, formerly owned by the Duke d'Orléans and midway between Paris and the Palace of Versailles. Following his proclamation as emperor in 1804, Bonaparte had established it as one of his main residences complete with a throne room. Had Charlotte visited Saint-Cloud when she was in Paris in 1802 and held on to her prized sheets of writing paper and her coloured sand since then, reserving them for only the most important missives she was to write? Perhaps her use of Bonaparte's writing paper was to demonstrate to Vansittart her ability to mix, unobserved, alongside the highest circles, all the while watching and recording her surroundings and the people she encountered? It certainly does not seem to have harmed Vansittart's estimation of Charlotte's character at all and their correspondence continued apace.

She was able to supply some interesting information to Vansittart regarding William Cobbett, a man who she had grown to hate as his values turned from loyalist to radical. Cobbett, much like Charlotte, had been lobbying for acknowledgement of his authorship and personal expenditure in the publication of his anonymous pamphlet *Important Considerations for the People of the Kingdom* in 1803. This was a work which, upon Windham's request, had been read by Charlotte and edited and amended by her; some parts of it were her own additions. Only Charlotte and a few ministers, including Windham, had known the identity of the author. Cobbett had tried to have the pamphlet vindicated at his trial for libel as proof of his loyalty but his request was refused and he had found himself behind bars. Now, free once again, he was making mischief. His fine of £1,500 had not been levied, perhaps in a subtle acknowledgement of his former loyalist writings, and Cobbett intended to embarrass the government by making this publicly known alongside, he hoped, official confirmation that *Important Considerations...* had stemmed from his pen. An MP was at risk of blackmail and Charlotte, although she did not name him, clearly knew about this. Her advice to Vansittart was that the MP in question should make the whole thing public. Intriguingly, she seems to suggest in her letter to Vansittart that she was still conversing with Cobbett, despite her dislike of the man. Was Charlotte double-dealing, pretending to Cobbett's face that she was his friend, his literary equal and then passing on information to government ministers? 'Mr Cobbett fancies he has the means of annoying him, & has often exposed this persuasion to me – he even thinks had that noble person been in office he should not so long have endured confinement.'[6]

Ultimately Charlotte's plans to travel to France in 1813 came to nothing; instead she made a visit to London, aiming to be there by 27 April. Despite still owning the two properties in Frith Street, Soho, when in London Charlotte lodged in rooms on the first floor of a house in noisy Suffolk Street, just off Pall Mall. She travelled from Bristol via Eton as she was escorting a boy back to the renowned public school. James Reeves Williams Protheroe, the elder brother of Charlotte and Sir James's goddaughter was a new boy there in the spring of 1813. His two middle names suggest that John Reeves and Charlotte were his godparents and, as the only son of the family who attended Eton, it appears that his education was paid for by his childless godfather John Reeves, who had been educated there himself.[7]

In 1813, a book was published in which there is a particularly curious circumstance relating to Charlotte. Mrs Julia Smith was a vicar's wife as well as an author (her husband, the Reverend Joseph Smith, held a living in Melksham at Wiltshire) and her first 'reflective tale', which she claimed was founded in fact, was titled *The Prison of Montauban; or, Times of Terror*. It had been published in 1810 and before that she had edited *Letters of the Swedish Court*. Her next work was *The Old School* which was published in two volumes and recounted the history of Sir William Jerningham and his family.[8]

Sir William Jerningham, 6th Baronet, had married Frances, daughter of Henry Dillon, 11th Viscount Dillon of Costello-Gallen. The Dillon family had a strong Jacobite heritage (the Hon. Arthur Dillon, Henry's father, was granted titles by James Francis Edward Stuart, the 'Old Pretender') and strong links with France. Lady Jerningham's younger brother was Arthur, General Dillon, who led a French regiment until he met his end on the guillotine in 1794, accused of being a royalist. In *A Residence in France*, Charlotte claimed she was present in Lille in August 1792 when one of the assassins of Théobald Dillon, a cousin to Lady Jerningham, was guillotined. Théobald, like Arthur, was a general with the French forces; after defeat by the Austrians he was set upon by his own men who believed him to be a traitor and Charlotte attended his funeral.

*The Old School* comprises anecdotes on the history of the family and a series of letters, supposedly written by a lady who signs herself A.S., that recount her conversations with Lady Jerningham to her unnamed correspondent. One letter contains a copy of a further epistle:

> A very intelligent sensible woman who called here yesterday, as we
> happened to fall upon French affairs, produced a letter she had

received, some considerable time since, from a friend of hers, well known to Lady Jerningham, who had been long detained in France; a story it contained interested me, and I begged leave to copy it for your perusal: *le voici*.

'Prior to the revolution, the daughter of a man of small fortune, Monsieur de Santerre, accepted the offer of Monsieur de St Evremond, at sixteen, to marry her, and to relinquish her fortune to her two younger sisters.'[9]

The letter went on to relate the history of Eugenia de Santerre almost word for word as it had appeared in *A Residence in France* which Charlotte had published anonymously some fifteen years earlier but with a little extra detail. While it is possible that the intelligent and sensible woman was Charlotte, it is more likely that she was instead the author of the letter the lady carried, the lady who had been 'long detained in France' and was well known to Lady Jerningham. It perhaps goes some way to confirming the validity of at least parts of *A Residence in France* and suggests that Charlotte did not simply take her friend La Marquise's recollections verbatim but instead meshed them with her own, making the whole much more interesting, if a little less authentic. How the tale came to the ears of Mrs Julia Smith is unknown, another of the many mysteries that Charlotte has left behind in her wake, but it is possible that as the two ladies were both published authors they were also friends and corresponded with each other.

By the end of the year Charlotte was suffering ill health and confined to bed in her Bristol home for six weeks with a severe pulmonary complaint. Her condition was exacerbated by the bitterly cold winter weather and the start of the greatest frost of the nineteenth century. The Thames was frozen solid and a frost fair held upon its glacial surface; Charlotte planned to be in London during February and if her health had mended in time then perhaps she witnessed the fair, which was the last one ever to be held on the river. Charlotte hated the cold, damp British winter and a dismal spring that year did not improve matters. For the sake of her health, as well as just for the pure enjoyment of travel, Charlotte once again planned to go to France, intending to be there by the late summer. First though, she had taken rooms at 12 Sion Row in Clifton, a suburb of Bristol. The house was owned by a Mrs Mary Morgan and overlooked open fields towards the River Avon and St Vincent's Rock. The air at Clifton was better than that in the centre of Bristol and Sion Row was close to the Hotwells where people 'took the waters', precisely the reason that Charlotte was there.[10]

Charlotte may still have been residing at Sion Row when she wrote to Vansittart on 2 May 1814, for she simply gave 'Bristol' as her address; she was on the eve of leaving for London and she wrote with a proposition. She offered to return to France, to report back on the differences she noticed in the state of the country from her first-hand experience before the revolution, under the republic and now, at the restoration of the Bourbon monarchy. Napoléon Bonaparte had been defeated and Paris had surrendered to the allied troops. When he realized there were no other options left to him, Napoléon abdicated his position of emperor, surrendered to his opponents and was exiled to Elba, a small island off the Italian coast. With France once more welcoming British tourists, Charlotte wanted to waste no time in availing herself of the chance to return to the country she loved and visit her old friends there. As Charlotte's contemporary, the writer Mary Berry was to say of travel to France, 'most thoroughly do I begin to feel the want of that *shake* out of English ways, English whims, and English prejudices, which nothing but leaving England gives one.' Travel represented independence, knowledge, adventure and enlightenment but it was cripplingly expensive. Charlotte just needed some ready cash with which to fund her journey and this was where Vansittart came in. Referring him to her friends, John Reeves and Colonel Disbrowe, Charlotte confessed to authorship of *A Residence in France* and stressed her long connection with the country before offering her services in return for some money to top up her own meagre funds:[11]

> I was partly educated in France before the subversion of the monarchy, I resided there during the whole of the first six years of the Revolution & for some months during the Peace of Amiens...
> I think I could, for about three hundred pounds, traverse the most interesting parts of France...[so] as to procure very essential information.[12]

It was the fruition of the idea germinated between Charlotte and her old friend William Windham; one that had been placed on hold due to his untimely death but that she was determined would go ahead. Charlotte intended to publish an account of her travels, but in a way that would be a useful propagandist tool to the government. In the end, Vansittart proved more generous than Charlotte expected. Whatever his surprise at receiving Charlotte's letter, he took her offer in good faith – perhaps helped by the testimony of Reeves and Disbrowe – and authorized £453 to be deposited into Mrs Biggs' account at Drummond's bank (Charlotte also had an account with Messrs Moreland on Pall Mall).[13]

Lieutenant Colonel Edward Disbrowe of the Staffordshire militia was another man close to the royal family whose good opinion Charlotte had cultivated. As well as serving as an MP, he was also vice-chamberlain to Queen Charlotte, a position gained when he became a trusted favourite of George III while stationed with his regiment at Windsor in the 1780s. All the royal family came to rely on him and enjoyed his friendship; he was exactly the sort of man Charlotte was drawn to and she more than likely came to his notice initially through her planning of the royal jubilee of 1809. Disbrowe was later to offer her a small favour, insignificant in the eyes of the world but one of great import to Charlotte as it concerned her one true love, the man for whom she still carried a flame in her heart: David Ochterlony, now a decorated major general.

David Ochterlony, like many other men in the employ of the EIC, had 'gone native' and fully embraced the Mughal culture and lifestyle. He had thirteen Muslim wives with whom he promenaded each evening, each wife atop an elephant, but chief among them was the young and beautiful Mubarak Begum, formerly a Brahmin slave and dancing girl (she had converted to Islam) who had captivated the now elderly general and reigned supreme within his household. The mother of his youngest children (Ochterlony had several, born to his various wives), she was socially and politically adventurous and 'the mistress of everyone within the walls'; while she referred to herself as Lady Ochterlony to the chagrin of the British, she was also known as 'Generallee Begum'. The Anglican primate of Kolkata, Bishop Reginald Heber, who described Ochterlony as a 'tall and pleasing looking old man' recalled meeting with the general who received him sitting on his *diwan* wearing Mughal dress with servants ranged behind fanning the general with peacock feather fans. Next to Ochterlony's own tent was that of his harem, made from red silk. His daughters had their own tent, 'hung around with red cloth and thus fenced in from the eyes of the profane'. Quite what Charlotte would have made of the general's domestic affairs is open to conjecture. While the newspapers reported on his military successes, they were silent on his wives and children, but it is possible that Charlotte, with her wide-ranging network of correspondents, had managed to glean some information.[14]

In London in anticipation of her imminent journey, Charlotte took the opportunity to visit Sir James's house and to meet with his wife and sister-in-law, Lady Anne Barnard. She wrote to Sir James, excusing herself from an intended trip to the theatre due to a continued cough – she was still not fully recovered from her illness – and apologizing as she had found her card intended for the ladies of Burges's house in the bottom of her carriage when it should have been residing on Sir James's mantelpiece. Charlotte's letters to Sir James are like no others she wrote. She became a little more informal with William Windham during her correspondence and always remained businesslike in tone towards Vansittart, but with Sir James she was playful, joking and laughing, a rare glimpse of the true woman behind her carefully-cultivated serious and blue-stockinged façade. With Vansittart and Windham, Charlotte was very much the 'female politician', although with Windham she did let him glimpse another side of her, but with Sir James she was simply a woman, one with a lively interest in his literary and theatrical works and in his domestic concerns. One could almost sometimes think that Charlotte was flirting with him.

Burges's wife, Lady Margaret, his daughters and Lady Anne Barnard all received Charlotte at their house on Upper Brooke Street and happily returned her visits by calling at her lodgings in Suffolk Street. Charlotte was forced to apologize; the ladies who usually lived on the floor above her had taken her rooms and on this particular sojourn in the capital Charlotte was forced to make do with their former apartment on the second floor which meant that her visitors had many stairs to climb. She consoled herself with the fact that she now had a much better view from her windows.

Charlotte had a lot in common with Lady Anne Barnard. The two ladies were both adventurous and well-travelled (Anne had been in Paris when the revolution broke out and subsequently sailed to the Cape with her husband when he was appointed to a position there), they both had an interest in politics, wrote extensively and both had a link with William Windham. Anne had conducted a love affair with Windham for many years, perhaps even going so far as to live with him as his mistress while they were both in Paris, and Windham was not the only statesman who had courted Anne. She engaged in her politicking over the dinner table and in the drawing room, although she said of herself, 'I am and ever was a poor politician.'[15]

There was another link too; one that perhaps ran deeper with Charlotte. Lady Anne Barnard and her sister, Lady Margaret Burges, were from a large Scottish family (their father was James Lindsay, 5th Earl of Balcarres) and had a brother who had served with the EIC in India. They had a large circle of friends at home, both in their native Scotland and in England and possibly proved a rich source of information for Charlotte about David Ochterlony's life in India.

Margaret had formed an attachment to Sir James Burges in her youth but had instead married the louche Alexander Fordyce, a Scottish banker who led her into debt and disaster. Anne penned a ballad titled *Auld Robin Gray* set to a tune she knew from her childhood about a girl who lost her first love, a man named Jamie who had gone to sea to seek his fortune. Instead the girl married Robin Gray, an older and wealthier man. She had her sister, Sir James and Alexander Fordyce in mind when she wrote it. There were also parallels with Charlotte's loss of Ochterlony when he sailed for India and her years as the enforced mistress of Heaviside, which may have resonated with Charlotte. However, Margaret's love story had a happier ending than Charlotte's; in 1812, after being widowed, she finally married Sir James as his third wife.

Now that Vansittart had supplied the necessary funds, Charlotte turned her full attention to her departure. Accompanied by servants, she planned to traverse mainland Europe. She was later to recall that during 1814 and 1815 she spent most of the months journeying not only in France but also through 'Holland – Germany – Italy – Switzerland – God knows where…'. She applied, via Vansittart, to the Foreign Secretary (Robert Stewart, Viscount Castlereagh and later the Marquess of Londonderry) for official recommendations to both the Duke of Wellington and to Sir Charles Stewart who was the British minister at the court of Berlin. Wellington had been in Toulouse when he heard of Napoléon Bonaparte's abdication, about to give a dinner. Days later it was Sir Charles Stewart who arrived to offer him the appointment of British ambassador in Paris.[16]

Charlotte and her servants embarked for France in August and, after visiting her old haunts of Amiens and Abbeville, she made directly for Paris to observe the ongoing celebrations there. Wellington arrived in Paris towards the end of the month and took up residence in a house on the Rue du Faubourg Saint-Honoré that had formerly been owned by Napoléon's sister Pauline. It was a round of festivities, with Wellington the fêted guest of honour, present at balls, dinners and salons where he enjoyed the attention of many beautiful women, but an undercurrent of tension ran beneath the glitzed façade; Wellington had been warned that his life was in danger and the newly-restored Bourbon monarchy was viewed with suspicion by many.

The rest of the year was an itinerant blur: Charlotte visited châteaux, attended balls, feasted with French peasants in a vineyard and dined at splendid fêtes, all the while passing almost as a Frenchwoman due to her perfect knowledge of the language and the country and gaining an insight that a general tourist could never hope to.

Despite her claims that her health was bad and that she benefited from spending the colder months further south, Charlotte braved a severely cold winter to return to England during November or December 1814 due to the death of someone she simply described (in a letter written in 1816 to Earl Fitzwilliam) as a family member. Perhaps it was someone over whose affairs she had some jurisdiction or from whom she hoped to inherit as she felt the need to be there personally. Her travels in France and mainland Europe had proved more expensive than she had expected and Charlotte was forced to write to Vansittart from Paris at the beginning of November 1814 to ask for £50 to be deposited in her bank account. Charlotte had spent more than £600 already; the atrocious state of the roads in France had nearly destroyed her carriage and the repairs had been costly. Vansittart duly obliged his pernicious female spy once again. Charlotte returned to England in the depths of winter, enduring a 'long & somewhat hazardous passage' across the Channel and made for London. There had been another death in December 1814, one that Charlotte, as she travelled home, was possibly unaware of for Lady Margaret Burges, Sir James's wife who had been ailing for some months, had finally succumbed to her illness. We are reminded of the almost flirtatious letters that Charlotte wrote to Sir James in the preceding years. Charlotte was a married lady, or at least she passed as such to the world, so she could have held out no hope of becoming the next Lady Burges if such a scheme was even in her mind, but she could perhaps hope to become an even closer female confidante to the widowed Burges after his bereavement. She called at the Burges's London residence, unaware that they were from home, and left a manuscript for Sir James before taking a seat in a coach bound for Bristol. She had arrived back in Pritchard Street before the end of the year as she spent some time on the first day of 1815 writing to her friend to offer her condolences on his loss and to apologize for importunely calling at his home.[17]

The cold weather and the terrible voyage across the Channel took their toll on Charlotte's always precarious health and she fell ill, spending the first weeks of 1815 confined to her home. Sir James and his sister-in-law were Charlotte's correspondents during her enforced stay in Bristol; Lady Anne Barnard sent two letters to Charlotte and Charlotte enlisted Sir James's help in acting as a go-between. She wanted Mr Croker to get young Samuel Rosser Protheroe moved to a different ship (there was 'a schism between the captain and officers' on board his ship HMS *Orontes* which had recently returned from the West Indies, and Captain Nathaniel Day Cochrane of the *Orontes* thought that it would be for Protheroe's 'good to separate him from the rest'). Sir James duly obliged and Mr Croker used his influence to get Charlotte's young friend transferred to the *Horatio* instead, captained by William Dillon and bound for the East Indies.[18]

Charlotte also wrote to Sir Nicholas Vansittart, enclosing a lengthy manuscript that contained all the observations she had made on her travels across mainland Europe and her travel itinerary. Her trip had been funded by the government with the intention that she would publish her account of it but Charlotte was now unable to uphold this part of the bargain. To her chagrin she had discovered that a large number of French people still held Napoléon Bonaparte in high reverence, noting that the French were 'odiously versatile'. This was not the narrative that she wanted to remit to the world at large:

> To you Sir, I may confess that I would not publish, which is that I am returned with the conviction, that if Buonaparté could have subdued his inordinate ambition & subjected his conduct to some moral principle he was in many respects well gratified to govern a great country – I found this opinion on the comparative state of France during all the periods in which I have seen it, namely under the ancient monarchy, the Republic & all its revolutionary anarchies, the Peace of Amiens, the present time. – I think it very possible to make what I have seen an amusing book, but I am doubtful whether without a great sacrifice of truth I could make it a useful one, & I cannot consider myself at liberty to render that which you so obligingly enabled me to perform with comfort, a source of mischief – much reflection therefore will be incumbent on me before I venture to communicate the results of my journey, & as I propose returning to the Continent in the spring in order to traverse France in another direction I may perhaps wait & publish both tours together. But should I deem it prudent to suppress the whole, I must disclaim all merit in the sacrifice, for far from desiring literary reputation I have the utmost repugnance to it, & as for any profit which I might desire from such a work I consider myself as already remunerated by your liberality in contributing to the expences [*sic*] of the journey.

A hefty manuscript was attached, a 'summary of the present state of France' covering religion, commerce, population, anything that Charlotte thought Vansittart would find useful in lieu of her promised work. She demonstrated a wide-ranging knowledge, for instance able to compare the industry of stocking manufacture at Nimes in southern France against that of Nottingham in the English Midlands and assuring Vansittart that England would not be able to compete with the continent unless the price of labour could be reduced. Charlotte was also particularly presentient in the information she transmitted to Vansittart:

> The writer never was dazzled by the military successes of Buonaparté – she went to France & she has returned, detesting his moral qualities & deploring their effects, she reports therefore the attachment of the French to him with regret & has never communicated it even to her nearest connections, but she solemnly asserts her perfect conviction of what she advances & is persuaded that could he (now the invading powers are withdrawn) enter France at the head of a very moderate army, the result would be fatal to the Bourbons.[19]

Another death occurred in the spring of 1815; one that Charlotte, if she was aware of it, would not mourn in the slightest. Richard Heaviside had carved out a respectable life for himself, albeit one lived largely unnoticed once the tempestuous years of his infatuation for Charlotte were at an end. After Heaviside had sold Peterborough House – he had let the house and estate fall into disrepair and part of the house had been torn down – he resided quietly on his estate at Sandhurst in Berkshire, making a fresh beginning as a country gentleman, sent his son to Eton for his education and lived out his twilight years in the Paragon Buildings at Bath. It was there that he died on 12 April 1815, intestate (i.e. he left no will), which seems unusual for a man of his age and standing. Perhaps, if he had continued to pay Charlotte the annuities he had settled upon her in her youth when he had held the upper hand over her, then dying without leaving a will was a way to obfuscate any future payments from his estate and to leave everything to his wife and son who survived him? A way to bury his past.[20]

Once she was fully recovered from her illness, Charlotte lost no time in recommencing her tour of Europe. She arrived in London in May preparatory to setting out for Switzerland with a female friend, Miss Maria Chavasse, and a relation (who, sadly, Charlotte neglects to name). The initial plan, as recorded in letters she wrote to Vansittart who was organizing passports for the small party, was for Charlotte and her friend to travel to Brussels under the escort of her relation where she would be met by her

Swiss servant who was in the employ of an English family and who would oversee the journey to Switzerland. The intrepid Mrs Biggs then intended to enter France either by way of Strasbourg or Switzerland 'according to the seat of war'; she had promised to perform some kind of 'engagement' for a dying friend, one that she declared in writing to Vansittart 'nothing short of personal danger would induce me to break'. However, these plans altered due to fast-moving events on mainland Europe and the Swiss servant was instead instructed to meet Charlotte and her companion at Calais. (It is not clear from Charlotte's letters if her relation accompanied the two ladies across the Channel or not, with their changed itinerary.) Earlier in the year, Bonaparte had managed to slip past his guards and, as Charlotte had predicted when she wrote to Vansittart a month before his escape from exile on Elba, the emperor was now reinstated in France and at the head of the army, but Charlotte felt safe enough to travel. It probably comes as no surprise to find that, upon hearing that Bonaparte was back in France, Charlotte wrote to Vansittart suggesting how the military forces could halt him in his tracks:

> [It would be] most desirable & might spare a vast expence [*sic*] of lives & money could [Bonaparte] be checked before he arrives within an hundred miles of Paris – it certainly is not within the competence of one of [my] sex to judge of the means of doing this, yet… we have troops at Antwerp, Bruxelles &c &c, they might be of the greatest use were they marched immediately across the country to Dijon – the distance is 70 posts, but cannot be more than 300 miles – & if Buonaparté experiences any opposition at Lyons they might still be in time to assist in interrupting his route to Paris.[21]

However, events had moved too quickly for Charlotte's advice to be the least bit useful. When she wrote, Bonaparte was already at Lyons and he advanced through France to Paris. Elections were to be held in Abbeville and Amiens and Charlotte proposed to make a stop in these towns, ostensibly to catch up with old friends there but in reality to view the proceedings and report back to Vansittart. She planned to be in Paris for the *Champ de Mai* on 26 May, delaying her visit to Switzerland in favour of witnessing this spectacle. It was to be a huge national assembly for Napoléon Bonaparte to modify the constitution of his empire, 'a piece of splendid pageantry – in the shadow of the darker theatre of war' as William Wilberforce was to record in his diary. As it turned out, the event was postponed until 1 June due to the elections;

all those eligible to do so were to vote on the new constitutional changes and it proved impossible to get the registers of electors to Paris by 26 May:[22]

> [Charlotte had] just received a letter from her friends there urging her to attend this solemn act, as a great show, in which light they appear to look forward to it. – They assure her she may come without the smallest apprehension & that she will be at liberty to leave France again the instant she wills it.[23]

Regardless of her opinion of the republic and its principles, it was, as Charlotte's friends insisted, a 'great show', despite the postponement. William Cobbett, somewhat predictably, thought it impressive, a 'ceremony which [spoke] for itself' and he castigated his fellow journalists who labelled the event a tragicomedic farce, branding them 'the vile hireling press'. He also lauded the bravery of Bonaparte for appearing unarmed and without guards on his 'elevated throne' when it had largely been suggested by the British press that he was, by this time, so reviled, even by a growing number of Frenchmen and women, that he dare not appear in public and travelled shut inside a closed carriage or at full gallop on his horse, constantly worried about an assassin ending his life. The *Champ de Mai*, Cobbett believed, proved that the French people still loved their emperor. Charlotte left Paris directly after the celebrations and she got out just in time to find herself – luckily – in neutral Switzerland for what was to be the pivotal battle of the Napoléonic Wars: Waterloo.[24]

The allied forces, led by Arthur Wellesley, Duke of Wellington, met the French across a muddy valley in Belgium on 18 June 1815; some of the British officers were still dressed for the ballroom, having come directly from the Duchess of Richmond's ball at Brussels that had been in full swing when a messenger arrived with news of the French advance. The duke was caught off guard: 'Napoleon has humbugged me, by God; he has gained twenty-four hours' march on me.'

The fighting was fierce but by the end of the day the field was Wellington's... just. His own opinion was that it had been 'the nearest run thing you ever saw in your life'. Napoléon was in retreat, eventually surrendering to the British who exiled him to the remote island of St Helena in the Atlantic Ocean. There was going to be no further chance of escape for him.

The Bourbon monarchy was once more upon the French throne in the person of Louis XVIII, the younger brother of the unfortunate Louis XVI, and Charlotte re-entered France via Switzerland, ending up in Paris where she stayed for many months.

Charlotte wrote a curious letter to Vansittart on 21 January 1816 from the French capital, which suggests that her involvement in espionage was deeper than we had previously imagined. Thus far, her activities had been limited to propagandist reporting on the state of France, the conditions in which the people lived, their attitudes and beliefs, the economy, etc. However, Charlotte now received a secret message that dramatically spontaneously combusted as soon as she read it! Charlotte had returned in her carriage alone except for her servant and the coachman and, as it was dark, she waited while the servant went to fetch a light from the porter's lodge. To Charlotte's surprise, a packet was surreptitiously thrown into her carriage and a Frenchman directed her, in strongly-accented English, to open it when she was alone. He instantly vanished, unobserved by either Charlotte's servant or the coachman. Once in her rooms Charlotte examined the suspicious package. It consisted of 'a square parchment envelope, enclosing two other envelopes all wafered closely; within was a small square of thick paper of a yellowish colour…' On this yellowed paper was written, in French, a warning:

> You must leave here by the 25th of March. If there is danger, you must leave earlier. You will be warned of it. A man who is not of your society but who esteems you, and admires you, watches over you. I know all but am able to do nothing. Be calm – don't worry, and do not forget me.

No sooner had Charlotte read the note than she 'beheld the written paper instantly consumed' and let out a cry of alarm. Luckily the letter had lain on a marble table and Charlotte, who had one hand on the envelopes, was certain that no spark from her fire or from her candle had touched the paper. Quickly regaining her composure, she realized that it was the work of 'some chemical operation neither difficult nor uncommon' and when her *femme de chambre* rushed to her side, Charlotte pretended that nothing untoward had happened.

She knew that she needed to let Vansittart know and hurriedly wrote a letter to be posted to London. It is not clear whether the writer of the note and Charlotte knew one another; the warning at the end – 'do not forget me' – could be construed as 'do not ignore my warning' rather than 'do not forget about me'. She went on to tell Vansittart about the public discontent she was witnessing daily on the streets of Paris. Louis XVIII was disliked and distrusted by many who said that he 'came into France with peace in his mouth, vengeance in his heart and war and famine at his heels'. As well as the king, three other parties were jostling for position, with rumours about their ascendancy fermenting throughout the Parisian boulevards. The republicans were joined to Napoléon's second wife, Marie Louise, Duchess of Parma and speculating about a regency around her son by Napoléon. The Duke of Orléans headed another party for whom speculation was rife as well as another who wanted to see Louis Antoine, the Duke of Angoulême and his duchess, Marie-Thérèse Charlotte of France (otherwise Madame Royale, Louis XVI and Marie Antoinette's eldest daughter) in the ascendancy.[25]

Charlotte knew the watchword of the Orléans party and had repeatedly heard allusions to an event expected to take place at the *premier chant du rossignol* (the first song of the nightingale), i.e. in the springtime. It was curious indeed then, that she was advised to leave Paris and warned of possible risks just before this time. Someone was expecting danger and wanted to see Charlotte safe. Was she intriguing for the Bourbon dynasty, or even for the Orléans party as she knew their watchword?[26]

Although she did not specifically ask Vansittart for more funds, Charlotte made it clear that she was happy to continue to divulge information to him, perhaps hoping that he would immediately respond with a further deposit to her bank account. If that was her hope then she was disappointed and instead approached William Wentworth-Fitzwilliam, 4th Earl Fitzwilliam. He had performed an 'essential service' for Charlotte during 1813 (Charlotte enlightens us no further) and now she prevailed upon his goodwill once more. Perhaps she approached him in his capacity as lord lieutenant of the West Riding of Yorkshire; although Theakston fell in the North Riding, it was very close to the boundary between the two divisions and Charlotte mentioned receiving rents on her house there to the earl.[27]

Did Charlotte leave Paris before the end of March, as instructed? Her movements in the early spring of 1816 remain unclear but she was certainly ensconced in the city during the middle of May, funds obviously having been advanced to her from one source or another. Lady Anne Barnard's younger sister Lady Hardwicke was resident in Paris at the same time as Charlotte, who would have made use of their connection with alacrity and all the more so as Lady Barnard was a source of information about someone from Charlotte's distant past. That someone was General Sir David Ochterlony.

Both Lady Barnard and Lady Hardwicke were in touch with Lady Mary Mackenzie Hood who lived in their native Scotland. Lady Hood knew Ochterlony, a man who also had Scottish roots, and regularly corresponded with him. Ochterlony penned chatty letters to Lady Hood telling her a little of his campaigns and promising to enlist the help of a female friend in India to choose shawls and white heron feathers to send across the ocean to her as he knew nothing of these items. He suggested – probably in jest – that he would retire from his service in the EIC army to a cottage on Lady Hood's estate, becoming 'one of her tenants in the land of his fathers'. Did Lady Hood recount her correspondence with the general to the Ladies Barnard and Hardwicke and, if so, did they then relate Ochterlony's words to an eager Charlotte? She had held a candle for her one true love throughout her life but had neither overtly mentioned nor demonstrated it until the spring of 1816. Charlotte herself attributed her renewed acquaintance with Ochterlony to be due to the mysterious and extremely wealthy Mr Charles Barber who had served, like Ochterlony, with the EIC's army on its Bengal establishment. Barber had died in the Adelphi at the Strand, London in August 1799 during a visit home and his will was disputed, the resulting case dragging on for more than twenty years.[28] 'I declare to you that I have many times wished Mr. Barber's property had sunk in the Bay of Bengal rather than have been brought home to occasion my writing to you – for I preferred being quite forgotten to the imputation of being intrusive.'[29]

Enthused by the opening of an avenue that led her to correspond directly with Ochterlony, as she had hoped to do some four decades earlier, Charlotte asked her old friends Colonel Disbrowe and John Hiley Addington to send copies of the *Gazette* and information about Ochterlony to her in Paris. It was in this way that she heard of Ochterlony's triumphs in India and read that he had been created a baronet.[30]

In the early 1800s, Ochterlony had held the position of British Resident at Delhi, a diplomatic role in which he was an advisor to the ruler Shah Alam II who gave him the honorary title of Nasir-ud-Daula (Defender of the State). Since then he had commanded a column of infantry in the Anglo-Nepalese Wars (1814–15) with his victories leading to promotion to command of a main force. When he brought the war to a successful conclusion, he was lauded with honours and received the baronetcy as his reward.

Charlotte decided to honour her hero and hosted a ball at Paris in celebration of his military success; an open declaration of her admiration for Ochterlony. Did she hope that he would get to hear of this event, perhaps relayed to him second- or third-hand via the Ladies Hardwicke and Hood? Benjamin Hunt Biggs was clearly not by Charlotte's side as she tentatively began to open channels of communication with the man she had loved and lost. 'The Hero of Nepaul [*sic*] little imagined that his early friend was on the 15th of May 1816 giving a Ball in celebration of the anniversary of his treaty after the reduction of Malown, to some of the prettiest women in Paris.'[31]

Did the ball achieve its object? Charlotte certainly seemed content to retreat to the shadows after these few exciting months full of espionage, intrigue and society. For the next few years both Charlotte and Benjamin Hunt Biggs vanish from view, glimpsed only occasionally as they toured mainland Europe. The *Gazzetta di Milano* newspaper recorded the arrivals and departures of people of note in the Italian city including the Biggses, only they were never in company with each other. In the summer of 1818 Mr Biggs arrived in Milan direct from London to meet with an Englishman named Mr Dixon who had travelled from Bern in Switzerland. The two men spent six days in the city before leaving together for Venice. Less than a fortnight later they both arrived back in Milan, possibly to witness the inauguration of Milan Cathedral. The next year it was Charlotte who arrived in the city at the beginning of June. Described as an English gentlewoman, she had crossed mainland Europe from London, travelling independently and with only servants for company. She remained in Milan for exactly a fortnight before she left in a coach bound for Turin.[32]

Where was Charlotte during the summer of 1818 and where was Benjamin Hunt Biggs during 1819? We are left only to guess at their reasons for travelling separately but, knowing that in the aftermath of the French Revolution the Biggses were in possession of a Swiss bank account, it is interesting that Benjamin met up with a man who had arrived in Milan directly from Bern in Switzerland. On the face of it, Mr Biggs and Mr Dixon appear to be just two gentlemen, perhaps friends, both embarked upon a tour of the continent who met up to spend time in each other's company. However, in 1820 it was not Charlotte who repeated her Italian tour, although she did embark on a two-month tour of the continent in the early summer months (she found herself in Marseilles at the same time as Miss Harris, daughter of Lord Harris, but made excuses not to travel home with her). Instead Benjamin once more arrived in Milan in the autumn months and it was he who, this time, arrived via Switzerland for the coach he arrived in had departed from Geneva. More interesting still, a Mr Blizard had arrived in Milan six days earlier, and – with growing impatience – had been awaiting the arrival of Mr Biggs. Joseph Blizard was Benjamin's 'money man', the stockbroker to whom he had entrusted his financial affairs some twenty years earlier. Did the two men have business to contract in Milan, and was it pertinent that Benjamin had travelled from Switzerland? With Benjamin arrived and the business swiftly concluded, Mr Blizard departed for the coastal town of Genoa on the same day, while Benjamin loitered in Milan for over a month before setting off for the delights of Florence.[33]

Meanwhile Charlotte, to all intents and purposes now living a separate life from the man known to the world as her husband, remained based in Bristol when she was home in England and by 1819 had moved some five houses further down Pritchard Street to no. 7.[34]

*Chapter Eleven*

# Love Rekindled

It was, therefore, from 7 Pritchard Street in Bristol, Charlotte's modest and unassuming terraced house, that she embarked upon a correspondence with the man who she had remembered with fondness for most of her life: General Sir David Ochterlony.

Unfortunately for us their early correspondence does not appear to have survived and we are left only to guess at the contents of the letters that passed between them, or how Charlotte first reminded him of her existence. We know that Charlotte told Ochterlony all about her 'marriage' and she was conscious enough of the possibly scandalous and reputation-damaging contents for her to be circumspect in signing her letters; she merely gave her name as Charlotte B. in case they fell into the wrong hands during their long transit to India.

Ochterlony, whatever his surprise at hearing from Charlotte again after so long an absence, replied to her. Encouraged by his response, she sat down at her desk on 26 February 1821 for a day of letter-writing to two old friends. One letter – a solemn affair – was to Sir James Bland Burges, commiserating with him on the death of his daughter, Clara Maria. The second was to Ochterlony, the letter that has survived to this very day and is the only record of Charlotte's victimization at the tyrannical hands of Richard Heaviside. Charlotte was unwell and, for the first time since 1814, she was spending the ensuing, often damp, early months of the year in England; she feared that this would kill her. She viewed her letter to Ochterlony as possibly her last-ever correspondence with him; her one and only chance to put forward her story and regain his favour and esteem. It was truly Charlotte's 'testament'.[1]

The letter, accompanying a miniature portrait of Charlotte – the present she refers to below – began thus:

Private

I fear, my dear General, your first impression on opening this packet will be that I am making you an extraordinary present & that I am taking a liberty with you which an acquaintance so long suspended does not authorise. – To this I have nothing to plead but the gratification I *myself* feel, & though I am aware this could be no plea to your reason or your justice, I think it will be one to your friendship & kindness: for you have told me you still take an interest in my happiness & I am no longer of an age to be the object of *professions* – I *must* believe you.[2]

Charlotte was vain, despite her advancing years, and thought the miniature unflattering but she sent it anyway, taking care to point out that she was actually much slimmer than she appeared. When Ochterlony gazed again upon her features, she wanted to present at least an echo of the pretty young girl full of confidence and hope that he had known all those years earlier. She reflected – somewhat ruefully and self-deprecatingly – that she had clearly never been as attractive as she would have liked to have been to Ochterlony, even in her youth (or he would not have forgotten her so easily) and now the portrait would prove her to be an old woman and not in the least desirable to him, although at the same time she did not hesitate to recall that she looked so youthful until she was almost 40 years of age that no one would believe her true years:

They say here the Miniature resembles, without doing me justice – of this I can be no judge – but it certainly conveys the idea of a *larger* woman than I am both in form & features – the lower part of the face is fuller than mine – & the Shoulders broader – with these exceptions I think there is a great likeness. When you read my story you will not wonder that the habitual turn of my countenance is pensive – The costume is exactly my usual afternoon dress when I am well, though the veil is ill done – the artist is a female & the best I could find – In Poetry & painting are not the *fine arts* of Bristol – You will find, dear General, that time which adds new verdure to the Laurel is fatal to the bloom of the Rose, & that while you have been gathering immortal wreaths for *your* brow, every charm has faded away from *mine* – yet my heart remains the same & my mind is I hope, something more worthy of your attachment… I know not why but time had passed lightly over me – since then I have gradually faded to the state you behold in the Miniature.[3]

The crux of her communication was, however, a manuscript which she enclosed with her letter and likeness, a manuscript in which – with a brutal and unflinching honesty – she laid bare the story of her life from Ochterlony's departure through to her escape from Heaviside's clutches. Her pen retraced the repeated kidnaps and rapes to which she had been subjected, her imprisonment and eventual acceptance of her fate, her escape to Briton Ferry and return to Peterborough House. With what aim did Charlotte write? News of her residence at Peterborough House had made its way to Ochterlony's ears in far-flung India and she now wished to dissuade him of the notion that she had lived willingly as Heaviside's mistress:

> I am the more anxious to leave my memory exonerated from the suspicion of my having been accessory to the horror which befell me. The friendship you have expressed for me, dear as it is – is less gratifying to me till I have recovered your esteem – Good God, what must you think of me, to believe that I who could so young & inexperienced resist the object of my first my fondest affections, & when I was eighteen months older, with my understanding more cultivated & a perfect notion of the consequences, voluntarily throw myself into the arms of a Libertine half mad & half fool – & who had been my ridicule and aversion.[4]

Charlotte gave her account of the destruction of her youthful hopes and of her peace of mind. In doing so, and while subtly pointing out to Ochterlony that he should have had more faith in her strength of character and moral rectitude, she also perhaps found the whole exercise therapeutic, allowing her to shake off some of the demons that had plagued her entire adult life. Did she hope that the general would return to her side after reading this letter? Ochterlony's had been a long and glorious career and now, in his later twilight years, retirement and a return home were a possibility.

Ochterlony, upon reading this startling 'testament' that had been shared with him by a woman who was now little more than a ghost from his past, must have been shocked. He had a new life in a faraway land, military duties to occupy his working day and a harem of wives including the much younger and exotic Mubarak Begum for his leisure hours. Then – suddenly – the past he had left behind confronted him head-on, made real by seeing Charlotte's image in miniature, only she was no longer the pretty young girl of his memory. He was confronted with an elderly and greying lady who had endured a life of catastrophe, triumph and adventure.

Knowing that it would be some time before she would hear anything back from the general in reply, Charlotte turned her attention to other events while she waited. King George III had died and his eldest son, the reprobate Prince Regent, had ascended to the throne as George IV. His coronation was to take place on 19 July 1821 and Charlotte, ever the ardent royalist, wanted a prime seat to view the spectacle. She enlisted the help of her trusted allies, John Reeves and Sir James Bland Burges, to get two seats, the second not for Benjamin Hunt Biggs but instead for Charlotte's goddaughter, 14 years of age and as tall as Charlotte but who had never travelled more than a dozen miles from her home. Reeves managed to get one seat in a gallery erected at the front of the Westminster Sessions House (the police magistrates who operated within had most of the seats for themselves and their friends) and Charlotte intended to let her goddaughter take this if they could not get seats together. She continued to press Sir James to get her two of the prime seats in Westminster Hall where the banquet following the coronation would be held with all due pomp and circumstance.[5]

George IV, when the Prince of Wales, had married his first cousin, Caroline of Brunswick, under duress and because his father promised to sort out his debts and increase his allowance once he was wed. The marriage, as may have been predicted, was a total disaster. The exuberant Caroline was tactless and had a poor grasp of personal hygiene (she boasted that her personal toilette was but a 'short' one). The prince was rolling drunk during the wedding ceremony, recovering enough to consummate his marriage on the wedding night before falling drunk into the grate of the fireplace where Caroline left him. Later he was to claim that he had been intimate with his wife on only three occasions, twice on their wedding night and once on the following night but it proved enough and nine months later Caroline gave birth to a daughter, Princess Charlotte of Wales. She was to be the couple's only child and subsequently husband and wife lived separately. Caroline, whose access to her child was severely and cruelly restricted, led an erratic and peripatetic lifestyle, rumoured to be the mistress of her Italian servant, Bartolomeo Pergami. Such was the state of marital disharmony between the royal couple when George became king and Caroline, whether he liked it or not, his queen, even if in name only. Caroline was always popular with the British public and hastily returned to England, determined to be crowned alongside her husband.[6]

This coronation was planned to be the costliest, most extravagant ever seen. George had viewed Napoléon Bonaparte as his great rival and, even though Bonaparte had recently died in exile on St Helena, he held his coronation as emperor in 1804 as the benchmark alongside which he would judge his own; George's had to be more spectacular. (When the new king had been given the news that his bitterest enemy was dead his first thought was that it was his wife, and he replied to the messenger: 'Is she, by God!')

With his love of costume and theatre, George planned a spectacle of pageantry, fashion and frippery which he was determined would never be outdone by any future monarch, personally overseeing the designs for the costumes that followed a Tudor theme. The total cost approached a quarter of a million pounds, around twenty times more than the cost of his more frugal father's coronation. A number of prize fighters were hired and dressed as Tudor pages, their job specifically to prevent Caroline from gaining access to Westminster Abbey during the coronation and when Caroline duly arrived, crying, 'Let me pass, I am your Queen', she was thwarted and dejectedly turned her carriage around.[7]

The day proved to be bright and sunny. The coronation procession left Westminster Hall, wending its way through bedecked streets decorated to convey the idea of old-fashioned feudal grandeur and chivalry and past packed public galleries that had been erected along the route, to cheers and jubilation. Charlotte would have seen a few familiar faces go by, or at least people with whom she had corresponded. Nicholas Vansittart was there, in his coronation robes as Chancellor of the Exchequer, and the Duke of Wellington in his state robes, attended by a page who carried his field marshal's baton. Finally came the perspiring monarch in robes adorned with jewels under a canopy of cloth of gold, his train carried by eight eldest sons of peers; the year had been generally chilly through the spring and early summer and the new king had failed to take account of how hot and heavy the elaborate costumes would be. By mid-afternoon and with George crowned, the procession retraced its steps to Westminster Hall for the banquet. The spectators in the stands had withstood the blazing sun rather than lose their place. They were perhaps just too far away to detect how overheated and distressed their newly-anointed king was, trussed up with elaborate stays underneath his ceremonial costume to hold in his ever-increasing girth. Lady Cowper wryly noted that 'several times he was at the last gasp; he looked more like the victim than the hero of the fête'. Another spectator, the diarist Mrs Arbuthnot, was less kind: 'Anybody who could have seen his disgusting figure, with a wig the curls of which hung down his back, and quite bending beneath the weight of his robes and his 60 years would have been quite sick.'[8]

If Charlotte had been successful in gaining seats within the hall then she would have witnessed the sumptuous banquet prepared for the coronation party and the farce into which it descended. Yet again, in the planning the heat of the summer's day had not been taken into consideration: there was a profusion of candles and chandeliers in which an estimated 2,000 lights gleamed, competing with the sun's rays streaming in through the windows. As the room grew hotter and hotter, great globules of melted wax from the candles fell, indiscriminately, onto the heads of the people below, causing havoc 'upon the curls of many of the ladies, several of whose heads had lost all traces of the friseur's skill long before the ceremony of the day was concluded.'[9]

There would have been a shadow cast on the day for Charlotte, however. If she had succeeded in getting tickets for the banquet she would have entered Westminster Hall via the platform erected at the corner of New Palace Yard and found herself facing the house in which she had been drugged and molested and then held captive. Charlotte had come so far and achieved so much in her life since then but she could never truly escape her past.

The spectacle of King George IV's coronation was to be the last major event to which Charlotte would bear witness. Now approaching her seventh decade, her zeal for acting as a 'female politician' or as a form of spy for the British government was diminished in relation to her advancing years and increasing frailty. She still travelled abroad but now it was for the sake of her health alone rather than for any other reason and when in England she lived quietly at her modest home in Pritchard Street that she shared with an elderly widowed lady named Mary Gifford whose son was the Bath and Bristol agent for the London Wine Company. It was a link with Charlotte's past as this company had, in 1821, taken over the premises at 141 Fleet Street in London formerly occupied by Faulkner and Radley whose address Charlotte had used as a forwarding one in 1800. The London Wine Company acted as importers of all wines except those from the Cape and Nathaniel Gifford, in advertisements for his business, used both 141 Fleet Street in London and 7 Pritchard Street in Bristol as his address. It seems that Charlotte, or at least her friends, were heavily involved in the wine trade and had been for most of her life from the Beaufoys of her Lambeth youth in the later eighteenth century, then Faulkner and Radley's raisin wine manufactory through to the Giffords and the London Wine Company during the first quarter of the nineteenth century.[10]

One more connection to Charlotte's youth was perhaps her involvement in the funeral of Captain John Hitchcock of the 8th Invalid Regiment who died aged 64 in lodgings in Exeter in October 1823 and was buried at East Stonehouse in Devon where there is a Royal Marines barracks and a Royal Naval Hospital. Charlotte paid for his funeral. There had been Hitchcocks in Lambeth who owned a timber yard on Narrow Wall; possibly this was a man who had formerly been a childhood friend of Charlotte's and with whom she had stayed in touch throughout her life.[11]

Charlotte would have been delighted to hear that General Sir David Ochterlony had been granted the additional title of Baronet of Ochterlony and perhaps even more pleased when, two years later, the British newspapers reported that he had resigned his command and had travelled to Kolkata in preparation for returning to England. Was it possible that she would see him once more? After all these years, was he was coming home to her?

Ochterlony's career in India had gone from strength to strength. Created a Knight Grand Cross of the Order of the Bath – the first recipient of this honour to be a British officer with the EIC – he subsequently proved his worth in the Pindari War (1817–18) to which he managed to negotiate a conclusion without the engagement of enemy troops. He had served as the British Resident at Delhi for a further two years, combined with the residency at Rajputana, but now his years were catching up with him and he wanted to step back and shoulder fewer responsibilities.

All too soon Charlotte realized what a cruel deception the news had played and her hopes were dashed. While she was reading the newspaper reports that suggested her long-lost love would return home, the ships carrying letters announcing his death were already sailing across the stormy seas, bearing down upon the British shores with their terrible news. Ochterlony, his health failing, had died in July 1825 at Meerut just outside Delhi, a broken man after his masters in Kolkata had humiliatingly rebuffed him, disregarding his years of experience and leading to his resignation. If Charlotte had hoped that her hero would return to England so that she could see him for one last time, then her dreams came to nothing. It was the last and fatal blow to Charlotte and one from which she never fully recovered. The following winter found the ailing Mrs Biggs living in Versailles at 24 Rue Saint-Honoré, and it was there that she passed away on 23 February 1827.[12]

Described in the information given to the Versailles deputy mayor on the evening of the day following her death as a *rentière*, a person living on an income from capital or property (which would be the rents she received from her properties in Frith Street, Soho and her father's old home in Theakston, North Yorkshire), she either looked much younger than her years or had given out that she was for she was declared to be only 56 years of age. Her maiden surname of Williams (albeit it as William) was included: she was Rachel Charlotte William and, intriguingly in the light of one further revelation to come, she was described as the widow of Henri Biggs, not the wife of Benjamin Hunt Biggs. Had she been passing in France as a widow to explain the absence of a husband by her side? The information was given to the French notaries by two men who knew Charlotte (Francis Hudson, a 42-year-old upholsterer and Nicolas Roussel, aged 71 and, like Charlotte, a *rentier*, both of whom lived nearby on Rue de la Pompe) and as well as the garbled information about her husband, this document also revealed her birthplace to be Caerleon in Wales.

Someone, possibly Benjamin Hunt Biggs, inserted a notice of Charlotte's death into the Bristol newspapers, replete with mistakes. 'Died, at Marseilles, Mrs. R. Biggs of this city, and late of Faringdon, Somerset.' Her will left everything to Benjamin and three days after this notice appeared in the newspaper he proved the document at London.[13]

Charlotte's story had one more surprise in store. Benjamin Hunt Biggs, as Charlotte's executor, had the task of going through her papers including the correspondence she most prized and that was kept locked in the writing desk given to her by Princess Elizabeth as a reward for her efforts in planning the jubilee. Among these papers, Benjamin found two packets for the princess that had been trusted to Charlotte some years earlier by the Dowager Queen of Württemberg, Princess Elizabeth's elder sister who was resident in Germany and happy to remain in her adopted country rather than return to England and be stifled once again within the confines of the royal family. Charlotte had been acting as a courier for the daughters of King George III but for some reason had not delivered her missives. Something of a wild goose chase ensued as royal officials tried to locate the elusive and reclusive Benjamin Hunt Biggs and reclaim the packet. A letter from Nicholas Vansittart, now Chancellor of the Duchy of Lancaster, addressed simply to Mr Biggs, lay unclaimed at the Southampton Post Office. Frederick Dawes Danvers who was the deputy clerk to the Duchy of Lancaster, on the insistence of Sir William Knighton, King George IV's private secretary, entered into correspondence with the Southampton postmistress. The postmistress did not know of any Mr Biggs who lived in Southampton and instead suggested that the possible recipient might be 'a Gentleman of the name of H. Biggs Esqr who resides in the neighbourhood of Romsey' who had his letters directed to the Southampton Post Office, routinely sending a carrier to collect them. As the Mr Biggs of Romsey always had his letters 'particularly directed to H Biggs Esqr' the letter had not been sent to him. The postmistress promised to make further enquiries as she had no further address.[14]

Why all the subterfuge and secrecy, for the gentleman going by the name of 'H Biggs Esqr' and living at Romsey was indeed Benjamin Hunt Biggs? Why would he choose not to use his first name and why be so circumspect about his address, not wanting to have correspondence sent directly to his home? Moreover, what was the 'H' in his name denoting; did it represent his middle name of Hunt or was he passing as Henry, or Henri, Biggs? It is one more riddle in the Biggs' secretive lives. Was Benjamin merely private almost to the point of paranoia or did he too, like Charlotte, engage in activities that necessitated a need to 'hide' from the world at large and remain under the radar?

The packets for the Princess Elizabeth were reclaimed by Frederick Dawes Danvers who, once Mr Biggs' identity had been established, visited him at Romsey to collect them. It is perhaps fitting that Charlotte's enigmatic and remarkable life, which involved so much secrecy, should end with yet more tantalizing titbits of information. Loyal to her country and to her monarch, she was brave in the face of danger, witnessed history being made first-hand but perhaps most remarkable of all, Charlotte, a woman in a man's world, overcame the brutal treatment she had received as a young woman to emerge as an author and playwright, a 'female politician', a spy and a propagandist and was successful in all her endeavours. If she had been born a man, then we are sure that her name would have gained the renown it deserves, both in her own lifetime and subsequently, but Charlotte was a woman who had to operate anonymously and use others as her mouthpiece and she has remained, until now,

**a forgotten Georgian heroine.**

# Appendix

## Benjamin Hunt Biggs

The man who passed to the world at large as Charlotte's husband lived a further six years after her death. Much as he always had, he lived quietly and continued to reside in Romsey in Hampshire with occasional trips to Bath for his health. In a similar way that Charlotte had written her own will directly after inheriting from her father, Benjamin Hunt Biggs penned the will that would remain his last, albeit with many codicils appended to it, almost as soon as he had proved Charlotte's will and inherited her properties and effects.

Two women make an appearance in Benjamin's will. One was an elderly, unmarried lady who lived at Chepstow: Jane Frances Morgan. Miss Morgan, originally from Somerset, was the sister of the Reverend Charles Henry Morgan who married Frances Williams of Tidenham House, the stepdaughter of Harriet Williams who had leased Boughwell's Green House to Charlotte in the early 1800s. A young Welsh lady was also left an inheritance. Elizabeth (née Parry) was the wife of a Frenchman, Joseph Lacorne, who was a customs official in the northern French port town of Saint-Valery-en-Caux. She had been born in Abergavenny in 1799, the daughter of William Parry, a carpenter. In late 1827, the year of Charlotte's death, the Lacornes had been in Bristol; they baptized their 3-week-old son, William, at St Philips and Jacob's church in the city, only about half a mile away from Charlotte's former Pritchard Street home. It is possible that Elizabeth lived with Charlotte as a companion, servant or to nurse her through her last years and had met Joseph Lacorne when she travelled to France with Mrs Biggs. It is of note that the Frenchman worked in customs and excise; did the Biggses know this man through Charlotte's work as a spy and courier?

Benjamin originally left £500 to Jane Frances Morgan and £100 to Elizabeth Lacorne but amended his will to reduce the latter bequest to just £50 following 'transactions' with Elizabeth.[1]

The Frith Street properties formerly owned by John Williams and then by Charlotte passed, via Benjamin's will, to a man named John Cole who lived at Odiham in Hampshire. Early in April 1833, Benjamin died at his home in Romsey and was buried at nearby Nursling.[2]

In his will, Benjamin Hunt Biggs also left a bequest for a charitable fund to be established to care for the poor of Putney. The charity continues to this day and is now known as the Biggs–Wymondesold Trust.

## Fantasist and enigma? How to read Charlotte's life

Charlotte's abduction and rape has parallels in a novel written some thirty years prior to her abduction; a novel written by Samuel Richardson coincidentally while he was living at Parson's Green in Fulham as a near neighbour of the 3rd Earl of Peterborough and his mansion, Peterborough House. *Clarissa* tells the story of Clarissa Harlowe, a young girl whose family are newly come into a fortune. First betrothed to Richard Lovelace in anticipation of the earldom he will inherit, she is then forced by her family to agree to marry a man she loathes, Roger Solmes. Lovelace, intent on avenging himself on her family as well as wanting to possess her, tricks Clarissa into running away with him before she can marry Solmes; she is subsequently held prisoner by him before being drugged and raped. Charlotte, unlike Clarissa, was not in possession of a fortune no matter how small or large but Heaviside undoubtedly wished to possess her, body and mind.

Marius Kociejowski published Charlotte's letter to General Sir David Ochterlony and his thoughts about it in a work titled *The Testament of Charlotte B* and as an abridged version in *London: City of Disappearances*, which is how we first made the acquaintance of Charlotte and her story when researching Peterborough House. While we have no reason to doubt Charlotte's words, in fairness to Richard Heaviside we must highlight that it is Charlotte's version of events only that has been preserved. Some aspects of her story do still puzzle us, despite our years of research.

Charlotte, in her *Testament*, referred to two people by initial only, Mr H___ and Mr B___. While Heaviside was easy to identify as Mr H___, Mr B___ was more problematic. Other people mentioned, such as Mr Saunders the apothecary, were given their full name. Throughout, Charlotte referred to both Mr Mark Beaufoy and Mr B___ and it could be that this is one and the same person. If this is the case, however, she did it for no one else; Mr H___ was never Mr Heaviside and the people referred to in full were never referred to only by their initial. Is Mr B___ someone else then, not Mark Beaufoy? If so, then to whom could Mr B___ possibly refer? There is only one other person who was a constant in Charlotte's story, a man whom

Ochterlony would have known who she referred to when she did not use his name in full and whose surname begins with the letter 'B' and this is Benjamin Hunt Biggs.

Charlotte, when she was writing in 1821, used Benjamin's surname as her own but did not sign it on the letter, worried as to whose hands her tale might fall into and wishing in such an event to remain anonymous; she signed herself only as 'Charlotte B'. It then follows that she would not wish to mention her married name elsewhere. The assumption we have made when telling Charlotte's story is that Mr B___ is Benjamin Hunt Biggs and not Mark Beaufoy in disguise.

One other man in Charlotte's story was not named at all and this was the man employed by Heaviside to fetch her away from the small cottage at Briton Ferry. Charlotte did not dare to name this man, not even using only the first initial of his surname; this man's identity she wanted to remain a secret. She told Ochterlony: 'I will not name him because he is now in high reputation – a favourite with the King – & I believe he did not at that time feel the disgrace of his mission – in fact he was poor & under great obligations to my persecutor.' She added further explanation at the end of her letter: the man who discovered her had poor relations at Neath that he occasionally visited and, whether by gossip or chance, it was in this way that Charlotte had been found. There were not many men who had family living in Neath who had risen to a high reputation and a favourite of King George IV by the 1820s when Charlotte was writing to Ochterlony. To narrow it down still further to men who were once poor and who had not yet gained that high reputation in the mid-1780s, to a man who was under obligations to Richard Heaviside…we are left with but one man who it could possibly be and that is John Nash, the childhood friend of Richard Heaviside from their early days in Lambeth.

There are times when Charlotte's story is difficult to believe; sometimes we suspect she is bending the truth to suit her own means. One such incident is the immediate aftermath of her second abduction. Her father was fully aware of what had passed between his daughter and Richard Heaviside, he had been instrumental in trying to bring the matter to court, had challenged Heaviside to a duel and been bound over to keep the peace with him and seen his daughter left degraded and distraught. Why would he then so easily accept and reconcile himself to the fact that his daughter had run away to 'live in sin' with this man? A few enquiries would have led him to Peterborough House, even if he was unaware of the location to which Heaviside had moved.

Benjamin Hunt Biggs was also in Fulham throughout the time Charlotte was held prisoner in Peterborough House. Given his involvement in Charlotte's story and later life, it is probable that he was fully aware of how, where and with whom she was living. Charlotte carefully placed Benjamin well away from her side when she wrote to Ochterlony, mentioning that she bribed the woman who was nursing her child to send letters to her father and to Mr B___; she received no answer to these appeals and concluded that her family had given her up but the woman had betrayed Charlotte and had not delivered these letters. It is entirely possible that Mr Biggs was in fact a near neighbour of Charlotte, possibly even spending time within the confines of Peterborough House during Charlotte's captivity there.

One further suspicion rests with her choice of Briton Ferry in south Wales as her place of sanctuary. Wales – especially that very area of Wales – was the place of choice with Richard Heaviside and his friend John Nash for sending away people from whom they wished to distance themselves. Did she then really escape, or was she sent away into Wales by Richard Heaviside in much the same manner as Nash had sent away his wife and indeed as Heaviside had sent away his servants after his first attack on Charlotte had been discovered? If we remember that, at this period, Heaviside had enrolled himself into the Inner Temple, that he had established himself as a justice of the peace and that he was moving away from his background in trade, was Charlotte, much as he was infatuated with her, an encumbrance to his ambitions? The truth generally falls between two extremes: perhaps rather than run away, rather than being sent away, it was mutually acceptable to them both that Charlotte should retire to the isolation of south Wales.

Questions remain about some 'trash' she wrote for an unnamed publication that was seen by Ochterlony in India. She confessed to Ochterlony that she had hoped the Miss Sibthorpes, if they replied, would mention him, so they were obviously mutual friends. Marius Kociejowski confirms that there were Sibthorpes in India; he too feels that this portion of Charlotte's *Testament* is full of unresolved questions. Mr Sibthorpe, presumably either father or brother to the Miss Sibthorpes, was a man to whom Charlotte could not apply for assistance. She stated that his 'behaviour to me had been so bad that I held him in abhorrence & I had known an instance of his acting with a sort of revenge towards me – merely perhaps from the fear of my exposing him.' What else had happened to Charlotte? Was this before or after she had been kidnapped by Heaviside? She seems to have been cruelly used and abused by more than one man of her society.

Charlotte's authorship of *A Residence in France* provides us with yet another problem. She published it anonymously and perhaps never intended to be known as the author, other than to the few government ministers and statesmen to whom she privately admitted it. Evidence found in archives in France places Charlotte and Benjamin Hunt Biggs (who does not appear within *Residence* under his own name) in different prisons to those in which she places herself within *Residence*'s pages. However, it is a fact that Charlotte was imprisoned during the revolutionary years and that her experience would have been akin to the one she describes for us. Our belief, and it can be no more than that, is that Charlotte had appropriated the memoirs of someone else and meshed them with her own, and that she and Mr Biggs appear within its pages as the shadowy Mr and Mrs D___ (it is entirely possible that this is some form of private joke on Charlotte's part), hence the continued need for anonymity in her authorship of this work.

What makes Charlotte's story even more remarkable is that after we have questioned the authenticity of *A Residence in France* and queried whether she has told the whole truth about her experience at Heaviside's hands, we come to her organization of the jubilee, her activities as a 'female politician' and her willingness to spy and pen propaganda for the British government, all of which sound equally if not even more far-fetched. Yet these activities are all a matter of fact. Charlotte did single-handedly instigate the royal jubilee of 1809; she did put words into the mouths of politicians such as Wilberforce and Windham; she penned propaganda and travelled France, reporting to ministers back home.

She was a unique and bold woman and it has been in equal measure a pleasure and a frustration to research her life. Where we doubt the authenticity of her words, we also applaud her aplomb in ordering the situation to suit her needs and to gain her ultimate objective, regardless of whether this was to seek the good opinion of a man she had loved to distraction or, in a scholarly vein, to work against the principles of republicanism and radicalism and to curry the favour of men high in government. Charlotte used particularly feminine wiles to succeed in what was a man's world on surprisingly equal terms.

# Endnotes

### Chapter One: Love, Loss and Abduction

1. In the eighteenth century Caerleon was a major port located on the busy River Usk. A convent education was not unusual for daughters of well-to-do families of that period and not solely limited to those who practised Catholicism. Charlotte and David Ochterlony met at some point between February 1775 and July 1777.

2. *White Mughals* by William Dalrymple. David Ochterlony was born in Boston, Massachusetts on 12 February 1758, the eldest of the four children of Katherine Tyler, an American, and David Ochterlony, a merchant sea captain who died, deeply in debt, at St Vincent's in the West Indies when his son was only 7 years of age. He was the grandson of Alexander Ochterlony, laird of Pitforthy. As a child, David was educated at the Dummer Charity School (now known as the Governor's Academy) in nearby Byfield, Massachusetts. After his father's death, he moved to England with his mother, where Katherine married Isaac (later Sir Isaac) Heard, a long-serving Officer of Arms at the College of Arms in London, at St Andrew-by-the-Wardrobe in the City of London on 7 March 1770. Young David split his time between his mother's new home and that of his Scottish paternal grandparents. Sir Isaac became both a father figure and close confidant to Ochterlony throughout his life and David, around the time he met Charlotte, assisted him in his work at the College of Arms.

3. *The Testament of Charlotte B* by Marius Kociejowski. Charlotte's parents seem to have played no part in Ochterlony's courtship of their daughter, nor did she seek their help when she wished to hear news of him. It all leads one to suspect that Charlotte was allowed a certain amount of unchaperoned independence in her private life.

4. The *Lord North*, with David Ochterlony on board, sailed in July 1777 from Gravesend for India, waiting for a fair wind at Spithead in the Solent in convoy with the *Besborough* Indiaman and the *Belle Isle* man-of-war which was conducting them to the Cape. *Caledonian Mercury*, 5 July 1777 and *Kentish Gazette*, 21 July 1777. It took nine months for letters to reach India from England and then the same time again for any reply to arrive back home.

5. The author and historian Hallie Rubenhold describes eighteenth-century Covent Garden as a 'visual carnival'. See *The Covent Garden Ladies: Pimp General Jack & the Extraordinary Story of Harris's List* by Hallie Rubenhold for further reading.

6. There was another daughter. Eleanor Heaviside married Josiah Hutchins on 7 February 1764 at St Stephen's Church in Coleman Street, City of London and on 6 October 1765 baptized a son named Richard in the church of St Katharine by the Tower. A son named Josiah was baptized in the same church on 20 January 1767. Eleanor's death occurred at some point between the birth of her son Josiah and her husband's remarriage in 1771. Sarah Prudden was the daughter of Simon Prudden and his wife Elizabeth, née Pottinger. Her grandfather George Pottinger, who died in 1747, had owned a timber yard in Lambeth; his obituary described him as 'one of the most considerable Timber-Merchants in the Kingdom'. It is possible that Richard Heaviside and James Morris took over the Pottinger timber yard upon George's death.

7. PROB 11/1014/167, The National Archives (hereafter TNA). Richard Heaviside's will is not dated but written between 1765 and his death in December 1775. It named his daughter Elizabeth Heaviside to whom he left £5,000 and also his grandson Richard Hutchins. The will also left money to his siblings back in County Durham: brothers Valentine, Ralph and John and a sister Mary from Bishop Auckland. He left a bequest to a cousin, yet another Richard Heaviside, this one a saddler from the parish of St Andrew's in Holborn, London. Richard Heaviside senior described his son as apprentice to him in his timber business.

8. The information given in Chapter One ('Love, Loss and Abduction') on Charlotte's treatment at the hands of Richard Heaviside and her opinion of him comes from the letter she wrote in 1821 to David Ochterlony, a letter that was subsequently discovered by Marius Kociejowski and published as *The Testament of Charlotte B.*

9. An eminent Quaker physician, Doctor Fothergill, suggested to Mark Beaufoy that he should produce raisin wine from the waste product left over from his vinegar-making, the stalks and skins of the raisin being the best way to obtain a product called 'rape' necessary to filter and clarify the vinegar but that left the best part of the raisin to be thrown away. As a dual vinegar and raisin wine operation the business quickly became successful, not least from the contracts secured from the Admiralty who used Beaufoy's vinegar to preserve food on board their ships and to wash the ships' decks.

## Chapter Two: Freemasonry, Theatres and Friends in High Places

1. John Nash called John Edwards his cousin. Edwards later owned Rheola House in the Neath valley, Glamorganshire. Information on Nash from William Porden's diary, 3 July 1812, Derbyshire Records Office, 03311/4/5.

2. Elizabeth Heaviside married Samuel Hill on 6 June 1774 at St Michael Bassishaw in the City of London. On 16 September 1775, at St Paul's Covent Garden, Samuel and Elizabeth Hill baptized a son, John William Hill.

3. Heaviside was initiated into the St Alban's Lodge on 21 March 1774. The Library and Museum of Freemasonry. Bartholomew (or Bartolomeo) Ruspini

had been born in 1730 in northern Italy. Qualified as a surgeon in his native country, by the early 1750s he was practising dentistry in England, first in Bath and Bristol where he became a Freemason and then from 1766 onwards in London.

4.  *Harris's List of Covent-Garden Ladies: Sex in the City in Georgian Britain* by Hallie Rubenhold.

5.  *The Memoirs of Mrs. Sophia Baddeley, late of Drury Lane Theatre* by Mrs Elizabeth Steele, vol. V, 1787.

6.  *Harris's List of Covent-Garden Ladies: Sex in the City in Georgian Britain* by Hallie Rubenhold. For more information on the men behind Harris's List, see also *The Covent Garden Ladies: Pimp General Jack and the Extraordinary Story of Harris's List* by the same author.

7.  *The Publications of the Selden Society*, vol. 49, 1932, Memorial of Annuities, Ewart v. Heaviside.

8.  Dodd was hung on 27 June 1777. The *Norfolk Chronicle*, 5 July 1777 and *Hampshire Chronicle*, 30 June 1777.

9.  John Dunning was created 1st Baron Ashburton in 1782. The *Douglas Cause or Case* (1769) concerned Archibald Douglas's attempt to prove his birth: his mother, the sister of the Duke of Douglas, had been 50 years of age when Archibald and his twin brother Sholto were born in Paris. As heir to the wealthy but childless Duke of Douglas he faced – and lost – a legal challenge to the legitimacy of his claim to the dukedom. It was suggested that he and his brother were spurious children and part of a deception. The Duchess of Kingston, formerly Elizabeth Chudleigh, had secretly and privately married Augustus Hervey in 1744 (he was later to become 3rd Earl of Bristol). The couple soon grew tired of each other and as the marriage was a secret and unrecorded, Elizabeth saw no need to admit to it: she travelled extensively in Europe and found love with Evelyn Pierrepoint, 2nd Duke of Kingston-upon-Hull, whose mistress she became. Once it became clear that Hervey would become Earl of Bristol, there was a financial benefit to proving herself his wife and she forged a record of their marriage. In 1769, the Consistory Court ruled that Elizabeth was a spinster and so she married her lover, the Duke of Kingston, only to face charges of bigamy from his nephew after the duke's death.

10. In *Eighteenth-Century Women: An Anthology*, Bridget Hill says that while rape was a frequent occurrence, successful prosecutions were not, except in cases where the victim was below the age of consent.

## Chapter Three: Debauchery at Peterborough House

1.  Benjamin Biggs was buried on 27 December 1766 at Monk Sherborne in Hampshire alongside several of his relations, indicating his ancestral origins from this small town. In his will (PROB 11/925/114, TNA) he ensured that his wife Mary was well provided for before naming his eldest son Benjamin

Hunt Biggs as the beneficiary of freehold land known as Peat Moor near Yately in Hampshire plus property in Frimley and Putney.

2. *Public Advertiser*, 5 May 1778.

3. Robinaiana, Countess of Peterborough was for many years the mistress of the 4th Earl of Peterborough, the couple only marrying upon the death of his first wife. Robinaiana was the maternal aunt of the celebrated eighteenth-century courtesan Grace Dalrymple Elliott. Grace, like Charlotte, would live to be caught up in the turmoil of the French Revolution. For more information on Grace and the Earl and Countess of Peterborough, see our previous work *An Infamous Mistress: The Life, Loves and Family of the Celebrated Grace Dalrymple Elliott*. Robert Carpenter left the stage under a cloud around the same time as he was accused of rape; dismissed, it was said, due to a forgery. Instead he found work as a navy agent at Gosport near Portsmouth but old habits die hard and he was accused and found guilty of forging seamen's wills. In 1785 he was hanged at Winchester for his crimes.

4. The heyday of the house had been in the early eighteenth century when the then owner, the celebrated 3rd Earl of Peterborough, entertained many of the leading wits and literati of the day including Alexander Pope, Jonathan Swift (who wrote praising the gardens), John Gay and Voltaire.

5. The information given in Chapter Three ('Debauchery at Peterborough House') on Charlotte's treatment at the hands of Richard Heaviside and her opinion of him comes from the letter she wrote in 1821 to David Ochterlony, a letter that was subsequently discovered by Marius Kociejowski and published as *The Testament of Charlotte B.*

6. There was indeed a Mary Belson living in the same Lambeth area as Charlotte. Mary Watkins had married John Belson in March 1773, shortly before the birth of her first child, William. A daughter, Frances, was born in 1779 and buried (as Francis) at St Mary's in Lambeth in 1785 when her address was given as [Narrow] Wall, exactly where the Belson family lived in Charlotte's account. A burial is recorded for both a John and Mary Belson on 26 March 1809 at St Mary's in Lambeth, with their address given as Cuper's Bridge. A mulatto is an historical term describing someone who is of mixed white and black ancestry.

7. John Churchill was chairman of the Westminster Committee of Association who met in the King's Arms Tavern in New Palace Yard, next door but one to Heaviside's house.

8. Heaviside still owned his house in New Palace Yard; on 27 October 1781, the *Morning Herald* newspaper reported that his house there had been broken into and a considerable amount of plate and goods was stolen. The report also mentioned that his compting house (where a business, in this case Heaviside's timber merchant operation, carried out its paperwork and accounting) had been robbed some weeks earlier too. *Whitehall Evening Post*, 8 January 1782. Robert Harrison was mentioned in Benjamin Hunt Biggs's will, proving their long friendship.

9. Lowndes's London Directory, 1783 and Inner Temple archives.
10. *White Mughals: Love and Betrayal in Eighteenth-Century India* by William Dalrymple. Charlotte, in a note added to her *Testament*, suggests that the colonel is indeed James Kirkpatrick.

## Chapter Four: Neath, of all Places!

1. John Nash and Jane Elizabeth Kerr were married on 28 April 1775 at St Mary Newington in Southwark. Their eldest son, John, was baptized just over a year later on 10 June 1776 at Lambeth and Hugh on 29 April 1778 at the same place. London Metropolitan Archives.
2. There is some ambivalence over whether the baby was born in 1779 or 1780; records pertaining to the Nashs' divorce suggest 1779 but the Neath parish baptism registers record her baptism on 18 January 1783 and her birth date as 29 December 1780. Welsh Archive Services.
3. William Porden's diary, 3 July 1812, Derbyshire Records Office, 03311/4/5.
4. Ibid. Nash grew weary of his lifestyle and subsequently applied himself industriously to his profession as an architect, with brilliant results. He became the favourite of the Prince Regent, later George IV, and was responsible for remodelling Buckingham Palace and the Brighton Pavilion among other projects.
5. Laki, or Lakagígar, in Iceland erupted on 8 June 1783 and continued for eight months, causing a global drop in temperatures.
6. Lambeth parish registers and the *Kentish Gazette*, 25 July 1786.

## Chapter Five: Residence in France

1. Thomas Poplett was appointed to the post of lieutenant in Captain Joseph Wall's African Corps in 1780, subsequently listed as on half-pay in 1783 when the corps disbanded.
2. The *Morning Herald*, 2 and 4 February 1788.
3. The *Morning Herald*, 5 February 1788 and the *Morning Post*, 7 February 1788. Around this time, both Heaviside and Poplett were listed among the subscribers to a scheme to found a school for daughters of Freemasons who were unable to provide for their children, a plan that was the brainchild of Heaviside's friend Bartholomew Ruspini and had the patronage of the Duchess of Cumberland.
4. Charlotte made the claim that she attended the Panthemont in the pages of *A Residence in France* but we have been unable to verify this.
5. We have been unable to verify Charlotte's information regarding Eugenia de Santerre.
6. In France, the title marquis can either denote the holder of a *marquisat* (marquessate), or can be bestowed upon someone of noble birth as a form of courtesy title.
7. The marriage took place at Topsham in Devon on 20 August 1789.

8. For quotes and information in this chapter regarding Charlotte's time in France without further source, please refer to *A Residence in France* by Charlotte Biggs.

9. Bibliothèques d'Amiens Métropole, d'archives révolutionnaire 4 I 5/1 – Providence, 1793 – AN 3.

10. See our previous work *An Infamous Mistress: The Life, Loves and Family of the Celebrated Grace Dalrymple Elliott* for more information. In that book we endeavour to separate fact from fiction, as it concerns Grace's journal.

11. The *Morning Post* of 26 June 1795 reported the arrival of the *Young Eagle*, an American ship from Le Havre, in the Thames the day before with several English passengers who had been prisoners of the revolution aboard. This fits with the dates of Charlotte and Benjamin Hunt Biggses' arrival back in England and it is likely they were two of the former prisoners on board.

12. *Fatal Purity: Robespierre and the French Revolution* by Ruth Scurr.

13. Bibliothèques d'Amiens Métropole, d'archives révolutionnaire 4 I 5/1 – Providence, 1793 – AN 3. Bulletin des citoyens détenus en la Maison dite de la Providence depuis le 7 septembre 1793.

14. *France in eighteen hundred and two, described in a series of contemporary letters* by Henry Redhead Yorke. The surrender of Valenciennes took place on 28 July 1793. *Le Réveil du Peuple*, an anthem adopted by the *jeunesse dorée* (gilded youth) which was a militia of minor officials and small tradesmen, was first sung in January 1794 according to *Gilded Youth of Thermidor* by François Gendron, so Yorke might not be strictly accurate in his account which dates almost a decade after the surrender of Valenciennes but his story does illustrate the horror with which Joseph Le Bon was regarded and remembered.

15. The charges were: 1. Having dilapidated and lavished the finances of the nation. 2. Having conspired against the Liberty of the French Nation. 3. Having sought to starve the People in 1789. 4. Having excited the murders of 5 and 6 October. 5. Having, in concert with BAILLY and LA FAYETTE, caused the Patriots to be butchered in the Champs de Mars. 6. Having prevailed upon the Swiss to fire on the people on 10 August. 7. Having, like another AGRIPPINA, forgotten that she was a mother, in order to commit incest with her son.

16. The Place de la Concorde in Paris was, between 1792 and 1795, renamed the Place de la Révolution.

17. General Custine was guillotined at Paris on 28 August 1793.

18. *Fatal Purity: Robespierre and the French Revolution* by Ruth Scurr.

## Chapter Six: Return to England

1. Grace put pen to paper to record her account in the early years of the 1800s when she was living in Twickenham with her elderly and ailing aunt. There may, therefore, be some truth in the rumour that the king's doctor requested Grace to record her experiences if he was also treating Grace's aunt and spending time with the ladies in Twickenham.

2. Description of John Williams' Theakston house from the *York Herald* of 16 January 1808, when the property was advertised for sale.

3. Wiltshire and Swindon History Centre, 9/35/271.

4. The *London Gazette*, 27 September 1794.

5. Free Library of Philadelphia, Rare Book Department. George III, King of Great Britain, 1738–1820. Document licensing Joseph Blizard to remit payment to B.H. Biggs in Abbeville, France. Court at St James's, London, 16 May 1795.

6. British Library (hereafter BL), Windham Papers, Add, MSS, 37915/02–03.

7. *History of Somersetshire* by the Reverend John Collinson, F.A.S., vol. II, 1791.

8. The mansion house has gone through a variety of names. Originally called The Elms (due to the trees at the front aspect), from 1892 it was known as Parsonage Farm. By 1927 it was The Parsonage and now is The Old Parsonage. Charlotte called it Farrington House. The historic building consultant J. Robert Sutcliffe remembers that as a young boy in the 1960s he would often pass the building and be intrigued by its appearance, as well as a rumour that it had been built by French masons, a rumour no doubt due to both the house's appearance and the first early medieval owners of the estate, the de Gournay family. Historical & Archaeological Building Report on The Stables, Coach House & Store, The Old Parsonage, Farrington Gurney, Somerset by The House Historians, May 2007. The Old Parsonage is now a fine bed and breakfast and self-catering establishment and information about the history of the house is given on their website.

9. BL, Windham Papers, Add, MSS, 37915/09–13.

10. *Politics and Genre in the Works of Elizabeth Hamilton, 1756–1818* by Claire Grogan.

11. At the 1807 poll for Yorkshire, John Williams, gentleman, was one of four people from Theakston who voted, and cast his vote for William Wilberforce Esq, Henry Lascelles and the RH Charles William Wentworth Fitzwilliam (Viscount Milton).

12. BL, Windham Papers, Add, MSS, 37915, folios 02–06.

13. The *Monthly Review*, March 1797.

14. *What Is She?* has traditionally been ascribed to the poet and novelist Charlotte (Turner) Smith due to a pencilled notation of Charlotte Smith's name in brackets against the title page of *What Is She?* in a copy of volume 10 of *The Modern Theatre* (1811), a work by the contemporary novelist, actress and dramatist Elizabeth Inchbald. Florence Hilbish, in *Charlotte Smith, poet and novelist (1749–1806)*, acknowledges that it is by no means certain that the authorship of *What Is She?* should be ascribed to Charlotte Smith. Mrs Smith never acknowledged *What Is She?* as one of her works. A later advertisement for an anonymous propagandist pamphlet written by Rachel Charlotte Biggs refers to the author's previous works, *A Residence in France* and *What Is She?*, revealing the author to be not Charlotte Smith but Rachel Charlotte Biggs.

15. Richard Heaviside's son, also named Richard, was born on 12 July 1793 at Braintree in Essex.

16. Sarah Prudden was buried at Lambeth on 27 August 1798, exactly a week after writing her will. The will was not proven until 23 February 1799, just a little over two months before *What Is She?* was first performed on the stage at Covent Garden. PROB 11/1319/227, TNA.

17. *The Critical Review: Or, Annals of Literature*, vol. 27, 1799 by Tobias George Smollett and the *Monthly Review*, vol. 29, 1799.

18. *Kentish Weekly Post*, 28 May 1799.

## Chapter Seven: A Female Politician

1. BL, Windham Papers, Add, MSS, 37889, folios 17–19. Charlotte merely gave Fleet Street on this first letter but subsequent letters identify the address as 141 Fleet Street. Faulkner and Radley's British Wine Manufactory is shown at 141 Fleet Street on Richard Horwood's 1799 map of London, Westminster and Southwark.

2. *A Maximum; or, the Rise and Progress of Famine, Addressed to the British People* by Rachel Charlotte Biggs.

3. *Hampshire Chronicle*, 1 December 1800.

4. BL, Windham Papers, Add, MSS, 37915, folios 9–13.

5. BL, Windham Papers, Add, MSS, 37915, folios 9–13. Charlotte was in London between 9 and 15 December and asked for post to be directed to her at 141 Fleet Street between these dates. From 16 December to 6 January she planned to be in Bedale.

6. *Salisbury and Winchester Journal*, 6 April 1801 and *York Herald*, 2 May 1801. *The British Critic* (1801), in a review, considered *A Maximum* to be a supplement to the 'celebrated' *A Residence in France*.

7. BL, Windham Papers, Add, MSS, 37915, folios 21–24. Letter dated 19 July 1801 and written from Farrington Gurney. William Windham resigned on 7 February 1801.

8. BL, Windham Papers, Add, MSS, 37915, folios 02–33. The letter, dated 26 July 1801, is written from Farrington Gurney following a few days in London during which Charlotte had been indisposed.

9. Sheffield Archives, WWM/F64, folio 101. In a letter written to Earl Fitzwilliam in 1816, Charlotte recalled that she had been in France for the whole period of the Peace of Amiens. BL, Windham Papers, Add, MSS, 37915, folios 09–13. In a letter to Windham on 5 December 1800, Charlotte referred to a small income that would be at her disposal '15 months hence'. She gives no further clues as to the source of this income but it would appear to be an annuity that had already been agreed prior to December 1800 to commence no later than March 1802. Lady Day, on 25 March, was one of the traditional 'quarter days' when rents were due, accounts settled and regular payments were made. *The Banks Letters*: a calendar of the manuscript correspondence of Sir Joseph Banks, preserved in the British Museum, the British Museum (Natural History) and other collections in Great Britain.

10. *Salisbury and Winchester Journal,* 2 July 1804.
11. Captain John Wesley Wright was captured by the French in May 1804 when HMS *Vincejo* was becalmed in Quiberon Bay after being blown off course. He was held in the Temple and questioned about putting the royalist *Chouans* ashore at Bivill but refused to answer. He was held until 27 October 1805 when he was reported to have committed suicide; the British authorities believed that he had, in fact, been murdered.
12. BL, Vansittart Papers, Add, MSS 31234, folio 51, 4 December 1812.
13. *William Cobbett: Englishman, A Biography* by Anthony Burton.
14. BL, Windham Papers, Add, MSS, MS37916, folios 02–05.
15. The Earl of Lauderdale (1759–1839) was a Scottish peer who appeared in parliament dressed in a Jacobin costume to mark the outbreak of the French Revolution and spent time during the revolution in Paris. Francis Seymour-Conway, 3rd Marquess of Hertford (1777–1842) was known by the title Earl of Yarmouth 1794–1822.
16. John Williams was buried on 28 December 1807. Gout was historically known as 'the disease of kings' or 'rich man's disease' and was associated with excessive eating and alcohol consumption. The bill to abolish the slave trade had been passed in the House of Commons in February 1807 and had received Royal Assent on 25 March 1807.
17. Yorkshire Probate Records, RD/AP1/164/2. The reference to the Reverend Mr James Williams, the son of the late Mr James Williams of Chepstow, Gentleman, is frustrating. We have traced a Reverend James Williams, who was indeed the son of a James Williams of Chepstow who had died prior to John Williams writing his will; they seem to fit. However, tracing back this Williams line in Chepstow we can see no definite link to our John Williams. We feel that they must be kin, however, as the bequests left – a diamond ring and the knee buckles set in gold and silver – are both valuable and personal items.
18. PROB 11/1722/428, TNA.
19. *York Herald,* 16 January 1808.

## Chapter Eight: The Royal Jubilee

1. Sarah Lowder née Williams was one of the sisters of the late James Williams of Chepstow mentioned in John Williams' will; James Williams was the father of both the Reverend James Williams and the Thomas Williams who married Harriett Maria Lowder. *Gloucester Journal,* 11 February 1811. The house was to be let from midsummer and would be the date upon which Charlotte left the property vacant.
2. William Cobbett in a letter to John Wright, 12 February 1809. *William Cobbett: An Englishman, A Biography* by Anthony Burton.
3. Colonel Wardle was prosecuted in 1810 for non-payment of a bill for furnishing Mary Anne Clarke's house; she said this had been the price of her testimony.

Mary Anne Clarke was prosecuted in 1813 for libel and spent nine months in prison. The novelist Daphne du Maurier is a direct descendant of Mary Anne Clarke.

4. *Kentish Gazette*, 18 April 1809.
5. Poplett's will revealed that he had entertained a lifelong love for a lady named Penelope Gale from whom he had been separated and thought dead. He married Louisa Augusta Bayly in 1789, daughter of the Duke of Uxbridge, by whom he seems to have behaved honourably even after finding out that his first love was still alive. Penelope remained a spinster and Poplett's will requested that she be buried in the same vault as he when she died. Both Louisa and Penelope were left bequests and were named joint executors of his will. PROB 11/1516/362, TNA.
6. R.C. Biggs to Lord Dartmouth, 14 October 1809, Staffordshire Record Office, 1778/1/ii/1737.
7. *The European magazine, and London review*, July 1809. Henry III had reigned for fifty-six years between 1216 and 1272. Although James I reigned as James VI of Scotland for fifty-seven years, as James I after the union of Scotland and England his reign was twenty-two years.
8. *Regency Spies: Secret Histories of Britain's Rebels & Revolutionaries* by Sue Wilkes, citing Hansard, Parliamentary Debates, Vol. XXXVI, pp.1007 and 1051.
9. BL, Vansittart Papers, Add, 31234, folio 05–11.
10. *The Alien Office, 1792–1806*. Historical Journal, 33: 361–84. JSTOR 2639462 by Elizabeth Sparrow, 1990. *Bristol Mirror*, 7 October 1809 and *Morning Chronicle*, 14 October 1809. The windows of Robert Waithman's shop were broken during the jubilee celebrations; *Examiner*, 29 October 1809. BL, Vansittart Papers, Add 31234, Folio 20.
11. R.C. Biggs to Lord Dartmouth, 14 October 1809, Staffordshire Record Office, 1778/1/ii/1737 and BL, Vansittart Papers, Add, MS31234, folio 05–11, 15 September 1812.
12. R.C. Biggs to Lord Dartmouth, 14 October 1809, Staffordshire Record Office, 1778/1/ii/1737.
13. Ibid.
14. Stuart Semmell argues this very point in his thesis *Radicals, Loyalists, and the Royal Jubilee of 1809*.
15. R.C. Biggs to Lord Dartmouth, 14 October 1809, Staffordshire Record Office, 1778/1/ii/1737.
16. *Leeds Intelligencer*, 25 September 1809, *Bristol Mirror*, 4 November 1809 and *Aberdeen Journal*, 8 November 1809.
17. *Hereford Journal*, 18 October 1809.
18. *Bristol Mirror*, as above.
19. BL, Vansittart Papers, Add 31234, folio 08. Frances Williams was the daughter of Thomas Williams of Tidenham House by his first wife, Frances Stevens.

## Chapter Nine: A New Life in Bristol

1. BL, Windham Papers, Add, MSS, 37907, folio 21.
2. Ibid.
3. BL, Vansittart Papers, Add 31234, folio 32.
4. *Morning Post*, 8 September 1810.
5. Sheffield Archives, Earl Fitzwilliam Papers, WWM, F64, folio 103. Aliens Entry Books, 1794–1921, HO 5/0013:1809–1910 (Aliens entry books: correspondence), TNA.
6. Sarrazin married Cecilia Charlotte Schwartz in 1799 at Livorno, then known as Leghorn. Cecilia Charlotte was born in October 1782 at Exeter to George Schwartz, a Presbyterian merchant who was possibly of Swiss extraction. The general's son Frederic had been born on 24 February 1805.
7. *Napoleon's Enfant Terrible: General Dominique Vandamme* by John G. Gallacher; *London Courier*, 12 and 13 June 1810; *Public Ledger*, 15 June 1810.
8. *The History of Parliament: the House of Commons 1754–1790*, eds L. Namier, J. Brooke and *Burges, Sir James Bland, first baronet (1752–1824)*, Oxford Dictionary of National Biography, by David Hill Radcliffe. Sir James Bland Burges's first wife was Elizabeth Noel, daughter of Edward Noel, 1st Viscount Wentworth. His sister-in-law, Judith Noel, was the mother of Byron's wife, Anne Isabella Milbanke (Anne Isabella later inherited the title Baroness Wentworth). In October 1821, Sir James took the surname Lamb and subsequently used that instead of Burges in compliance with the will of John Lamb, Esquire, late of Golden Square. *Hampshire Chronicle*, 29 October 1821.
9. Bodleian Library Oxford University (hereinafter BLOU), Dep Bland Burges 28, folio 38 and Dep Bland Burges 25, folio 40.
10. *Bristol Mirror*, 7 July 1810. The inauguration took place on 3 July 1810.
11. The ascent at Oxford in 1810 was Mr Sadler's fifteenth aerial voyage. BLOU, Dep Bland Burges 25, folio 40. *Hampshire Chronicle*, 2 and 16 July 1810; *Kentish Weekly Post*, 3 July 1810; *Kentish Gazette*, 6 July 1810.
12. Hansard 1803–2005, Parochial Schools Bill, HC Deb 04 August 1807, vol. 9, cc1050–5.
13. BLOU, Dep Bland Burges 25, folio 44.
14. PROB 11/1525/307, TNA. The bequest is further evidence that Reverend James Williams was close kin to the family. Sarah's will named two more people who shared her marital surname. Mr William Williams of Nash near Newport in Monmouthshire, south Wales received a bequest of £20 and an A.M. Williams put their name to the will as a witness.
15. General Jean Sarrazin also published several other works.
16. Preface to *The Philosopher; or Historical and Critical Notes* by General Jean Sarrazin.
17. In the summer of 1814, Charlotte, writing from Bristol, sent Sir James Bland Burges some sweet lemons she had received from the West Indies, with an apology that there would be nothing else until the autumn arrival of the next

cargo. BLOU, Dep Bland Burges 25, folio 30. *The Glenbervie Journals*, edited by Walter Sichel, London, 1910.

18. BLOU, Dep Bland Burges 28, folio 46. We have so far been unable to trace the baptism of the young Protheroe girl. Perhaps the intended baptismal name was something of a jest between Charlotte and Sir James Bland Burges and her name did not reflect those of her intended godparents.

19. Charlotte did not specify who the relation was, whose death had left her asking for financial aid. Perhaps she had expected to be left something by her stepmother. Her father's old house in Theakston was rented out to Edward Carter Esq. (as referenced in his will PROB 11/1733/279, TNA).

20. Samuel Rosser Protheroe was baptized on 1 January 1794 at Abbots Leigh. In 1801 a younger brother was baptized at the same place and given the name James Reeves Williams Protheroe; it is possible that Charlotte and John Reeves were godparents of this boy, given his middle names and Charlotte's obvious closeness to the family. Although we have been unable to locate the baptism of the girl Charlotte describes as her and Sir James Bland Burges's goddaughter, she does confirm, in letters to Sir James, that the goddaughter and Samuel Rosser Protheroe are brother and sister. The *Swiftsure* had taken part in the Battle of Trafalgar. Samuel Rosser Protheroe entered the Royal Navy on 22 September 1811; First Class Volunteer was also known as Boy First Class.

## Chapter Ten: Espionage in France

1. BL, Vansittart Papers, Add 31234, folio 04.

2. Ibid.

3. BL, Vansittart Papers, Add 31234, folio 34. The Westminster election was held on 8 October 1812 and returned the radical Sir Francis Burdett and Thomas Cochrane, 10th Earl of Dundonald, both Whigs who were unopposed.

4. BL, Vansittart Papers, Add 31234, folio 42.

5. BL, Vansittart Papers, Add 31234, folio 46.

6. BL, Vansittart Papers, Add 31234, folio 51.

7. BL, Vansittart Papers, Add 31234, folio 42. James Reeves Williams Protheroe was listed in the first form at Eton in 1814. Speaking to Sir James Bland Burges in a letter written the following year, Charlotte told him that she was not sure if she could 'bear the din' of Suffolk Street. BLOU, Dep Bland Burges 25, folio 63.

8. In the preface to *The Prison of Montauban*, Julia declared of her work that she would 'most manfully maintain with this my goose quill, that it is not a novel, since it consists neither of swoonings, idolatry, or seduction; nor of expressions, and situations bordering upon blasphemy and indecency. I am then at a loss of a name to my little harmless book; and must, I believe, call it *a Reflective Tale.*'

9. This letter is dated 8 July in *The Old School*; the year is missing but is probably 1811.

10. BLOU, Dep Bland Burges 25, folio 61. Charlotte's pulmonary complaint took hold at the end of October 1813. The frost fair on the Thames was held at the beginning of February 1814. Mrs Mary Morgan née Flowers married Philip Morgan on 12 January 1785 at St Philip and St Jacob, Bristol; their son John Flower Morgan (who became a naval surgeon) was born c.1786. The Clifton suspension bridge now stands in the area overlooked by the Morgans' Sion Row house. It was at Sion Row that Charlotte heard news regarding the death of a man who had stood as both patron and benefactor to her family, Thomas Brudenell-Bruce, Earl of Ailesbury.

11. *Ladies of the Grand Tour* by Brian Dolan. Mary Berry, writing in 1798, was at risk of being accused of Jacobin sympathies with her condemnation of 'English ways' but was actually referencing the confinement she felt as a woman, both intellectually and physically.

12. BL, Vansittart Papers, Add 31234, folio 93.

13. Royal Bank of Scotland, Drummond Bank archives.

14. *White Mughals* by William Dalrymple. Kolkata was formerly known by the British as Calcutta.

15. *Defiance: The Life and Choices of Lady Anne Barnard* by Stephen Taylor.

16. *Testament of Charlotte B* by Marius Kociejowski. BL, Vansittart Papers, 31234, folio 114. Sir Charles Stewart was Viscount Castlereagh's half-brother; on 27 August 1814, shortly after Charlotte wrote to Vansittart, he was appointed ambassador at Vienna. He later took the surname Vane and succeeded his half-brother as Marquess of Londonderry. It was on 11 May 1814, following his successes in the Peninsular War, that Arthur Wellesley was created Duke of Wellington.

17. BLOU, Dep Bland Burges 25, folio 82. BL, Vansittart Papers, Add 31234, folio 126.

18. BLOU, Dep Bland Burges 25, folios 54 and 87. HMS *Horatio*, a 38-gun frigate (fifth-rate), was strictly speaking the first Royal Navy ship to commemorate Lord Nelson but the only one ever called *Horatio* (apart from a couple of twentieth-century armed trawlers). Royal Museums, Greenwich.

19. BL, Vansittart Papers, Add 31234, folios 126–157.

20. *Peterborough House* by Sue Pierson. Richard Heaviside's widow, Ann, was granted administration of his effects in May 1815. As she left this unadministered, in 1873 administration was granted to her grandson Richard William Spicer who had been named as an executor in Ann Heaviside's own will when she died in 1855 (in 1853 her grandson, Richard Heaviside, was granted the right to change his surname to William Spicer in order to inherit from his maternal great-uncle William Francis Spicer). National Probate Calendar (Index of Wills and Administrations), 1858–1966, probate date 3 March 1873 and *Morning Post*, 30 April 1853. A memorial plaque in Heaviside's memory stands in Bath Abbey, where he is buried.

21. BL, Vansittart Papers, Add 31234, folios 158–161.

22. Diary of William Wilberforce, MP, 13 May 1815. *Kentish Weekly Post*, 2 June 1815.
23. BL, Vansittart Papers, Add 31234, folios 169, 194 and 82.
24. *Cobbett's Weekly Political Register*, 10 June 1815.
25. BL, Vansittart Papers, Add 31234, folios 228–230.
26. BL, Vansittart Papers, Add 31234, folio 231.
27. Sheffield Archives, WWM/F64/101.
28. National Records of Scotland, GD46/15/6/13, Papers of the Mackenzie Family, Earls of Seaforth (Seaforth Papers), Personal Letters, mainly addressed to Mary, Lady Hood, 1816.
29. *The Testament of Charlotte B* by Marius Kociejowski.
30. Ibid. David Ochterlony was created Sir David Ochterlony, 1st (and last) Baronet of Pitforthy on 7 March 1816.
31. Ibid.
32. Benjamin Hunt Biggs, recorded as Mr Hunt, and Mr Dixon arrived in Milan on 23 July 1818, leaving for Venice on 29 July (Benjamin still listed as Mr Hunt). On 9 August they returned, this time leaving no doubt of Benjamin's identity for he was recorded as Mr Hunt Biggs. Charlotte arrived there on 4 July 1819 and left for Turin on the 18th of the same month. *Gazzetta di Milano*, 25 and 31 July and 11 August 1818, and 6 and 20 June 1819. Charlotte had also passed through Milan in 1814.
33. Mr Blizard arrived in Milan from London on 4 October 1820 and Benjamin, as Mr Smitt Biggs, English gentleman, arrived from Geneva on 10 October; Blizard left Milan on the same day. On 9 November Benjamin Hunt Biggs left for Florence, the Italian newspaper mistakenly listing him as Mr Vigg-H. *Gazzetta di Milano*, 6 and 12 October and 11 November 1819. For details of Charlotte's two-month tour, BLOU, Dep Bland Burges 26, folio 126 and for the information on not bringing Miss Harris back from Marseilles, *The Testament of Charlotte B* by Marius Kociejowski. Miss Harris was possibly Phoebe Frances Harris (1787–1862), daughter of the 1st Baron Harris of Seringapatam and Mysore, a man who would be known to General Sir David Ochterlony through their shared service in the armed forces in India. Margaret Woodall, Belmont House archivist, advised that Phoebe Frances Harris travelled in the Low Countries and France during July to December 1814 in company with her sister-in-law; perhaps this is how she encountered Charlotte?
34. Bristol Archives, Matthew's Directories of Bristol.

**Chapter Eleven: Love Rekindled**

1. Clara Maria Burges died on 4 February 1821. It was Marius Kociejowski who first described Charlotte's letter as her 'Testament'.
2. *The Testament of Charlotte B* by Marius Kociejowski.
3. Ibid. The miniature was possibly painted by either Ellen or Rolinda Sharples, two of the most prominent artists in Bristol at the time and is sadly now lost.

4. Ibid.
5. King George III died on 29 January and was buried on 16 February 1820 in St George's Chapel in Windsor. BLOU, Dep Bland Burges 25, folios 32 and 41.
6. Princess Charlotte of Wales, the daughter of George IV and Caroline of Brunswick, died in childbirth in 1817 following the stillbirth of a son.
7. Caroline fell ill and died less than three weeks after the coronation.
8. *George IV, Regent and King, 1811–1830*, Christopher Hibbert and *The Mistresses of King George IV*, M.J. Levy. Harriet Fane married, as his second wife, the diplomat and politician Charles Arbuthnot.
9. *Bell's Weekly Messenger*, 23 July 1821 and *Morning Post*, 25 July 1821.
10. *Bell's Weekly Messenger*, 25 November 1821 and *Bristol Mirror*, 16 September 1826.
11. When Marius Kociejowski discovered Charlotte's 'Testament' several other documents were with it, including several military commissions in Hitchcock's name and an account of the expenses incurred in his funeral.
12. David Ochterlony died on 15 July 1825. *Morning Post*, 18 October 1825 and *Evening Mail*, 21 December 1825.
13. *Bristol Mercury*, 26 March 1827. Charlotte's will was proved by Benjamin Hunt Biggs at London on 29 March 1827.
14. The Southampton postmistress at the time was Mary Ann Watson (British Postal Service Appointments Book, 1737–1969). Royal Archives, RA GEO/ MAIN/31780–31781. The Queen of Württemberg was the former Charlotte, Princess Royal.

### Appendix

1. PROB 11/1815/192, TNA. William Lacorne, who was baptized at Bristol in 1827, died in Saint-Valery-en-Caux in France early in 1832. Another child, a daughter named Eléonore Anastasie, was born c.1830. Elizabeth Parry and Joseph Lacorne did not marry until 1828, after William's birth; their marriage took place during October at Saint-Valery-en-Caux (Elizabeth's parents were still living at Abergavenny). Archives départementales de Seine-Maritime. While Benjamin Hunt Biggs recorded the properties on Frith Street in his will, the Theakston house is not specifically mentioned and it may be, as there was a question mark over John Williams' entitlement to it, that he did not inherit that particular property. The tenant of the Theakston house was Edward Carter, and his will had the following bequest: 'I give and bequeath the messuage or dwelling house garden stable buildings and lands in Theakston aforesaid which I hold by lease under Mrs Biggs to my said wife during all my estate and interest there she paying the rent and performing the covenants to become due or to be performed for or in respect of the same premises from the time of my death.' PROB 11/1733/279, TNA (Edward Carter died late in 1827, not long after Charlotte).
2. *Hampshire Telegraph*, 15 April 1833. Benjamin was buried at Nursling on 16 April 1833.

# Bibliography

## Printed Sources

A Lady, the wife of a naval officer, *An account of the celebration of the Jubilee, on the 25th October, 1809* (Birmingham, 1809)

Arnold, Catharine, *City of Sin: London and its Vices* (Simon & Schuster, 2010)

Biggs, Rachel Charlotte, *A Maximum; or, the Rise and Progress of Famine, Addressed to the British People* (1801)

Biggs, Rachel Charlotte, *A Residence in France, during the years 1792, 1793, 1794, and 1795; described in a series of letters from an English Lady; with general and incidental remarks on the French character and manner* (1797)

Biggs, Rachel Charlotte, *What Is She?* (1799)

Blanc, Oliver, *Last Letters: Prisons and Prisoners of the French Revolution* (André Deutsch, 1987)

Burton, Anthony, *William Cobbett: Englishman, A Biography* (Aurum Press, 1997)

Colley, Linda, *Britons: Forging the Nation, 1707–1837* (Yale University Press, 2005)

Collinson, Reverend John, *History of Somersetshire in three volumes*, vol. II (1791)

Cornwell, Bernard, *Waterloo: The History of Four Days, Three Armies and Three Battles* (Lulu Press, 2015)

Dalrymple, William, *White Mughals: Love and Betrayal in Eighteenth-Century India* (HarperCollins, 2002)

Dalrymple, William and Sharma, Yuthika (eds), *Princes & Painters in Mughal Delhi 1707–1857* (Penguin, 2013)

Dawson, Warren Royal, *The Banks Letters: a calendar of the manuscript correspondence of Sir Joseph Banks*, preserved in the British Museum, the British Museum (Natural History) and other collections in Great Britain (1958)

Dinwiddy, J.R., *Radicalism and Reform in Britain, 1780–1850* (The Hambledon Press, 1992)

Dolan, Brian, *Ladies of the Grand Tour* (Flamingo, 2002)

Dwyer, Philip, *Citizen Emperor: Napoleon in Power, 1799–1815* (Bloomsbury, 2013)

Dyck, Ian, *William Cobbett and Rural Popular Culture* (Cambridge University Press, 1992)

Elliott, Grace Dalrymple, *Journal of My Life during the French Revolution* (Richard Bentley, 1859)

Fletcher, Loraine, *Charlotte Smith: A Critical Biography* (Palgrave Macmillan, 1998)

Fraser, Antonia, *Marie Antoinette, The Journey* (Phoenix, 2002)

Fraser, Flora, *Princesses: The Six Daughters of George III* (John Murray, 2004)

Fraser, Flora, *The Unruly Queen: The Life of Queen Caroline* (Macmillan, 1996)

Gallaher, John G., *Napoleon's Enfant Terrible: General Dominque Vandamme* (University of Oklahoma Press, 2008)

Gendron, François, *Gilded Youth of Thermidor* (McGill-Queen's Press, 1993)

Gilleir, Anke, Montoya, Alicia A. and van Dijk, Suzanna (eds), *Women Writing Back/Writing Women Back: Traditional Perspectives from the Late Middle Ages to the Dawn of the Modern Era* (BRILL, 2010)

Gray, Denis, *Spencer Perceval: The Evangelical Prime Minister, 1762–1812* (Manchester University Press, 1963)

Grogan, Claire, *Politics and Genre in the Works of Elizabeth Hamilton, 1756–1816* (Routledge, 2016)

Hibbert, Christopher, *George IV, Regent and King, 1811–1830* (Harper & Row, 1975)

Hibbert, Christopher, Weinreb, Ben, Keay, Julia and Keay, John, *The London Encyclopaedia* (Pan Macmillan, 2008)

Highfill, Philip H, Burnim, Kalman A. and Langhans, Edward A., *A Biographical Dictionary of Actors, Actresses, Musicians, Dancers, Managers, and other Stage Personnel in London, 1660–1800, volume 3: Cabanel to Cory* (SIU Press, 1975)

Highfill, Philip H., Burnim, Kalman A. and Langhans, Edward A., *A Biographical Dictionary of Actors, Actresses, Musicians, Dancers, Managers, and other Stage Personnel in London, 1660-1800, volume 14: Siddons to Thynne* (SIU Press, 1991)

Hilbish, Florence May Anna, *Charlotte Smith, Poet and Novelist (1749–1806)* (Philadelphia: University of Pennsylvania, 1941)

Hill, Bridget, *Eighteenth-Century Women: An Anthology* (George Allen & Unwin, 1984)

Holmes, Richard, *Wellington: The Iron Duke* (Harper Collins, 2002)

Howarth, David, *Waterloo: A Near Run Thing* (Phoenix, 1997)

Huish, Robert, *An Authentic History of the Coronation of George IV* (London, 1821)

Hutton, James, *Selections from the Letters and Correspondence of Sir James Bland Burges, Bart., sometime under-secretary of state for Foreign Affairs. With notices of his life* (John Murray, 1885)

Kelly, Gary, *Women, Writing and Revolution, 1790–1827* (Clarendon Press, 1993)

Kociejowski, Marius (ed.), *The Testament of Charlotte B* (Libanus Press, 1988)

Kociejowski, Marius, *The Testament of Charlotte B* in '*London: City of Disappearances*', ed. by Iain Sinclair (Penguin, 2007)

Kociejowski, Marius, *The Pebble Chance: Feuilletons and Other Prose* (Biblioasis, 2014)

Levy, M.J., *The Mistresses of King George IV* (Peter Owen, 1996)

Major, Joanne and Murden, Sarah, *An Infamous Mistress: The Life, Loves and Family of the Celebrated Grace Dalrymple Elliott* (Pen & Sword History, 2016)

Montluzin, Emily Lorraine de, *Anti-Jacobins: The Early Contributors to the Anti-Jacobin Review* (Macmillan Press, 1998)

Moore, Wendy, *The Knife Man* (Random House, 2010)

Namier, L. and Brooke, J. (eds), *The History of Parliament: the House of Commons 1754–1790* (Boydell and Brewer, 1964)

O'Byrne, William R., *A Naval Biographical Dictionary: comprising the life and services of every living officer in Her Majesty's Navy, from the rank of Admiral of the Fleet to that of Lieutenant, inclusive*, vol. 3 (John Murray, 1849)

Pierson, Sue, *Peterborough House* (Fulham and Hammersmith Historical Society, 2013)

Preston, Thomas, *Jubilee Jottings: The jubilee of George the third. 25th October, 1809. A record of the festivities with the proclamations, congratulatory addresses, etc.* (Whittaker & Co., 1887)

Rubenhold, Hallie, *Harris's List of Covent Garden Ladies: Sex in the City in Georgian Britain* (Tempus, 2005)

Rubenhold, Hallie, *The Covent Garden Ladies: Pimp General Jack & the Extraordinary Story of Harris's List* (Tempus, 2006)

Sarrazin, General Jean, *The Philosopher; or, Historical and Critical Notes* (London, 1811)

Scurr, Ruth, *Fatal Purity: Robespierre and the French Revolution* (Chatto & Windus, 2006)

Sichel, Walter (ed.), *The Glenbervie Journals* (London, 1910)

Smith, Julia Bernard, *The Old School*, vols I and II (London, 1813)

Smith, Julia Bernard, *The Prison of Montauban; or, Times of Terror. A Reflective Tale* (London, 1810)

Smith, Captain Thomas, *Narrative of Five Years' Residence at Nepaul*, vols 1 and 2 (London, 1852)

Steele, Elizabeth, *The Memoirs of Mrs Sophia Baddeley, late of the Drury Lane Theatre* vol. V (London, 1787)

Summerson, John, *The Life and Work of John Nash, Architect* (Allen & Unwin, 1980)

Taylor, Stephen, *Defiance: The Life and Choices of Lady Anne Barnard* (Faber & Faber, 2016)

Thorne, R. (ed.), *The History of Parliament: the House of Commons 1790–1820* (Boydell and Brewer, 1986)

Uglow, Jenny, *In These Times: Living in Britain through Napoleon's Wars 1793–1815* (Faber & Faber, 2015)

Vickery, Amanda, *The Gentleman's Daughter: Women's Lives in Georgian England* (Yale University Press, 1998)

Watkins, Walter Kendall, *The Ochterlony Family of Scotland and Boston, in New England* (1902)

Wilkes, Sue, *Regency Spies: Secret Histories of Britain's Rebels and Revolutionaries* (Pen & Sword History, 2015)

Williams, Kate, *Becoming Queen* (Arrow Books, 2009)

Williams, Kate, *Josephine: Desire, Ambition, Napoleon* (Random House, 2013)

Yorke, Henry Redhead, *France in eighteen hundred and two, described in a series of contemporary letters* (William Heinemann, 1906)

## Online Sources

Barker, Hannah, 'Stockdale, John (c.1749–1814)', *Oxford Dictionary of National Biography* (Oxford University Press, 2004)

British Listed Buildings, The Old Parsonage, Farrington Gurney

Cavell, Samantha A., Bachelor of Business, Queensland University of Technology, 1990, Brisbane, Australia, 'Playing at Command:

Midshipmen and Quarterdeck Boys in the Royal Navy, 1793–1815', A thesis submitted to the Graduate Faculty of the Louisiana State University and Agricultural and Mechanical College, May 2006

Hansard 1803–2005 (www.hansard.millbanksystems.com)

'House of Lords Journal Volume 37: March 1787 21–30', in *Journal of the House of Lords Volume 37, 1783–1787* (London, 1767–1830), pp.625–644. British History Online.

Inner Temple admissions database (www.innertemplearchives.org.uk)

Kennedy, Deborah F., 'Williams, Helen Maria (1759–1827)', *Oxford Dictionary of National Biography* (Oxford University Press, 2004)

Lloyd, E.M., 'Vane [Stewart], Charles William, third marquess of Londonderry (1778–1854)', rev. A.J. Heesom, *Oxford Dictionary of National Biography* (Oxford University Press, 2004)

Morgan, Kathleen and Smith, Brian S., 'Tidenham including Lancaut: Introduction', in *A History of the County of Gloucester*: Volume 10, Westbury and Whitstone Hundreds, ed. C.R. Elrington, N.M. Herbert and R.B. Pugh (London, 1972), pp.50–62. British History Online.

Plowright, John, 'Vansittart, Nicholas, first Baron Bexley (1766–1851)', *Oxford Dictionary of National Biography* (Oxford University Press, 2004); online edn, Jan. 2008

Radcliffe, David Hill, 'Burges, Sir James Bland first baronet (1752–1824)', *Oxford Dictionary of National Biography* (Oxford University Press, 2004)

Schofield, Philip, 'Reeves, John (1752–1829)', *Oxford Dictionary of National Biography* (Oxford University Press, 2004); online edn, Jan. 2008

Special Collections, University of Southampton, *The road to Waterloo: Week 14* (www.specialcollectionsuniversityofsouthampton.wordpress.com)

The Old Parsonage, Farrington Gurney (www.theoldparsonagebandb.co.uk)

Three Decks – Warships in the Age of Sail (www.threedecks.org)

Tyack, Geoffrey, 'Nash, John (1752–1835)', *Oxford Dictionary of National Biography* (Oxford University Press, 2004)

Wilkinson, David, 'Windham, William (1750–1810)', *Oxford Dictionary of National Biography* (Oxford University Press, 2004)

## Manuscript Sources and Journals

A Statement of Architectural and Historic Significance and a justification of works relating to the alteration and extension of the existing kitchen [at The Old Parsonage] by J. Robert Sutcliffe, IHBC ICOMOS, Historic Buildings Consultant (26 February 2015)

An Account of the Lodge of the Nine Muses No. 235 from its foundation in 1777 to the present time, compiled from the Minute Books & other Sources by Past Masters of the Lodge (London, 2012)

Authentic and interesting memoirs of Mrs. Clarke, from her infancy to the present time. Likewise, a brief account of Mr. Wardle's charges, relative to His Royal Highness the Duke of York: together with the minutes of evidence as taken in the House of Commons, 1809

Historical & Archaeological Building Report on The Stables, Coach House & Store, The Old Parsonage, Farrington Gurney, Somerset by The House Historians (May 2007)

Rose, R.B., International Review of Social History, volume 4, issue 3, pp.432–445 – 18th-Century Price-Riots, the French Revolution and the Jacobin Maximum (December 1959)

Semmel, Stuart, Radicals, Loyalists, and the Royal Jubilee of 1809 in the Journal of British Studies 46 (July 2007)

Sparrow, Elizabeth, *The Alien Office, 1792–1806*. Historical Journal. 33: 361–84. JSTOR 2639462 (1990)

*The Critical Review, Or, Annals of Literature* (1799)

The Eton School Lists, from 1791 to 1850, London (1863)

The Jubilee of George the Third, an account of the celebration in the towns and villages throughout the United Kingdom of the forty-ninth anniversary of his reign, 25th October, 1809. Compiled from authentic sources, John Bumpus (1887)

The *Monthly Review* (1799)

The Publications of the Selden Society, volume 49 (1932)

The Transactions of the Honourable Society of Cymmrodorion, 2008

## Contemporary Newspapers and Magazines

As referenced in the text and endnotes.

## Archival Sources

Archives départementales de Seine-Maritime
Archives départementales de Yvelines
Bibliothèques d'Amiens Métropole, d'archives révolutionnaire
Bodleian Library
Bristol Archives
British Library

Derbyshire Records Office
Free Library of Philadelphia, Rare Book Department
Inner Temple archives
London Metropolitan Archives
National Records of Scotland
Royal Archives, Windsor
Sheffield Archives
Staffordshire Record Office
The Library and Museum of Freemasonry
The National Archives
Welsh Archive Services
Wiltshire and Swindon History Centre
Yorkshire Probate Records

# Index